أَسَاسِيَّات

فِي

التَّرْبِيَةِ الإِسْلَامِيَّة

حقوق الطبع محفوظة

First Edition in Arabic: ©

ISBN No: 978 – 977 – 6241 – 77 – 0

LD. No: 13616 / 2009

الطبعة الخامسة
التاريخ : 1443هـ — 2022 م

الترقيم الدولي : 0 — 77 — 6241 — 977 — 978

رقم الإيداع : 2009/13616

Translated by:

Al-Andalus Group LTD

Islamic Translation, Voice Over & Training

www.alandalusgroup.co.uk

ترجمة:

مجموعة الأندلس
للترجمة الإسلامية والتعليق الصوتي والتدريب

www.alandalusgroup.co.uk

مكتبة إقرأ للنشر والتوزيع
كلومبس ـ أوهايوا
ت : 6145000626 **(1)**

Basics of Islamic Upbringing

Questions and Answers

Compiled and Arranged by   جمع وترتيب

'Abdullah Hassan Fareh (San'aani)   عبدالله حسن فارح (صنعاني)

Introduction

All perfect praise is due to Allah, we praise Him, seek His Aid and ask Him for forgiveness. We seek refuge with Allah from the evil of our souls and the bad consequences of our misdeeds. Whoever Allah Guides none can lead astray and whoever Allah Sends astray none can guide. I testify that there is none truly worthy of worship except Allah and I testify that Muhammad is His Slave and Messenger.

{O you who have believed, fear Allah as He Should Be Feared and do not die except as Muslims [in submission to Him]} [Aal 'Imraan:102].

[O mankind, fear your Lord, Who Created you from one soul and Created from it its mate and Dispersed from both of them many men and women. And fear Allah, through Whom you ask one another, and the wombs. Indeed Allah Is ever, over you, an Observer] [An-Nisaa':1].

مُقَدِّمَةٌ

إِنَّ الحَمـدَ للهِ، نَحمَـدُهُ وَنَسـتَعِينُهُ وَنَستَغفِرُهُ، وَنَعُوذُ بِاللهِ مِن شُرُورِ أَنفُسِـنَا وَسـيِّئَاتِ أَعمَالِنَا، مَن يَهدِهِ الله فَلا مُضِلَّ لَهُ، وَمَن يُضلِلِ فَلا هَادِيَ لَهُ، وَأَشـهَدُ أَن لا إِلَه إِلاَّ الله وَحـدَه لا شَـرِيكَ لَـهُ، وَأَشـهَدُ أَنَّ مُحَمَّدًا عَبدُهُ وَرَسُولُهُ ﷺ.

﴿يَٰأَيُّهَا ٱلَّذِينَ ءَامَنُوا۟ ٱتَّقُوا۟ ٱللَّهَ حَقَّ تُقَاتِهِۦ وَلَا تَمُوتُنَّ إِلَّا وَأَنتُم مُّسلِمُونَ﴾ [آل عمران: ١٠٢]

﴿يَٰأَيُّهَا ٱلنَّاسُ ٱتَّقُوا۟ رَبَّكُمُ ٱلَّذِى خَلَقَكُم مِّن نَّفسٍ وَٰحِدَةٍ وَخَلَقَ مِنهَا زَوجَهَا وَبَثَّ مِنهُمَا رِجَالًا كَثِيرًا وَنِسَآءً ۚ وَٱتَّقُوا۟ ٱللَّهَ ٱلَّذِى تَسَآءَلُونَ بِهِۦ وَٱلأَرحَامَ ۚ إِنَّ ٱللَّهَ كَانَ عَلَيكُم رَقِيبًا﴾ [النساء: ١]

[O you who have believed, fear Allah and speak words of appropriate justice. He Will [then] Amend for you your deeds and Forgive you your sins. And whoever obeys Allah and His Messenger has certainly attained a great attainment]
[Al-Ahzaab: 70-71]

﴿يَـٰٓأَيُّهَا ٱلَّذِينَ ءَامَنُوا۟ ٱتَّقُوا۟ ٱللَّهَ وَقُولُوا۟ قَوْلًا سَدِيدًا ۝ يُصْلِحْ لَكُمْ أَعْمَـٰلَكُمْ وَيَغْفِرْ لَكُمْ ذُنُوبَكُمْ وَمَن يُطِعِ ٱللَّهَ وَرَسُولَهُۥ فَقَدْ فَازَ فَوْزًا عَظِيمًا ۝﴾

[الأحزاب: ٧٠ – ٧١]

The most truthful speech is that of Allah, The Almighty. The best guidance is that of Muhammad, sallallaahu ‘alayhi wa sallam. The most evil of matters are those invented in religion. Every invented matter in religion is a religious innovation. Every religious innovation is an error and every error is in Hellfire.

فَـإِنَّ أَصْـدَقَ الحَـدِيثِ كَـلَامُ الله، وَخَيرَ الهَدي هَدْيُ مُحَمَّدٍ ﷺ، وَشَرَّ الأُمُـورِ مُحـدَثَاتُهَا، وَكُـلَّ مُحْدَثَـةٍ بِدعَـةً، وَكُـلَّ بِدعَـةٍ ضَـلَالَةٌ وَكُلَّ ضَلَالَةٍ فِي النَّارِ.

Coming to the point,

I tried, in this book, to introduce to our young students in a simple way the religious knowledge they need and present it to them in a manner that is easy enough for them to grasp, using the simplest methods and shortest statements.

In fact, I lived with such youth who are living in non-Islamic countries and felt their dire need for such an educational series. Therefore, I decided to compile and abridge some of this knowledge for such youth to benefit from it since they need it more than others.

I used the question-and-answer form in most of the subjects, since most of the curricula in the countries where they live depend on the dialogue style, which most likely takes the question-and-answer form.

I spent much time in dealing with such youth, whereby I came to know that caring for them is of great importance. This is because they are the future generation, the Ummah's glory makers and the founders of its history. There is no

أما بعد،

فَإِنَّنِي حَاوَلْتُ أَنْ أُبَسِّطَ لِلنَّشْءِ مِنْ طُلّابِنَا مَا يَحْتَاجُونَهُ مِنْ عُلُومِ دِينِهِمْ، وَأَعْرِضَ لَهُمْ مَا يُقَرِّبُهُمْ فَهُمَهَا مُسْتَخْدِمًا أَيْسَرَ الأَسَالِيبِ وَأَقْصَرَ العِبَارَاتِ.

وَإِنَّنِي عَاشَرْتُ مَعَ هَؤُلاءِ النَّشْءِ الَّذِينَ يَعِيشُونَ فِي بِلادٍ غَيْرِ إِسْلامِيَّةٍ وَعَرَفْتُ أَنَّهُمْ فِي أَمَسِّ الحَاجَةِ إِلَى مِثْلِ هَذِهِ السِّلْسِلَةِ؛ لِذَا كَانَ هَدَفِي مِنْ جَمْعِ هَذِهِ العُلُومِ وَاخْتِصَارِهَا؛ لِيَسْتَفِيدَ هَؤُلاءِ الَّذِينَ هُمْ أَشَدُّ احْتِيَاجًا مِنْ غَيْرِهِمْ.

وَقَدِ اسْتَعْمَلْتُ فِي مُعْظَمِ المَوْضُوعَاتِ أَسَالِيبَ الأَسْئِلَةِ وَالأَجْوِبَةِ؛ لِأَنَّ مُعْظَمَ المَنَاهِجِ فِي البُلْدَانِ الَّتِي يُقِيمُونَ فِيهَا تَعْتَمِدُ بِأُسْلُوبِ الحِوَارِ الَّذِي يَسُودُهُ غَالِبًا أُسْلُوبُ الأَسْئِلَةِ وَالأَجْوِبَةِ.

وَقَدْ أَوْلَيْتُ وَقْتًا لِمُعَامَلَةِ هَؤُلاءِ، وَعَلِمْتُ أَنَّ العِنَايَةَ بِهِمْ ذَاتُ أَهَمِّيَّةٍ عَظِيمَةٍ؛ لِأَنَّهُمْ جِيلُ المُسْتَقْبَلِ وَصَانِعُو مَجْدَ الأُمَّةِ وَبَانُو تَارِيخِهَا، وَلا غَرَابَةَ فِي ذَلِكَ إِذْ تَقَدُّمُ الأُمَمِ نَاشِئِهَا بِكُلِّ مَا لَدَيْهَا مِنْ إِمْكَانَاتٍ، وَهَذَا يَعْنِي بِنَاءَ

wonder then that we find nations preparing their youth for all possible capacities, for this simply means the construction of their civilization, the restoration of their history, the immortalization of their glory and the integrity and coherence of their societies.

Should those youth be neglected and deprived of an upbringing that is connected to the culture of their Ummah and education that qualifies them for the standard that they are hoped to reach, then the Ummah will never realize the sought-after progress and will never have its academic reality connected to the civilization and history of the past.

That is why nations raise their generations on glory, confidence, dignity, pride and a strong sense of belonging to their creed, history and civilization. If such principles are not deeply instilled in their hearts, the generation will not be preserved and nothing could be maintained.

For the sake of this, I present herein this upbringing-related

حَضَارَتِهَا وَتَرْمِيمِ تَارِيخِهَا وَتَخْلِيدَ مَجدِهَا وَتَآلُفَ مُجتَمَعِهَا وَتَمَاسُكَهُ.

فَإِنْ أُهْمِلَ هَؤُلَاءِ الشَّبَابُ وَلَمْ يَتَلَقَّوا تَرْبِيَةً تَرْتَبِطُ بِثَقَافَةِ أُمَّتِهِم وَتعليمًا يُؤَهِّلُهُم إِلَى تَطَلُّعِ المُسْتَوى المطلوبِ مِنْهُم؛ فَلن يَتَحَقَّقَ لِلأُمَّة مَا تَنْشده مِن رُقِيّ وَمَا تَصبُوا إِلَيه مِنَ ارْتِبَاطِ الوَاقِعِ العِلمِيِّ إِلَى تَارِيخ وَحَضَارةِ مَاضِيهَا.

لِذا تُنَشِّئُ الأُمَمُ أَجيَالَهَا عَلَى العِزَّةِ وَالثِّقَةِ وَالكَرَامَةِ وَالأَنفَةِ وَقُوةِ الانْتِمَاءِ إِلَى العَقِيدةِ وَالتَّارِيخ وَالحَضَارَةِ، فَإِذا لَمْ يُغْرَسْ كُلُّ ذَلِكَ فِي قُلُوبِهِم فَلن يُحْفَظَ الجِيلُ ولن يُحمَي شَيئًا.

وَهَا أَنَا أُقَدِّمُ لَهُم هَذِهِ السِّلْسِلَةَ

series in its first issue under the title *"Asaasiyyaat Fil Tarbiyah Al-Islaamiyyah- As'ilah wa Ajwibah"* (Basics of Islamic Upbringing - Questions and Answers). It was anciently said, «Questions are the keys to knowledge».

In this educational series, the beginner can find what he is looking for regardless of his age. It is also a reminder for those who have completed their study. Even Though we believe that knowledge has no end to stop at.

I find it necessary, in our current time when many Muslims are ignorant about their religion, to advise myself as well as my Muslim brothers and sisters to be primarily concerned with the Quran; the Book of Allah, and secondly to seek religious knowledge and apply it. They also have to be engrossed in taking action and providing sound Islamic upbringing, exerting their utmost effort and investing all their time in what serves the interest of Islam and its Da'wah.

Allah, The Almighty, Says (what means): [*And who is bet-*

التَّربَوِيَّــةِ فِــي إِصْــدَارِهَا الأَوَّلِ المُسَــمَّى «أَسَاسِــيَّاتٌ فِي التَّرْبِيَــةِ الإِسْلَامِيَّةِ ـ أَسْئِلَةٌ وَأَجْوِبَةٌ» وَقَــدْ قِيــلَ قَــدِيمًا: «الأَسْــئِلَةُ مَفَــاتِيحُ العِلمِ».

وَفِي هَذِهِ السِّلسِــلَةِ التَّربَوِيَّــةِ يَجِدُ الطَّالِــبُ المُبتَدِئُ مُبتَغَاهُ مَهْمَا كَانَ عُمــرُهُ، كَمَــا أَنَّهَــا تَــذكِيرٌ لِلطَّالِــبِ المُنتَهِــي، وَإِن كُنَّــا نَعتَقِــدُ أَنَّ طَلَبَ العِلمِ لَيسَ لَهُ نِهَايَة.

وَفِي هَذِهِ الفَترَةِ الحَرِجَةِ الَّتِي جَهِلَ فِيهَا كَثِيرٌ مِــنَ المُسلِمِينَ أُمُــورَ دِينِهِم أَرَى لِزَامًــا عَلَــيَّ أَنْ أَنصَحَ نَفسِي وَإِخوَانِي المُسلِمِينَ الاهتِمَامَ بِكِتَابِ اللهِ وَالعِنَايَةِ بِهِ أَوَّلًا: وَطَلَبَ العِلمِ الشَّــرعِيِّ وَالعَمَــلَ بِــهِ ثَانِيًا: وَالانحِــرَاطَ فِــي العَمَــلِ وَالتَّربِيَــةِ الإِسْــلَامِيَّةِ الصَّــحِيحَةِ، وَبَــذْلَ كُلَّ الجُهْدِ واستِغلَالِ كُلَّ الوَقتِ لِمَا فيهِ خِدمَةُ الإِسلَامِ وَالدَّعوَةُ إِلَيهِ.

﴿وَمَنْ أَحْسَنُ قَوْلًا مِّمَّن دَعَآ إِلَى ٱللَّهِ

ter in speech than one who invites to Allah and does righteousness and says, «Indeed, I am of the Muslims»] [Fussilat: 33]

This series contains eight branches of Sharee'ah knowledge. Of each I selected the most significant points. I hope I can accomplish the task in future issues by the Permission of Allah, The Almighty.

Issue content:

Part I:

1- Islamic creed ('Aqeedah) - Question and answer

2- Islamic manners and morals.

3- Prophetic supplications and invocations - Question and answer.

4- Prophetic Seerah - Question and answer.

5- Islamic Fiqh - Question and answer.

Part II:

6- Stories of the Prophets - Question and answer.

7- Men and women around the Messenger of Allah, sallallaahu 'alayhi wa sallam, - Question and answer.

8- Forty Hadeeths cited from

وَعَمِلَ صَالِحًا وَقَالَ إِنَّنِي مِنَ الْمُسْلِمِينَ ﴾ [فصلت: ٣٣]

وَتَحْتَوِي هَذِهِ السِّلْسِلَةَ عَلَى ثَمَانِيَةِ فُرُوعٍ مِنَ العِلْمِ الشَّرْعِيِّ، واخْتَرْتُ مِنْ كُلِّ قِسْمٍ مِنْهَا أَهَمَّهُ؛ آمِلًا أَنْ أُكْمِلَ المَسِيرَةَ فِي الإِصْدَارَاتِ القَادِمَةِ بِمَشِيئَةِ اللهِ تَعَالَى.

مَحْتَوَيَاتُ الإصْدَارِ:

الجزء الأول

١- العَقِيدَةُ الإِسْلَامِيَّة – سُؤَالٌ وَجَوَاب.

٢- آدَابٌ وأَخْلَاقٌ إِسْلَامِيَّة.

٣- أَدْعِيَةٌ وَأَذْكَارٌ نَبَوِيَّةٌ – سُؤَالٌ وَجَوَاب.

٤- السِّيرَةُ النَّبَوِيَّةُ – سُؤَالٌ وَجَوَاب.

٥- الفِقْهُ الإِسْلَامِيُّ – سُؤَالٌ وَجَوَاب.

الجزء الثاني:

٦- قَصَصُ الأَنْبِيَاء – سُؤَالٌ وَجَوَاب.

٧- رِجَالٌ وَنِسَاءٌ حَوْلَ الرَّسُولِ ﷺ – سُؤَالٌ وَجَوَاب.

٨- أَرْبَعُونَ حَدِيثًا مِنَ الصَّحِيحَيْنِ.

Al-Bukhaari and Muslim.
Finally, I shouldn't miss the opportunity to express my thanks and gratitude to all those who contributed to this effort and helped produce this issue. I would particularly mention, from among my venerated Shaykhs and honorable brothers who did me a favor by reviewing this issue, the honorable venerated Shaykh/ Yoosuf Aadam 'Adani, the honorable professor/ Fu'aad Basheer Dool, the noble brother/ 'Umar Muhammad Warasmah.

I implore Allah, The Almighty, Lord of the Mighty Throne to Accept our humble efforts with good acceptance, to Reward us for it by the good reward and to Forgive us for mistakes should there be any. Indeed, He Is over all things Competent.

'Abdullah Hassan Fareh
San'aa', the 7th of Sha'baan
1429 A.H. (9/8/2008 A.D.)

وَلَا يَفُوتُني أَنْ أَتَقَدَّمَ بِالشُّكْرِ وَالعِرفَانِ لِكُلِّ مَنْ سَاهَم وسَاعَدَني بِعَمَلِ هَذَا الإِصْدَارِ، وَأَخُصُّ بِالذِّكْرِ مِنْ مشَايِخِي وإِخْوَاني الأَفَاضِلِ الَّذِينَ تَفَضَّلُوا بِمُرَاجَعَةِ هَذَا الإِصْدَارِ، الشَّيخ الفَاضِلِ الوَالِدِ يُوسُف آدَم عَدَنِي، والأُسْتَاذِ الفَاضِلِ/ فُؤَاد بَشِير دول، والأخِ الفَاضِلِ/ عُمَر مُحَمَّد وَرَسَمَة.

أَسْأَلُ اللهَ العَظِيمَ، رَبَّ العَرشِ العَظِيمِ أَنْ يَتَقَبَّلَ مِنَّا جُهدَ المُقِلِّ بِقَبُولٍ حَسَنٍ، وَأَن يَأجُرَنَا عَلَيهِ بِالثَّوَابِ الحَسَنِ، وَأَن يَغفِرَ لَنَا مَا كَانَ فِيهِ مِن خَطَأٍ إنَّهُ عَلَى كُلِّ شَيءٍ قَدِيرٍ.

عَبد الله حَسَن فارح
صنعاء في 7 شعبان 1429هـ
المُوافِق: 2008/8/9م

العَقِيدَةِ الإسلامِيَّة
'Aqeedah (Islamic Creed)

'Aqeedah (Islamic Creed) Questions and Answers in Islamic Creed

1- What is 'Aqeedah?

Answer: It is the firm and doubtless belief in Allah, The Almighty, and in the Oneness of His Lordship, the Oneness of His Divinity and the Oneness of His Names and Attributes as is due to Him.

2- What are the three fundamental principles that a slave of Allah must know?

Answer: Knowing his Lord, his religion and his Prophet; Muhammad, sallallaahu 'alayhi wa sallam.

3- Who is your lord?

Answer: My Lord is Allah.

4- How did you come to know your Lord?

I knew Him by His Signs and Creatures.

5- Mention two of the Signs of Allah.

Answer: The night and day.

6- Mention two of the Creations of Allah.

Answer: The earth and the heaven.

7- What is your religion?

Answer: My religion is Islam.

العَقِيدَة الإسلاميَّة
أَسْئِلَةٌ وَأَجْوِبَةٌ
فِي العَقِيدَةِ الإسلاميَّةِ

1- مَا العَقِيدَةُ؟

الجواب: هِيَ الإيَمانُ الجَازِمُ الَّذِي لَا يَتَطَرَّقُ إِلَيهِ شَكٌّ لَدَى مُعتَقِدِهِ فِي الإيمَانِ بِاللهِ تعالى، وَمَا يَجِبُ لَهُ مِنَ التَّوحِيدِ بِرُبُوبِيَّتِهِ وَأُلُوهِيَّتِهِ وَأَسمَائِهِ وَصِفَاتِهِ.

2- مَا الأُصُولُ الثَّلاثَةُ الَّتِي يَجِبُ عَلَى العَبدِ مَعْرِفَتُهَا؟

الجواب: مَعرِفَةُ العَبدِ رَبَّهُ، وَدِينَهُ، وَنَبِيَّهُ مُحَمَّدًا ﷺ.

3- مَن رَبُّكَ؟

الجواب: رَبِّيَ اللهُ.

4- بِمَ عَرَفتَ رَبَّكَ؟

الجواب: بِآيَاتِهِ وَمَخلُوقَاتِهِ.

5- اذكُر آيَتَينِ مِن آيَاتِ اللهِ؟

الجواب: اللَّيلُ والنَّهَارُ.

6- اذكُر مَخلُوقَينِ مِن مَخلُوقَاتِ اللهِ؟

الجواب: السَّمَاءُ والأرضُ.

7- مَا دِينُكَ؟

الجواب: دِينِيَ الإسلامُ.

8- What is Islam?

Answer: It is to submit to Allah Alone through monotheism and full obedience and to disassociate oneself from polytheism and its people.

9- What are the pillars of Islam?

Answer: They are five pillars:

1- To testify that there is no deity except Allah and that Muhammad is the Messenger of Allah.

2- To establish prayers.

3- To pay Zakaah (the obligatory charity).

4- To fast the month of Ramadhaan.

5- To perform Hajj to the House of Allah for whoever is healthy enough and can afford to do so.

10- What are the (spiritual) levels of Islam?

Answer: They are three levels:
1- Al-Islaam.
2- Al-Eemaan (faith).
3- Al-Ihsaan.

11- What is Eemaan (faith)?

Answer: It means to believe by the heart, confess by the tongue, and act accordingly by the bodily organs.

8- ومَا الإسلام؟

الجَـــواب: هُـــوَ الاستِســلَامِ للهِ بِالتَّوحِيدِ وَالانقِيَــادُ لَــهُ بِالطَّاعَــةِ وَالبَرَاءَةُ مِنَ الشِّرْكِ وَأهلِهِ.

9- مَا أَرْكَانُه؟

الجواب: أَرْكَانُه خَمْسَة وَهِي:

1- شَــهَادَةِ أَنْ لاَ إِلــهَ إلاَّ اللهُ وَأَنَّ مُحَمَّدًا رَسُولُ اللهِ.

2- وَإِقام الصَّلاةِ.

3- وَإِيتَاءَ الزَّكاةِ.

4- صَوْمِ رَمَضَانَ.

5- حِجُّ البَيتِ مَنِ استَطَاع إِلَيهِ سَبِيلا.

10- ما مَرَاتِبُ الإسلام؟ وَمَا هِي؟

مَرَاتِبُ الإسلام ثَلَاثَةٌ وَهِيَ:

1- الإِسلامُ.
2- الإِيمَانُ.
3- الإِحسَانُ.

11- ما الإِيْمَانُ؟

الجواب: الإِيمَانُ: هَـوَ الاعتِقَــادُ بِالقَلْبِ، وَالقَـولُ بِاللِّسَـانِ وَالعَمَـلُ بِالجَوَارِح.

12- What are the pillars of Eemaan (faith) and how many are they?

Answer: They are six pillars:

1- To believe in Allah

2- To believe in the angles.

3- To believe in the Divinely revealed Books.

4- To believe in the Messengers.

5- To believe in the Last Day.

6- To believe in the Predestination good or bad.

13- Is one's level of faith stable?

Answer: No, one's level of faith is not stable. It increases by obedience and decreases by disobedience.

14- What is Ihsaan?

Answer: Ihsaan is to worship Allah as if you see Him, for if you cannot see Him, indeed He Sees you.

15- Are there any pillars of Ihsaan?

Answer: No, Ihsaan has no pillars, it is only as we mentioned.

16- What is the meaning of La Ilaaha Illa Allah (There is no deity except Allah)?

Answer: It means that none is truly worthy to be worshipped

12- مَا أَرْكَانُ الإِيمَانِ؟ وَمَا عَدَدُهَا؟

أَرْكَانُ الإِيمَانِ سِتَّةٌ وَهِيَ:

1- الإِيمَانُ بِاللهِ.

2- الإِيمَانُ بِالمَلَائِكَةِ.

3- الإِيمَانُ بِالكُتُبِ.

4- الإِيمَانُ بِالرُّسُلِ.

5- الإِيمَانُ بِاليَوْمِ الآخِرِ.

6- الإِيمَانُ بِالقَدَرِ خَيْرِهِ وَشَرِّهِ.

13- هَلْ لِلإِيمَانِ ثُبُوتٌ؟

الجواب: لَا، لَيْسَ لِلإِيمَانِ ثُبُوتٌ، لَكِنَّهُ يَزِيدُ بِالطَّاعَةِ وَيَنْقُصُ بِالمَعصِيَةِ.

14- مَا الإِحْسَانُ؟

الجواب: الإِحْسَانُ: أَنْ تَعبُدَ اللهَ كَأَنَّكَ تَرَاهُ، فَإِنْ لَمْ تَكُنْ تَرَاهُ فَإِنَّهُ يَرَاكَ.

15- هَلْ لِلإِحْسَانِ أَرْكَانٌ؟

الجواب: لا، لَيسَ لَهُ أَركَانٌ وَإِنَّمَا لَهُ رُكنٌ وَاحِدٌ وَهوَ كَمَا ذَكَرنَاه.

16- ما مَعْنَى لا إلَهَ إلا اللهُ؟

الجواب: مَعنَاهَا: لَا مَعبُودَ بِحقٍّ إلَّا الله.

except Allah.

17- What are the prerequisites of (la Ilaaha Ilaa Allah)?

Answer: They are seven prerequisites:

1- Certainty.

2- Love.

3- Truthfulness.

4- Sincerity.

5- Knowledge.

6- Submission.

7- Acceptance.

18-What are the pillars of the testimony of Tawheed (Monotheism)?

Answer: They are two pillars: negation and affirmation.

19- What is the greatest thing that Allah Commanded?

Answer: The greatest thing that Allah Commanded is Tawheed (Monotheism).

20- What is Tawheed?

Answer: It is to single out Allah, The Almighty, with the Lordship, Worship and Names and Attributes that are exclusive to Him.

21- How many are the divisions of Tawheed? What are they?

17- ما شُرُوطُ لا إِلَهَ إلا الله؟

الجواب: شُرُوطُها سِبْعَةٌ وَهِيَ:

1- اليَقِينُ.

2- المَحبَّةُ.

3- الصِّدقُ.

4- الإِخَلَاصُ.

5- العِلمُ.

6- الانقِيَادُ.

7- القَبُولُ.

18- ما أركَانُ كَلِمةِ التَّوحِيدِ؟

أَركَانُهَا اثنَانِ، وَهُمَا: النَّفيُ، وَالإِثبَاتُ.

19- مَا أعظَمُ مَا أَمَرَ اللهُ بِهِ؟

الجَواب: أعظَمُ مَا أمَرَ اللهُ بِهِ التَّوحِيدُ.

20- مَا التَّوحِيد؟

هُوَ إِفرَادُ اللهِ تعالى بِمَا يَختَصُّ بِه مِنَ الرُّبُوبِيَّةِ وَالأُلُوهِيَّةِ وَالأسمَاءِ وَالصِّفَاتِ.

21- كَم قِسمًا للتَّوحِيد؟ وَمَا هِيَ؟

Answer: Tawheed has three divisions:

1- Tawheed Ar-Ruboobiyyah (Oneness of Lordship).

2- Tawheed Al-Uloohiyyah (Oneness of Worship)

3- Tawheed Al-Asamaa' was-Sifaat (Oneness of The Names and Attributes of Allah).

22- What is Tawheed Ar-Ruboobiyyah, (Oneness of Lordship)?

Answer: It is to admit with certainty that the creation, the sovereignty and the administration of the creation are exclusive to Allah.

23- What is Tawheed Al-Uloohiyyah, (Oneness of Worship)?

Answer: It is to dedicate all kinds of worship exclusively to Allah.

24- What is Tawheed Al-Asmaa' was-Sifaat (Oneness of The Names and Attributes of Allah)?

Answer: It is to believe that the Names and Attributes of Allah are exclusive to Him alone.

25- What is the benefit of Tawheed?

الجَوَاب: لِلتَّوحِيدِ أَقسَامٌ ثَلَاثَةٌ وَهِيَ:

1- تَوحِيدُ الرُّبُوبِيَّةِ.

2- تَوحِيدُ الأُلُوهِيَّةِ.

3- تَوحِيدُ الأَسمَاءِ وَالصِّفَاتِ.

22- مَا تَوحِيدُ الرُّبُوبِيَّةِ؟

الجَوَاب: هُوَ إِفرَادُ اللهِ تَعَالَى بِالخَلقِ وَالمُلكِ وَالتَّدبِيرِ.

23- مَا تَوحِيدُ الأُلُوهِيَّةِ؟

الجَوَاب: هُوَ إِفرَادُ اللهِ تَعَالَى بِالعِبَادَةِ.

24- مَا تَوحِيدُ الأَسمَاءِ وَالصِّفَاتِ؟

الجَوَاب: هُوَ إِفرَادُ اللهِ تَعَالَى بِمَا لَهُ مِنَ الأَسمَاءِ وَالصِّفَاتِ.

25- مَا فَائِدَةُ التَّوحِيدِ؟

Answer: Its benefit is that it grants protection from an everlasting punishment in the Hereafter, provides guidance in the worldly life and causes the sins to be forgiven.

الجواب: فَائِدَتُهُ: هِيَ الأَمْنُ فِي الآخِرَةِ مِنَ العَذَابِ المُؤَبَّدِ، وَالهِدَايَةُ فِي الدُّنْيَا وَتكفِيرُ الذُّنُوب.

26- What is the gravest sin in the Sight of Allah, The Almighty?

26- مَا أَعْظَمُ الذُّنُوب عِندَ الله تَعَالَى؟

Answer: It is Shirk (to associate partners with Allah).

الجواب: الشِّركُ بِالله.

27- What does Shirk mean?

27- وَمَا الشِّركُ بِالله؟

Answer: It is to dedicate an act of worship to others other than Allah, The Almighty[1].

الجواب: الشِّركُ بِاللهِ هُوَ أَن تَجعَلَ إِحْدَى العِبَادَاتِ لِغَيرِ اللهِ تَعَالَى.

28- How many are the divisions of Shirk?

28- كَم قِسمًا لِلشِّركِ؟

Answer: There are two divisions of Shirk:
1- Major Shirk.
2- Minor Shirk.

الجواب: لِلشِّركِ قِسمَان:

1- الشِّركُ الأَكبَرُ.

2- الشِّركُ الأَصغَرُ.

29- What is the major Shirk? Give an example.

29- مَا الشِّركُ الأَكبَرُ؟ وَمَا مِثَالُهُ؟

Answer: It is to set an equal to Allah regarding something that is exclusive to Him, like supplicating to other than Allah and slaughtering in the name of other than Him.

الجواب: هُوَ تَسوِيَةُ غَيرِ الله بِالله فِيمَا هُوَ مِن خَصَائِصِ الله. كَالدُّعَاءِ بِغَيرِ اللهِ، وَالذَّبحِ لِغَيرِ الله.

30- What is the minor Shirk? Give an example?

30- مَا الشِّركُ الأَصغَرُ؟ وَمَا مِثَالُهُ؟

---

(1) Also it is to associate partners with Allah in your supplications, obedience, intentions, and your love for Him.

Answer: It is all that is described by the Quran and the Sunnah as an act of Shirk but it does not reach the degree of major Shirk. An example of it is swearing by other than Allah or saying, «Had it not been for Allah and so-and-so».

الجواب: هُوَ مَا وَرَدَ فِي الكِتَابِ وَالسُّنَّةِ بِأَنَّهُ شِركٌ وَلَم يَصِلْ إِلَى حَدِّ الشِّركِ الأَكبَرِ، مَثلَ الحَلفِ بِغَيرِ اللهِ، وَقَولِ: لَوْلَا اللهُ وَفُلَان.

31- Why Did Allah Send the Messengers?

31- لِمَ أَرسَلَ اللهُ الرُّسُلَ؟

Answer: Allah Sent the Messengers to call for worshipping Him and to forbid associating partners with Him.

الجواب: أَرسَلَ اللهُ رُسُلَهُ لِلدَّعوَةِ إِلَى عِبَادَتِهِ، وَنَفيَ الشِّركِ بِهِ.

32- What is the result of committing major Shirk?

32- مَا نَتِيجَةُ الشِّركِ الأَكبَرِ؟

Answer: It results in entering Hellfire and abiding therein.

الجواب: نَتِيجَتُهُ الدُّخُولُ فِي النَّارِ وَالإِقَامَةُ فِيهَا.

33- What is the benefit of Tawheed?

33- مَا فَائِدَةُ التَّوحِيدِ؟

Answer: Tawheed grants protection in the Hereafter from an everlasting punishment. It provides guidance in the worldly life and causes the sins to be forgiven.

الجواب: فَائِدَتُهُ هِيَ الأَمنُ فِي الآخِرَةِ مِنَ العَذَابِ المُؤَبَّدِ، وَالهِدَايَةُ فِي الدُّنيَا وَتكفِيرُ الذُّنُوبِ.

34- Is Allah Present with us by His Self or by His Knowledge?

34- هَلِ اللهُ مَعَنَا بِذَاتِهِ أَم بِعِلمِهَ؟

Answer: Allah Is Present with us by His Knowledge and He Hears and Sees us.

الجواب: اللهُ مَعَنَا بِعِلمِهِ يَسمَعُنَا وَيَرَانَا.

35- Where Is Allah?

35- أَينَ اللهُ؟

Answer: Allah Is above the 7 Heavens[1].

36- Why Did Allah Create us?

Answer: Allah Created us to affirm His Oneness and to worship Him Alone without ascribing partners to Him.

37- What is worship?

Answer: Worship means all the sayings and actions, apparent and hidden, which are loved and approved of by Allah.

38- What are the types of worship?

Answer: There are many types of worship including: supplication, fear, hope (for the Mercy of Allah), reliance on Allah, love (for Allah), awe, slaughtering (in the name of Allah), vowing and so many other types of worship that are valid under Sharee'ah.

39- How should we worship Allah?

Answer: We should worship Allah according to the way that Allah and His Messenger ordered us to follow.

40- What is the greatest right to be observed after that of Allah and His Messenger?

الجواب: اللهُ فِي السَّمَاءِ.

36- لِمَاذَا خَلَقَنَا اللهُ؟

الجواب: خَلَقَنَا اللهُ لِتَوحِيدِهِ وَعِبَادَتِهِ وَعَدَمِ الإِشْرَاكِ بِهِ شَيئًا.

37- مَا العِبَادَة؟

الجواب: العِبَادَةُ: هِيَ كُلُّ مَا يُحِبُّهُ اللهُ وَيَرضَاهُ مِنَ الأَقْوَالِ وَالأَفْعَالِ الظَّاهِرَةِ وَالبَاطِنَة.

38- مَا أَنوَاعُ العِبَادَة؟

الجواب: أَنوَاعُ العِبَادَةِ كَثِيرَةٌ مِنهَا: الدُّعَاءُ وَالخَوفُ وَالرَّجَاءُ وَالتَّوَكُّلُ، وَالرَّغْبَةُ وَالرَّهبَةُ وَالذَّبحُ وَالنَّذرُ، وَغَيرُ ذَلكَ مِنْ أَنوَاعِ العِبَادَاتِ المَشرُوعَة.

39- كَيفَ نَعبُدُ اللهَ؟

الجواب: كَمَا أَمَرَنَا اللهُ وَرَسُولُه.

40- مَا أَعظَمُ حَقٍّ بَعدَ اللهِ وَرَسُولِهِ؟

---

(1) Above His Throne in a manner befitting His Majesty.

Answer: It is the right of the parents.

41- What are the conditions of Allah accepting your deeds?

Answer:

1- Belief in Allah and His Oneness.

2- Sincerity: That is to worship Allah with neither Riyaa' (ostentation: showing off), nor Sum'ah (seeking fame).

3- Compliance with the guidance of the Messenger of Allah, sallallaahu 'alayhi wa sallam.

42- What is the meaning of Al-Walaa' and Al-Baraa'?

Answer: Al-Walaa' means loving Allah, His Messenger, his Companions and the monotheistic believers.

Al-Baraa' means hating anyone who opposes Allah, His Messenger, his Companions and the monotheistic believers.

43- Who are the allies of Ar-Rahmaan (The Most Merciful)?

Answer: They are the pious believers who hold fast to the Quran and the Sunnah.

44- Who are the allies of the devil?

الجَوَابُ: حَقُّ الوَالِدَيْنِ.

41- مَا شُرُوطُ قَبُولِ العَمَلِ؟

الجَوَابُ:

1- الإِيمَانُ بِاللهِ وَتَوحِيدِه.

2- الإِخْلاصُ: وَهُوَ العَمَلُ للهِ مِن غَيرِ رِيَاءٍ وَلَا سُمعَةٍ.

3- المُوَافَقَةُ لِمَا جَاءَ بِهِ الرَّسُولُ ﷺ.

42- مَا الوَلَاءُ وَالبَرَاءُ؟

الجَوَابُ: الوَلَاءُ: هُوَ حُبُّ اللهِ وَرَسُولِهِ وَصَحَابَتِهِ وَالمُؤمِنِينَ المُوَحِّدِينَ.

البَرَاءُ: هُوَ بُغضُ مَن خَالَفَ اللهَ وَرَسُولَهُ وَصَحَابَتَهُ وَالمُؤمِنِينَ المُوَحِّدِينَ.

43- مَن أَولِيَاءُ الرَّحمَنِ؟

الجَوَابُ: أَولِيَاءُ الرَّحمنِ هُمُ المُؤمِنُونَ المُتَّقُونَ المُتَمَسِّكُونَ بِالكِتَابِ وَالسُّنَّةِ.

43- مَن أَولِيَاءُ الشَّيطَان؟

Answer: They are those who disobey Ar-Rahmaan (The Most Merciful) and do not adhere to the Quran and the Sunnah.

45- What is hypocrisy?

Answer: It is to declare Islam while hiding disbelief.

46- How many are the divisions of hypocrisy?

Answer: There are two divisions of hypocrisy: belief-related hypocrisy and action-related hypocrisy.

47- What is the belief-related hypocrisy?

Answer: It is to declare Islam while hiding disbelief.

48- What is the action- related hypocrisy?

Answer: Falling in action-related hypocrisy constitutes a grave major sin and it may be committed by the believers. Lying and cheating are some forms of action-related hypocrisy.

49- What is the Taaghoot?

Answer: It is any entity through which a slave transgresses his limits (of slavery) by worshipping, following or obeying.

الجواب: هُمُ المُخَالِفُونَ لِلرَّحمَنِ، الَّذِينَ لَا يَلتَزِمُونَ بِالكِتَابِ وَالسُّنَّةِ.

45- مَا النِّفَاقُ؟

الجواب: هُوَ إِظهَارُ الإِسلَامِ وَإِبطَانُ الكُفرِ.

46- كَم قِسمًا لِلنِّفَاقِ؟

الجواب: لِلنِّفَاقِ قِسمَانِ هُمَا: النِّفَاقُ الاعتِقَادِيُّ وَالنِّفَاقُ العَمَلِيُّ.

47- مَا النِّفَاقُ الاعتِقَادِيُّ؟

الجواب: هُوَ إِظهَارُ الإِسلَامِ وَإِبطَانُ الكُفرِ.

48- وَمَا النِّفَاقُ العَمَلِيُّ؟

الجواب: هُوَ كَبِيرَةٌ مِنَ الكَبَائِرِ وَقَد يَصدُرُ مِنَ المُؤمِنِينَ مِثلَ الكَذِبِ وَالخِيَانَةِ.

49- مَا الطَّاغُوتُ؟

الجواب: الطَّاغُوتُ: هُوَ مَا تَجَاوَزَ بِهِ العَبدُ حَدَّهُ مِن مَعبُودٍ أَو مَتبُوعٍ أَو مُطَاعٍ.

50- From what Did Allah Create the angels?

Answer: Allah Created the angels from light.

51- From what Did Allah Create Aadam?

Answer: Allah Created Aadam from clay.

52- From what Did Allah Create the Jinn?

Answer: Allah Created the Jinn from fire.

53- Mention some of the names of the angels and the tasks assigned to them.

Answer:

1- Jibreel: He is entrusted with delivering the Revelation.
2- Meekaa'eel: He is entrusted with sending down rain.
3- Israafeel: He is entrusted with blowing the Horn.
4- The angel of death: He is entrusted with taking the souls.

54- How many heavens are there?

Answer: There are seven heavens.

55- How many layers of the earth are there?

Answer: There are seven layers

50- مِمَّ خَلَقَ اللهُ الْمَلَائِكَةَ؟

الجواب: خَلَقَ اللهُ الْمَلَائِكَةَ مِن نُورٍ.

51- مِمَّ خَلَقَ اللهُ آدَمَ؟

الجواب: خَلَقَ اللهُ آدَمَ مِن طِينٍ.

52- مِمَّ خَلَقَ اللهُ الْجِنَّ؟

الجواب: خَلَقَ اللهُ الْجِنَّ مِن نَارٍ.

53- أذكُرْ أَسْمَاءَ بَعْضِ الْمَلَائِكَةِ وَالأعمَالِ الْمُوكَلةِ إِلَيهِم؟

الجواب:

1- جِبْريلُ العَليْهِ: وَهُوَ مُكَلَّفٌ بِتَبْلِيغِ الوَحي.
2- ميكائيل العَليْهِ: وَهُوَ مُكَلَّفٌ بِإنزَالِ الْمَطَرِ.
3- إسرافيل العَليْهِ: وَهُوَ مُكَلَّفٌ بِالنَّفْخ فِي الصُّورِ.
4- ملك الموت العَليْهِ: وَهُوَ مُكَلَّفٌ بِقَبْضِ الأرْوَاح.

54- مَا عَدَدُ السَّمَاوَات؟

الجواب: عَدَدُ السَّمَاوَات سَبْع.

55- مَا عَدَدُ الأرَضِين؟

الجواب: عَدَدُ الأرَضِينَ سَبَع.

of the earth.

56- How many are the gates of Paradise?

Answer: They are eight gates.

57- How many are the gates of Hellfire?

Answer: They are seven gates.

58- Who is the first human created by Allah?

Answer: It is our father, Aadam.

59- What is the devil?

Answer: It is every Jinni or human who is far from good and close to evil.

60- How many are the sects of the Jews?

Answer: They are seventy-one sects.

61- How many are the sects of the Christians?

Answer: They are seventy-two sects.

62- How many are the sects of our Ummah?

Answer: They are seventy-three sects.

63- What is the saved sect?

Answer: The saved sect is the one that holds fast to the methodology of the Messenger of Allah, sallallaahu ‘alayhi wa

56- مَا عَدَدُ أَبْوَابِ الجَنَّةِ؟

الجواب: ثَمَانِيَةُ أَبْوَاب.

57- مَا عَدَدُ أَبْوَابِ النَّارِ؟

الجواب: سَبْعَةُ أَبْوَاب.

58- مَنْ أَوَّلُ إِنْسَانٍ خَلَقَهُ اللهُ؟

الجواب: أَبُونَا آدَمُ عَلَيْهِ السَّلَام.

59- مَا الشَّيْطَانُ؟

الجواب: كُلُّ مَا هُوَ بَعِيدٌ عَنِ الخَيْرِ قَرِيبٌ مِنَ الشَّرِّ، مِن جِنٍّ أَو إِنْسٍ.

60- كم فِرق اليَهود؟

الجواب: وَاحِد وَسَبْعُونَ فِرقَة.

61- كَم فِرقُ النَّصَارَى؟

الجواب: فِرقُ النَّصَارَى اثْنَانِ وَسَبْعُونَ فِرقَة.

62- كَم فِرقُ هَذِهِ الأُمَّةِ؟

الجواب: فِرقُ هَذِهِ الأُمَّةِ ثَلَاثٌ وَسَبْعُون فِرقَة.

63- ما الفِرقَةُ النَّاجِيَةَ؟

الجواب: الفِرقَةُ النَّاجِيَةُ، هِيَ المُتَمَسِّكَةُ بِمِنْهَاجِ الرَّسُولِ ﷺ وَصَحَابَتِهِ، وَهُوَ الكِتَابُ وَالسُّنَّة.

sallam, and his Companions, which is the Quran and the Sunnah.

64- What is the difference between the believer's and the disbeliever's perspective on the worldly life?

Answer: The believer regards the worldly life as a mean to please His Lord and do righteous deeds. Allah, The Almighty, Says (what means): [*O you who have believed, fear Allah and seek the means [of nearness] to Him and strive in His Cause that you may succeed*] [Al-Maa'idah: 35]

The disbeliever, however, lives to satisfy his physical and moral desires.

Allah, The Almighty, Says (what means): [*Indeed, Allah will admit those who have believed and done righteous deeds to gardens beneath which rivers flow but those who disbelieve enjoy themselves and eat as grazing livestock eat, and the Fire will be a residence for them*] [Muhammad: 12]

64- مَا الْفَرْقُ بَيْنَ نَظْرَةِ الْمُؤْمِنِ وَنَظْرَةِ الْكَافِرِ فِي الدُّنْيَا؟

الجَوَاب: نَظْرَةُ الْمُؤْمِنِ فِي الحَيَاةِ إِرْضَاءُ خَالِقِهِ وَمَعْبُودِهِ، وَوَسِيلَتُهُ الأَعْمَالُ الصَّالِحَة. قَالَ تَعَالَى: ﴿يَٰٓأَيُّهَا ٱلَّذِينَ ءَامَنُواْ ٱتَّقُواْ ٱللَّهَ وَٱبْتَغُوٓاْ إِلَيْهِ ٱلْوَسِيلَةَ وَجَٰهِدُواْ فِي سَبِيلِهِۦ لَعَلَّكُمْ تُفْلِحُونَ﴾ [المائدة: 35]

وَأَمَّا الكَافِرُ فَيَعِيشُ إِرْضَاءً لِرَغَبَاتِهِ الجَسَدِيَّةِ وَالنَّفْسِيَّةِ. قَالَ اللهُ تَعَالَى: ﴿إِنَّ ٱللَّهَ يُدْخِلُ ٱلَّذِينَ ءَامَنُواْ وَعَمِلُواْ ٱلصَّٰلِحَٰتِ جَنَّٰتٍ تَجْرِي مِن تَحْتِهَا ٱلْأَنْهَٰرُ وَٱلَّذِينَ كَفَرُواْ يَتَمَتَّعُونَ وَيَأْكُلُونَ كَمَا تَأْكُلُ ٱلْأَنْعَٰمُ وَٱلنَّارُ مَثْوًى لَّهُمْ﴾ [محمد: 12]

الأَخْلاق المَشْرُوعَةُ لِكُلّ مُسلِم

Morals Enjoined
by Sharee'ah
on Every Muslim

Morals enjoined by Sharee'ah on every Muslim

الأَخْلَاقُ المَشْرُوعَة لِكُلِّ مُسلِم

Some of these morals are:

مِن هَّذِه الأَخْلَاقِ:

1- Truthfulness

1- الصِّدقُ.

2- Honesty

2- الأَمَانَةُ.

3- Chastity

3- العَفَافُ.

4- Bashfulness

4- الحَيَاءُ.

5- Courage

5- الشَّجَاعَةُ.

6- Generosity

6- الكَرَمُ.

7- Loyalty

7- الوَفَاءُ.

8- Maintaining good relations with neighbors

8- حُسنُ الجِوَارِ.

9- Helping those in need according to one's capacity

9- مُسَاعَدَةُ ذَوِي الحَاجَاتِ حَسبَ المَقْدِرَة.

10- Abstinence from all that which Allah Prohibits.

10- التَّنزُهَ عَن كُلِّ مَا حَرَّمَ الله.

(Including the like of such morals that are enjoined by Sharee'ah with evidence from the Quran and the Sunnah).

وَغَيرَ ذَلِكَ مِنَ الأَخلَاقِ الَّتِي دَلَّ الكِتَابُ وَالسُّنَّةُ عَلَى مَشرُوعِيَّتِهَا.

Manners of Mounting:

آدَابُ الرُّكُوب:

1- If you want to mount anything, be it a car, a horse, a ship or a plane, you should say, «Bismillaah, Al-Hamdu Lillaah, Subhaan Al-Lathi Sakhkhara Lana Haatha Wa Ma Kunna Lahu Muqrineen, Wa Inna ila Rabbina Lamunqaliboon:

1- إِذَا أَرَدْتَ أَنْ تَركَبَ أَيَّ دَابَّةٍ كَالسَّيَّارَةِ أَوِ الحِصَانِ أَوِ السَّفِينَةِ أَوِ الطَّائِرَةِ تَقُولُ:

(In the Name of Allah, all praise be to Allah, Exalted Is

«بِسمِ اللهِ ، الحَمْدُ للهِ، سُبْحَانَ الَّذِي سَخَّرَ لَنَا هَذَا وَمَا كُنَّا لَهُ مُقْرِنِينَ،

He Who Has Subjected this to us, and we could not have [otherwise] subdued it, and indeed to Our Lord we shall return)».

2- Adhere to order, sit politely and do not crowd others.

3- Do not throw trash inside the vehicle.

4- Do not get out of the vehicle while it is still moving but you should wait until it completely stops.

5- Do not poke your head out the vehicle's window.

Manners of Eating:

1- You should say, «Bismillaah» (In the Name of Allah).

2- Eat with your right hand because the devil eats with his left hand.

3- Eat from that which is in front of you, and do not reach out to eat from what is in front of others.

4- Do not criticize the food you are served.

5- Wash your hands carefully before you eat.

6- Do not blow on the hot food.

7- If you forget to mention the Name of Allah at the beginning

وَإِنَّا إِلَى رَبِّنَا لَمُنقَلِبُونَ».

2- حَافِظْ عَلَى النِّظَامِ وَاجْلِسْ فِي أَدَبٍ، وَلَا تُزَاحِمْ أَحَدًا.

3- لَا تُلْقِ شَيْئًا مِنَ المُهمَلَاتِ دَاخِلَ السَّيَّارَةِ.

4- لَا تَنزِلْ مِنَ السَّيَّارَةِ أَثْنَاءَ سَيرِهَا، بَلِ انتَظِرْ حَتَّى تَتَوَقَّفَ تَمَامًا.

5- لَا تُخْرِجْ رَأَسَكَ مِنْ نَافِذَةِ السَّيَّارَةِ.

آدَابُ الطَّعَامِ:

1- تَقُولُ: «بِسْمِ الله».

2- كُلْ بِيَمِينِكَ؛ لِأَنَّ الشَّيطَانَ يَأكُلُ بِالشِّمَالِ.

3- كُلْ مما أَمَامَكَ وَمِمَّا يَلِيكَ، وَلَا تَتَعَدَّ مَا أَمَامَ غَيرِك.

4- لَا تَعِبْ مَا قُدِّمَ لَكَ مِنْ طَعَامٍ.

5- اغسِلْ يَدَكَ جَيِّدًا قَبْلَ أَن تَأكُلَ.

6- لَا تَنفُخْ فِي الطَّعَامِ السَّاخِنِ.

7- إِذَا نَسِيتَ أَن تَذكُرَ الله فِي أَولِ

of the meal you should say, «Bismillaahi Awwalahu wa Aakhirahu (In the Name of Allah at the beginning and at the end)» once you remember.

8- After eating you should say, «Al-Hamdu Lillaahi Al-Lathi At'amani Haatha wa Razaqaneeh Min Ghayri Hawlin Minni Wa La Quwwah (Praise be to Allah Who Fed me this and Provided me with it without neither power nor strength on my part)».

Manners of Gatherings:

1- Do not sit except with the righteous and good people.

2- Greet the attendees when you enter upon them with the greeting of Islam: «Assalaamu 'Alaykom wa Rahmatullaahi wa Barakaatuh (May Peace and Blessings of Allah be upon you)».

3- Sit in a quiet and peaceful manner and do not speak loudly.

4- Do not interrupt others' speech, but listen to them carefully and attentively.

5- At the end of the gathering, you should say, «Subhaanak Allaahumma Wa Bihamdik, Ash-hadu Alla ilaaha illa Ant,

الطَّعَـامِ فَقُـلْ: «بِسْــمِ اللهِ أوَّلَــهُ وَآخِرَهُ».

8- قُلْ بَعْدَ الِانْتِهَاءِ مِنَ الطَّعَامِ: «الْحَمْدُ للهِ الَّذِي أَطْعَمَنِي هَـذَا وَرَزَقَنِيهِ مِن غَيْرِ حَوْلٍ مِنِّي وَلَا قُوَّةٍ».

آداب المجلس:

1- لَا تُجَالِسْ إِلَّا الصَّالِحِينَ وَأَهْلَ الخَيْرِ.

2- حَيِّ أَهْلَ المَجْلِسِ عِندَ دُخُولِكَ عَلَيْهِم بِتَحِيَّةِ الإِسْلَامِ: «السَّلَامُ عَلَيْكُم وَرَحْمَةُ اللهِ وَبَرَكَاتُه».

3- اجْلِسْ بِهُدُوءٍ وَسَكِينَةٍ وَلَا تَتَكَلَّمْ بِصَوتٍ عَالٍ.

4- لَا تَقطَعْ كَلَامًا مِن أَحَدٍ، بَلِ استَمِعْ لَهُ بِإِنصَاتٍ وَاهتِمَامٍ.

5- عِنـدَ خِتَـامِ المَجْـلِسِ قُـلْ: «سُبْحَانَكَ اللَّهُمَّ وَبِحَمْدِكَ، أَشْهَدُ أَن لَا إِلَـهَ إِلَّا أَنـتَ، أَستَغْفِرُكَ وَأَتُوبُ

Astaghfiruka Wa Atoobu ilayk (Exalted and Praised Be Allah, I testify that there is none worthy of worship except You, I seek Your Forgiveness and turn to You in repentance)».

Manners of Asking Permission:

1- Do not enter others' homes except after asking permission.

2- Knock on the door gently for no more than three times.

3- If you are asked who you are don't say, «It's me», but mention your name.

4- If you are granted permission to enter, then start by the greeting of peace[1] and lower your gaze upon entering.

5- Do not enter your parents' room (uninvited) at these times: before the Fajr Prayer, at noon and after the 'Ishaa' Prayer.

Manners of the Student in the Classroom:

Among the beautiful characteristics of the Muslim student are the following:

1- Going to bed early in order

إِلَيْكَ».

آدابُ الاستئذانِ:

1- لَا تَدخُلْ عَلَى البُيُوتِ حَتَّى تَستَأْذِنَ.

2- اطْرِقِ البَابَ بِرِفقٍ وَلَا تَزِدْ عَن ثَلَاثِ طَرَقَاتٍ.

3- إِذَا سُئِلتَ: مَنِ الطَّارِقُ؟ لَا تَقُلْ: أَنَا، لَكِن قُل بِاسْمِكَ.

4- إِذَا أَذِنَ لَكَ بِالدُّخُولِ، فَابْدَأْ بِالسَّلَامِ مَعَ غَضِّ البَصَرِ.

5- لَا تَدخُلْ غُرْفَةَ وَالِدَيْكَ قَبْلَ: صَلَاةِ الفَجرِ – ووَقتَ الظَّهِيرَةِ – وَبَعدَ العِشَاءِ.

آدابُ الطَّالِبِ فِي الفَصْلِ:

مِنَ الصِّفَاتِ الجَمِيلَةِ الَّتِي يَتَحَلَّى بِهَا الطَّالِبُ المُسْلِمُ مَا يَلِي:

1- أَنْ يَنَامَ مُبَكِّرًا؛ لِيَقُومَ لِصَلَاةِ

---

(1) You can say before entering «Bismillaahi walajna, wa bismillaahi kharajna, wa' ala Allahi Rabbana tawakkalna» With the name of Allah we enter, with the name of Allah we leave, and upon Our Lord we relayed.

to wake up for the Fajr Prayer.

2- Maintaining a good appearance and taking care of his hygiene.

3- On entering the classroom, he should greet the attendees with the greeting of Islam: Assalaamu 'Alaykom Wa Rahmatullaahi Wa Barakaatuh.

4- Being polite and humble with his classmates, he must never harm them or shout at them.

5- He should neither laugh without a reason, speak so much nor look here and there, rather, he should look at his teacher and listen to him attentively.

6- He should not speak without permission.

7- He should not throw trash on the floor, but should always keep the classroom clean.

8- If anyone hurts him, he should not retort and hurt him back, but he should address the offender saying, «Saamahaka Allaahu Wa Ghafara Lak (May Allah Pardon and Forgive you)».

9- If anyone does him a favor, he should say to him, «Jazaaka

الفَجْرِ.

2- أَنْ يَحْرِصَ عَلَى جَمَالِ مَظْهَرِهِ وَنَظَافَةِ جِسْمِهِ.

3- إِذَا دَخَلَ الفَصْلَ يُحَيِّي الحَاضِرِينَ بِتَحِيَّةِ الإِسْلَامِ: «السَّلَامُ عَلَيْكُم وَرَحمَةُ اللهِ وَبَرَكَاتُه».

4- أَنْ يَتَأَدَّبَ مَعَ زُمَلَائِهِ، وَيَتَوَاضَعَ لَهُم وَلَا يُؤْذِيَهُم، وَلَا يَرْفَعَ صَوتَهُ عَلَيهِم.

5- لَا يَضحَكُ فِي الفَصْلِ بِدُونِ سَبَبٍ، وَلَا يُكْثِرُ الكَلَامَ وَلَا يَلْتَفِتُ، بَل يُقْبِلُ عَلَى مُعَلِّمِهِ مُصغِيًا إِلَيهِ.

6- لَا يَتَكَلَّمُ بِدُونِ إِذْنٍ.

7- لَا يُلْقِي الفَضَلَاتِ عَلَى الأَرْضِ، بَل يَحْرِصُ دَائِمًا عَلَى نَظَافَةِ الفَصْلِ.

8- إِذَا أَسَاءَ إِلَيهِ أَحَدٌ لَا يَرُدُّ الإِسَاءَةَ بِمِثْلِهَا بَلْ يَقُولُ: «سَامَحَكَ اللهُ وَغَفَرَ لَكَ».

9- إِذَا قَدَّمَ إِلَيهِ أَحَدٌ مَعرُوفًا فَليَقُلْ لَهُ: «جَزَاكَ اللهُ خَيرًا».

Allaahu Khayran (May Allah Reward you best)».

10- He always respects his teachers.

Manners of Greeting:

There are many manners pertaining to greeting, of which we mention the following:

1- Greeting others with peace before initiating any speech is an act of Sunnah for the Muslim and its wording is: Assalaamu 'Alaykom. It is obligatory for the Muslim to answer back the greeting of peace.

2- When the Muslim is greeted, he has to answer the greeting back with one equal to or better than it.

3- The young should greet the old, the mounting should greet the walking, the walking should greet the sitting and the many should greet the few.

4- It is recommended to raise one's voice with the greeting of peace. He should, however, lower his voice if the greeted person is asleep.

Manners of Answering the Call of Nature:

If the Muslim wants to answer

10- يَحْرِصُ دَائِمًا عَلَى احْتِرَامِ مُعَلِّمِيه.

آدَابُ السَّلَامِ:

آدَابُ السَّلَامِ كَثِيرَةٌ نَذكُرُ مِنهَا:

1- السَّلَامُ سُنَّةُ المُسْلِمِ قَبْلَ الشُّرُوعِ بِأَيِّ كَلَامٍ آخَرَ، وَصِيغَتُهَا: السَّلَامُ عَلَيْكُمْ، وَرَدُّهَا وَاجِبٌ.

2- إِذَا سَلَّمَ عَلى المُسْلِمِ أَحَدٌ فَلْيَرُدَّ بِمِثْلِهِ أَوْ بِأَفْضَلَ مِمَّا سُلِّمَ عَلَيهِ.

3- يُسَلِّمُ الصَّغِيرُ عَلَى الكَبِيرِ، وَالرَّاكِبُ عَلَى المَاشِي، وَالمَاشِي عَلَى القَاعِدِ، وَالقَلِيلُ عَلَى الكَثِيرِ.

4- يُستَحَبُّ رَفعُ الصَّوتِ بِالسَّلَامِ، فَإِنْ كَانَ المُسَلَّمُ عَلَيهِ نَائِمًا فَلْيَخْفِضْ صَوْتَهُ.

آدَابُ قَضَاءِ الحَاجَةِ:

إِذَا أَرَادَ المُسْلِمُ قَضَاءَ حَاجَتِه فَعَلَيْه

the call of nature, he has to follow the following steps:

1- Before entering the toilet, the Muslim has to check if there is a Mus-haf, or anything that has verses of the Quran or Hadeeths written on it inside his pockets. If there is any, he has to leave it outside the toilet.

2- As he enters, he should mention the Name of Allah and say, «Allaahumma Inni A'oothu Bika Min Al-Khubuthi Wal Khabaa'ith (O Allah, I seek refuge with You from the male and female devils)».

3- He enters with his left leg and closes the door firmly.

4- He should not speak while answering the call of nature.

5- He should make Istinjaa' [1] using his left hand.

6- After finishing, he should wash his hands carefully with water and soap.

7- He gets out with his right leg and says, «Ghufraanak (I seek Your Forgiveness)».

Manners of Dealings:

1- The dealing should be initiated with the greeting of peace before discussing

أَنْ يَتَّبِعَ الْخُطُواتِ التَّالِيَةِ:

1- قَبْلَ أَنْ يَشْرَعَ فِي دُخُولِ الخَلَاءِ فَلْيُفَتِّشْ جُيُوبَهُ، إِنْ كَانَ فِيهَا مُصْحَفٌ أَوْ مَا هُوَ مَكْتُوبٌ فِيهِ القُرآنُ أَو الأَحَادِيثِ فَلْيَضَعْهُ خَارِجَ الخَلَاءِ.

2- يُسَمِّ اللهَ وَيَقُولُ: «اللَّهُمَّ إِنِّي أَعُوذُ بِكَ مِنَ الْخُبثِ والخَبَائِثِ».

3- ثُمَّ يُقَدِّمُ قَدَمَهُ اليُسْرَى عِنْدَ الدُّخُولِ وَيُغْلِقُ البَابَ جَيِّدًا.

4- لَا يَتَكَلَّمْ أَثْنَاءَ قَضَاءِ حَاجَتِهِ.

5- يَسْتَنْجِي بِيَدِهِ اليُسْرَى.

6- يَغْسِلُ يَدَه بِالمَاءِ وَالصَّابُونِ بَعْدَ الفَرَاغِ.

7- يُقَدِّم قَدَمَهُ اليُمْنَى عِنْدَ الخُرُوجِ وَيَقُولُ: «غُفْرَانَكَ».

آدَابُ المُعَامَلَةِ:

1- المُعَامَلَةُ تَبْدَأُ بِالسَّلَامِ قَبْلَ التَّطَرُّقِ لِأَيِّ شَيْءٍ آخَر.

---

(1) Cleansing oneself from urine or feces with water.

anything.

2- The Muslim should be cheerful and smiling as the dealing goes on.

3- He should adhere to truthfulness and avoid lying.

4- He should address people using the best names and avoid the titles that his addressee dislikes.

5- He should use the nicest words and statements.

6- He should avoid talking so much and abstain from useless speech and arguing. Moreover, he should hold off from uttering insults and curses.

7- He should abstain from talking about that which does not concern him and never say that which negatively affects his integrity.

2- فِي أَثْنَاءِ الْمُعَامَلَةِ يَنْبَغِي عَلَى الْمُسْلِمِ أَنْ يَكُونَ طَلِيقَ الْوَجْهِ مُبْتَسِمًا.

3- أَنْ يَكُونَ مُتَحَرِّيًا لِلصِّدْقِ ومُتَجَنِّبًا لِلكَذِبِ.

4- أَنْ يُخْتَارَ أَحَبَّ الأسْمَاءِ وَأَنْ يَبْتَعِدَ عَنِ الْأَلْقَابِ الْمَكروهةِ لَدَى الْمُخَاطَبِ.

5- أَنْ يَسْتَخْدِمَ أَطْيَبَ الْأَلْفَاظِ وَالعِبَارَاتِ.

6- أَنْ لَا يُكْثِرَ الْكَلَامَ وَأَنْ يَبْتَعِدَ عَنِ اللَّغوِ وَالجِدَالِ، وَأَنْ يُنَزِّهَ لِسَانَه عَنِ الشَّتْمِ وَالسِّبَابِ.

7- أَنْ لَا يَتَكَلَّم بِمَا لَا يَعنِيهِ، وَأَنْ لَا يَتَحَدَّث بِمَا يُخِلُّ بِالمُرُوءَةِ عُمُومًا.

* * *

فَضْلُ الذِّكر

Virtue of Thikr
(Remembrance of Allah)

Virtue of Thikr (Remembrance of Allah)

فَضْلُ الذِكر

Allah, The Almighty, Says (what means): [*Therefore remember Me; I Will Remember you, and be grateful to Me and never be ungrateful to Me*] [Al-Baqarah: 152]

قَالَ تَعَالَى: ﴿فَاذْكُرُونِي أَذْكُرْكُمْ وَاشْكُرُوا لِي وَلَا تَكْفُرُونِ﴾

[البقرة: 152].

- [*O you who believe! Remember Allah with much remembrance*] [Al-Ahzaab: 41]

قَالَ تَعَالَى: ﴿يَا أَيُّهَا الَّذِينَ آمَنُوا اذْكُرُوا اللهَ ذِكْرًا كَثِيرًا﴾

[الأحزاب: 41].

-[*Indeed, the Muslim men and Muslim women, the believing men and believing women, the obedient men and obedient women, the truthful men and truthful women, the patient men and patient women, the humble men and humble women, the charitable men and charitable women, the fasting men and fasting women, the men who guard their private parts and the*

وَقَالَ تَعَالَى: ﴿إِنَّ الْمُسْلِمِينَ وَالْمُسْلِمَاتِ وَالْمُؤْمِنِينَ وَالْمُؤْمِنَاتِ وَالْقَانِتِينَ وَالْقَانِتَاتِ وَالصَّادِقِينَ وَالصَّادِقَاتِ وَالصَّابِرِينَ وَالصَّابِرَاتِ

women who do so, and the men who remember Allah often and the women who do so – for them Allah has prepared forgiveness and a great reward.] [Al-Ahzaab: 35]

[الأحزاب: 35].

وَقَالَ ﷺ: «أَلَا أُنَبِّئُكُم بِخَيْرِ أَعْمَالِكُم، وَأَزْكَاهَا عِنْدَ مَلِيكِكُم، وَأَرْفَعِهَا فِي دَرَجَاتِكُم، وَخَيْرٍ لَكُمْ مِنْ إِنْفَاقِ الذَّهَبِ وَالفِضَّةِ، وَخَيْرٍ لَكُمْ مِنْ أَنْ تَلْقَوْا عَدُوَّكُم، فَتَضْرِبُوا أَعْنَاقَهُم، وَيَضْرِبُوا أَعْنَاقَكُم؟» قَالُوا: بَلَى، قَالَ: «ذِكْرُ اللهِ تَعَالَى».

The Prophet, sallallaahu 'alayhi wa sallam, said: "'Shall I not inform you about the best of your deeds, the purest in the Sight of your Lord, that raise your ranks most and that is better for you than spending gold and silver (in The Cause of Allah) and better for you than meeting your enemy, striking their necks and them striking your necks?' They said, 'Certainly (inform us).' He said, 'It is the Remembrance of Allah, The Almighty.'"

وَقَالَ ﷺ: «مَا جَلَسَ قَوْمٌ مَجْلِسًا لم يَذْكُرُوا اللهَ تَعَالَى فِيهِ وَلَمْ يُصَلُّوا عَلَى نَبِيِّهِم فِيهِ إِلاَّ كَانَ عَلَيْهِمْ تِرَةً، فَإِنْ شَاءَ عَذَّبَهُم، وَإِنْ شَاءَ غَفَرَ لَهُمْ».

The Prophet, sallallaahu 'alayhi wa sallam, also said: "No people sit in a gathering in which they do not remember Allah or send blessings upon their Prophet, but they will regret it; if He wills, He will punish them and if He wills He will forgive them."

وَقَالَ ﷺ: «مَا مِنْ قَوْمٍ يَقُومُونَ مِنْ مَجْلِسٍ لا يَذْكُرُونَ اللهَ تَعَالَى فِيهِ إلا قَامُوا عَنْ مِثْلِ جِيفَةِ حِمَارٍ وَكَانَ لَهُمْ حَسْرَةً».

And said: "There is no people who sit in a gathering in which they fail to remember Allah except that they will leave it as if it had a foul odor as that of a rotten carcass of a donkey and it will be a cause of regret for them".

1- What do you say when you wake up?

Answer: I say: "Al-Hamdu lillaahi Al-Lathi Ahyaana Ba'da Ma Amaatana wa ilayhi An-Nushoor
(Praise be to Allah Who Brings us to life after He Has Caused us to die, and to Him is the Resurrection)."

2- What do you say when you put on a garment?

Answer: I say: "Al-Hamdu Lillaahi Al-Lathi Kasaani Haatha Ath-Thawb wa Razaqaneeh Min Ghayri Hawlin Minni wala Quwwah (Praise be to Allah Who Clothed me with this garment and Provided me with it without neither power nor strength on my part)."

3- What do you say when you put on a new garment?

Answer: I say: «Allaahumma Laka Al-Hamdu Anta Kasawtaneeh, As'aluka min Khayrihi wa Khayri ma Suni'a lah, Wa A'oothu Bika Min Sharrihi wa Sharri Ma Suni'a lah

١- مَاذَا تَقُولُ عِندَ الاسْتِيقَاظِ مِنَ النَّوْمِ؟

الجواب: الحمْدُ لِلهِ الَّذِي أَحْيَانَا بَعدَ مَا أَمَاتَنَا وَإِلَيْهِ النُّشُورُ.

٢- مَاذَا تَقُولُ عِندَمَا تَلبَسُ الثَّوبَ؟

الجواب: الحَمدُ لله الَّذِي كَسَانِي هَذَا الثَّوبَ وَرَزَقْنِيهِ مِنْ غيْرِ حَوْلٍ مِنِّي وَلا قُوّةٍ.

٣- مَاذَا تَقُولُ عِندَمَا تَلبَسُ الثَّوبَ الجَدِيدَ؟

الجواب: اللَّهُمَّ لكَ الحَمْدُ أَنْتَ كَسَوْتَنِيهِ، أَسْأَلُكَ خَيْرَهُ وَخَيْرَ مَا صُنِعَ لَهُ، وأَعُوذُ بِكَ مِنْ شَرِّهِ وشَرِّ مَا صُنِعَ لَهُ.

(Praise be to You O Allah. You Clothed me with it. I ask You for the good of it and the good for which it was made, and I seek refuge with You from the evil of it and the evil for which it was made)}».

4- What do you say when you see someone wearing a new garment?

Answer: I say: «Ilbas Jadeedan wa 'Ish Hameedan wa Mut Shaheedan (May you wear new (clothes), live commendably and die as a martyr)»

5- What do you say when you put off your clothes?

Answer: I say: «Bismillaah (In the Name of Allah)».

6- What do you say on entering the toilet?

Answer: I say: «Bismillaah, Allaahumma inni A'oothu Bika minal Khubuthi wal Khabaa'ith (In the Name of Allah. O Allah, I take refuge with You from the male and female devils)».

7- What do you say on leaving the toilet?

Answer: I say: «Ghufraanak (I seek Your Forgiveness)».

٤- مَاذَا تَقُولُ حِينَمَا تَرَى مِن يَلْبَسُ ثَوْبًا جَدِيدًا؟

الجواب: البَسْ جَدِيدًا وَعِشْ حَمِيدًا وَمُتْ شَهِيدًا.

٥- مَاذَا تَقُولُ إِذَا أَرَدْتَ أَن تَضَعَ ثِيَابَكَ؟

الجواب: بِسْمِ اللهِ.

٦- مَاذَا تَقُولُ عِندَ دُخُولِ الحَمَّامِ؟

الجواب: بِسْمِ اللهِ، اللهُمَّ إِنِّي أَعُوذُ بِكَ مِنَ الخُبْثِ وَالخَبَائِثِ.

٧- مَاذَا تَقُولُ عِندَ الخُرُوجِ مِنَ الحَمَّامِ؟

الجواب: غُفْرَانَكَ.

8- What do you say before Wudhoo'?

Answer: I say: «Bismillaah (In the Name of Allah)».

٨- مَاذَا تَقُولُ قَبْلَ الوُضُوءِ؟

الجواب: بِسْمِ اللهِ.

9- What do you say after finishing Wudhoo'?

Answer: I say: «Ash-hadu allaa ilaaha illa Allah, Wahdahu la Shareeka lah, wa Ash-hadu anna Muhammadan 'Abduhu wa Rasooluh (I testify that there is no deity but Allah Alone; He Has no partner and I testify that Muhammad is His Slave and Messenger)».

٩- مَاذَا تَقُولُ بَعْدَ الفَرَاغِ مِنَ الوُضُوءِ؟

الجواب: أَشْهَدُ أَنْ لا إِلَـهَ إِلاَّ اللهُ وحْـدَهُ لا شَـرِيكَ لَـهُ، وأَشْـهَدُ أَنَّ مُحَمَّدًا عَبْدُهُ وَرسُولُهُ.

10- What do you say when leaving your home?

Answer: I say: «Bismillaahi Tawakkaltu 'Ala Allah, La Hawla wa la Quwwata Illa Billaah (In the Name of Allah,
I place my trust in Allah, and there is no might nor power except with Allah)».

١٠- مَاذَا تَقُولُ عَنْدَ الخُرُوجِ مِنَ المَنْزِلِ؟

الجواب: بِسْمِ اللهِ توكَّلْتُ عَلَى اللهِ، ولا حوْلَ ولا قُوةَ إِلاَّ بِاللهِ.

11- What do you say when entering your home?

Answer: I say: «Bismillaahi walajna, wa Bismillaahi Kharajna, wa 'Ala Rabbina Tawakkalna (In the Name of Allah we enter and in the Name of Allah we leave and

١١- مَاذَا تَقُولُ عَنْدَ دُخُولِ المَنْزِلِ؟

الجواب: بِسْمِ اللهِ وَلَجْنَا وبِسْمِ اللهِ خَرَجْنَا وَعَلَى رَبِّنَا تَوَكَّلْنَا.

upon our Lord we rely)».

12- What do you say when entering the Masjid?

Answer: I say: «Bismillaah was Salaatu was Salaamu 'Ala Rasoolillaah, Allaahumma Iftah li Abwaaba Rahmatik (In the Name of Allah, and peace and blessings be upon the Messenger of Allah. O Allah, Open the Gates of Your Mercy for me)».

13- What do you say on leaving the Masjid?

Answer: I say: «Bismillaah, was Salaatu was Salaamu 'Ala Rasoolillaah. Allaahumma inni as'aluka min Fadhlik. Allaahumma i'simni min Ash-Shaytaan Ar-Rajeem (In The Name of Allah, and peace and blessings be upon the Messenger of Allah. O Allah, I ask You from Your Bounty. O Allah, Protect me from the accursed devil)».

14- What is the Du'aa of Istiftaah (starting the prayer)?

Answer: It is to say: «Subhaanak Allaahumma wa Bihamdik, wa Tabaaraka

١٢- مَاذَا تَقُولُ عَنْدَ دُخُولِ المسجد؟

الجَوَاب: بِسْمِ اللهِ، وَالصَّلَاةُ وَالسَّلَامُ عَلَى رَسُولِ اللهِ، اللَّـهُمَّ افتَحْ لِي أَبوَابَ رَحَمتِكَ.

١٣- مَاذَا تَقُولُ عَنْدَ الخُرُوجِ مِنَ المَسجِدِ؟

الجَـوَاب: بِسْمِ اللهِ، وَالصَّـلَاةُ وَالسَّلَامُ عَلَى رَسُولِ اللهِ، اللَّـهُمَّ إِنِّي أَسْأَلُكَ مِن فَضلِكَ، اللَّـهُمَّ اعصِمنِي مِن الشَّيطَانِ الرَّجِيمِ.

١٤- مَا هُو دُعَاءُ الاستِفتَاح؟

الجَوَاب: سُبْحَانَكَ اللَّهُمَّ رَبَّنَا وَبِحَمْدِكَ وَتَبَارَكَ اسمُكَ وَتَعَالَى

Ismuka wa Ta'aala Jadduka wa la Ilaaha Ghayruk (Exalted and Praised Is You, O Allah. Blessed Is Your Name and lofty Is Your Might, and none has the right to be worshipped except You)».

15- What is the Du'aa' to be said during bowing?

Answer: It is: «Subhaana Rabbiya Al-'Atheem (Exalted Is my Lord, The Most Great)».

16- What is the Du'aa' to be said when rising from bowing?

Answer: It is: «Sami'a Allaahu Liman Hamidah, Rabbana wa laka Al-Hamdu Hamdan Katheeran Tayyiban Mubaarakan Feeh (Allah Listens to him who praises Him. Our Lord, all praise be to You, an abundant good and blessed praise)».

17- What is the Du'aa' to be said in prostration?

Answer: It is: «Subhaana Rabbiya Al-A'la (Exalted Is my Lord, The Most High)».

18- What is the Du'aa' to be said between the two

جَدُّكَ ولَا إِلَهَ غَيْرُكَ.

15- مَا دُعَاءُ الرُّكُوعِ؟

الجواب: سُبْحَانَ رَبِّيَ العَظِيم.

16- مَا دُعَاءُ الرَّفعِ مِنَ الرُّكُوعِ؟

الجواب: سَمِعَ اللهُ لِمَن حَمِدَه، رَبَّنَا وَلَكَ الحَمـدُ، حَمـدًا كَثِيـرًا طَيِّبًـا مُبَارَكًا فِيه.

17- مَا دُعَاءُ السُّجُودِ؟

الجواب: سُبْحَانَ رَبِّيَ الأَعْلَى.

18- مَا دُعَاءُ الجَلسةِ بَينَ السَّجدَتَينِ؟

prostrations?

Answer: It is: «Rabbi Ighfir li, Rabbi ighfir li (O my Lord, Forgive me, O my Lord, Forgive me)».

19- What do you say in the prostration due to the recitation of the Quran?

Answer: I say: "Sajada Wajhi Lillathi Khalaqahu Fa Ahsana Khalqahu, Wa Shaqqa Sam'ahu wa Basarah Bihawlihi wa Quwwatih, Fatabaarak Allaahu Ahsan Al-Khaaliqeen (My face fell in prostration to Him Who Created it and Brought forth its faculties of hearing and seeing by His Might and Power. So Blessed Is Allah, The Best of Creators).

20- What do you say in Tashahhud?

Answer: I say: «At-Tahiyyaatu Lillaahi was Salawaatu wat Tayyibaat, As-Salaamu 'alayka Ayyuha An-Nabiyyu wa Rahmatullaahi wa Barakaatuh, As-Salaamu 'alayna wa 'ala 'Ibaadillaahi As-Saaliheen, Ash-hadu Allaa Ilaaha Illa Allaahu wa Ash-hadu Anna

الجواب: رَبِّ اغْفِرْ لِي، رَبِّ اغْفِرْ لِي.

19- مَاذَا تَقُولُ فِي سُجُودِ التِّلاوَةِ؟

الجواب: سَجَدَ وَجْهِي لِلَّذِي خَلَقَهُ وَشَقَّ سَمْعَهُ وَبَصَرَهُ بِحَوْلِهِ وَقُوَّتِهِ فَتَبَارَكَ اللهُ أَحْسَنُ الخَالِقِينَ.

20- مَاذَا تَقُولُ فِي التَّشَهُّدِ؟

الجواب: التَّحِيَّاتُ لِلهِ وَالصَّلَوَاتُ وَالطَّيِّبَاتُ، السَّلامُ عَلَيْكَ أَيُّهَا النَّبِيُّ وَرَحْمَةُ اللهِ وَبَرَكَاتُهُ، السَّلامُ عَلَيْنَا وَعَلَى عِبَادِ اللهِ الصَّالِحِينَ، أَشْهَدُ أَنْ لَا إِلَهَ إِلَّا اللهُ وَأَشْهَدُ أَنَّ مُحَمَّدًا عَبْدُهُ وَرَسُولُهُ.

Muhammadan 'Abduhu wa Rasooloh (All reverence is for Allah, all worship and good deeds and words are for Him. Peace and the Mercy and Blessings of Allah be upon you O Prophet. Peace be upon us and all the righteous salves of Allah. I testify that none is truly worthy to be worshipped except Allah and I testify that Muhammad is His Slave and Messenger)».

21- How do we ask Allah to Confer peace and blessing upon the Prophet, sallallaahu 'alayhi wa sallam, after Tashahhud?

Answer: We say: «Allaahumma Salli 'ala Muhaammadin wa 'ala Aali Muhammad Kama Sallayta 'ala Ibraaheem wa 'Ala Aali Ibraaheem Innaka Hameedun Majeed, wa Baarik 'ala Muhammadin wa 'ala Aali Muhammad Kama Baarakta 'ala Ibraaheem wa 'ala Aali Ibraaheem Innaka Hameedun Majeed (O Allah, Confer Your prayer upon Muhammad and the family of Muhammad, just as You

٢١- كَيْفَ نُصَلِّي عَلَى النَّبِيِّ ﷺ بَعْدَ التَّشَهُّدِ؟

الجَوَابُ: اللَّهُمَّ صَلِّ عَلَى مُحَمَّدٍ وَعَلَى آلِ مُحَمَّدٍ، كَمَا صَلَّيْتَ عَلَى إِبْرَاهِيمَ وَعَلَى آلِ إِبْرَاهِيمَ، إِنَّكَ حَمِيدٌ مَجِيدٌ، اللَّهُمَّ بَارِكْ عَلَى مُحَمَّدٍ وَعَلَى آلِ مُحَمَّدٍ، كَمَا بَارَكْتَ عَلَى آلِ إِبْرَاهِيمَ، وَعَلَى آلِ إِبْرَاهِيمَ، إِنَّكَ حَمِيدٌ مَجِيدٌ.

Conferred Your prayer upon Ibraaheem and the family of Ibraaheem. Verily, You Are Praiseworthy and Honorable. O Allah, Confer Your blessings upon Muhammad and the family of Muhammad, just as You Conferred your blessings upon Ibraaheem and upon the family of Ibraaheem. Verily, You Are Praiseworthy and Honorable)».

22- What is the Du'aa' to be said after the last Tashahhud and before Tasleem?

Answer: It is to say: «Allaahumma inni A'oothu Bika min 'Athaabi Al-Qabr, wa min 'Athaabi Jahannam, wa min fitnati-l-Mahya wa-l-Mamaat, wa min Sharri fitnati-l-Maseeh Ad-Dajjaal (O Allah, I seek refuge with You from the punishment of Hellfire, from the torment of the grave, from the tribulations of life and death and from the evil trial of the Anti-christ)».

23- What is the Athkaar to be recited after Tasleem?

22- كَيفَ نَدعُو بَعدَ التَّشَهُّدِ الأَخِيرِ وَقَبلَ السَّلامْ؟

الجواب: اللّهُمَّ إِنّي أَعُوذُ بِكَ مِنْ عَذابِ جهَنَّمَ، وَمِنْ عَذَابِ القَبرِ، وَمِنْ فِتْنَةِ المحْيَا والمَمَاتِ، وَمِنْ شَرِّ فِتْنَةِ المَسِيحِ الدَّجَّالِ.

23- مَا الأَذْكَارُ الَّتِي بعدَ السَّلام مِنَ الصَّلاةِ؟

Answer: «Astaghfirullaah (I seek the Forgiveness of Allah)» three times.

"Allaahumma anta As-Salaam, Wa Minka As-Salaam, Tabaarakta Ya Tha Al-Jalaali wal Ikraam (O Allah, You are As-Salam (The Perfection) and from You is peace, Blessed Is You, O Possessor of Majesty and Honor)».

To say SubhaanAllah (Exalted is Allah), Al-Hamdulillaah (Praise be to Allah) and Allaahu Akbar (Allah is the Greatest).

24- What are the morning Athkaar?

Answer: «Allaahumma Bika Asbahna wa Bika Amsayna wa Bika Nahya wa Bika Namootu wa Ilayka An-Nushoor (O Allah, by Your Permission we have reached the morning and by Your Permission we have reached the evening, by Your Permission we live and die and To You is The Resurrection)." "Radheetu Billaahi Rabban, wa Bil Islaami Deenan, wa Bi Muhammadin, sallallaahu

الجواب: أَسْـتَغْفِرُ اللهَ. (ثَـلَاثَ مَرَّات).

اللَّهُمَّ أَنْتَ السَّلَامُ، ومِنْكَ السَّلَامُ، تَبارَكْتَ ياذَا الجلالِ والإكْرامِ.

سُـبْحَانَ اللَّهِ، وَالحَمْـدُ لله وَاللهُ أَكْـبَـرُ (ثَلَاثًا وَثَلَاثِين).

٢٤- مَا أذكَارُ الصَّبَاح؟

الجواب: اللَّهُـمَّ بِـكَ أَصْـبَـحْنَا وبِـكَ أَمْسَـيْنَا وبِـكَ نَحْيَـا، وبِـكَ نَمُـوتُ، وَإِلَيْكَ النُّشُورُ.

رَضِـيتُ بِـاللهِ رَبًّـا، وبالإسْلَامِ دِينًـا وبِمُحَمَّدٍ رَسُولاً (ثَلَاثَ مَرَّات).

'alayhi wa sallam, a Rasoola (I am pleased with Allah as Lord, Islam as religion and Muhammad, sallallaahu 'alayhi wa sallam, as Prophet)." [Three times]

25- What are the evening Athkaar?

Answer: It is to say: «Allaahumma Bika Amsayna wa Bika Asbahna wa Bika Nahya wa Bika Namootu wa Ilayka Al-Maseer (O Allah, by Your Permission we have reached the evening and by Your Permission we have reached the morning, by Your Permission we live and die and to You is the Return)».

26- What is the Du'aa' to be said when one experiences unrest and fear during sleep and the one who is afflicted with alienation?

Answer: It is to say: "A'oothu Bikalimaat-i-llaahi At-Taammaati min Ghadhabihi wa 'Iqaabihi wa Sharri 'Ibaadihi wa min Hamazaat Ash-Shayaateeni wa an Yahdhuroon (I seek refuge in the Perfect Words of Allah from His Anger and

25- مَا أَذْكَارُ المَسَاءِ؟

الجَوابُ: اللَّهُمَّ بِكَ أَمْسَيْنَا، وَبِكَ أَصْبَحْنَا وَبِكَ نَحْيَا، وَبِكَ نَمُوتُ وَإِلَيْكَ المَصِيرُ.

26- مَا دُعَاءُ القَلَقِ وَالفَزَعِ فِي النَّومِ وَمِن بُلِيَ بِالوَحْشَةِ؟

الجَوابُ: أَعُوذُ بِكَلِمَاتِ اللهِ التَّامَّاتِ مِنْ غَضَبِهِ وَعِقَابِهِ، وَشَرِّ عِبَادِهِ وَمِنْ هَمَزَاتِ الشَّيَاطِينِ وَأَنْ يَحْضُرُونِ.

Punishment, and from the evil of His slaves, and from the incitements of the devils and lest they be present with me)."

27- What is the Du'aa' to be said when encountering the enemy and people of power (tyrants)?

Answer: It is to say: "Allaahumma inna Naj'aluka fi Nuhoorihim, wa Na'oothu Bika min Shuroorihim (O Allah, we seek Your Help to repel them and we take refuge with You from their evil)."

28- What do we say in supplication against the enemy?

Answer: We say: "Allaahumma Munzil Al-Kitaab, Saree'-al-Hisaab, Ihzim Al-Ahzaab, Allaahumma Ihzimhum wa zalzilhum (O Allah, Revealer of the Book, Who Is Swift in reckoning, Defeat the confederates. O Allah, Defeat them and Convulse them)."

29- What is the Du'aa' to be said when fearing some people?

27- مَـاذَا نَـدعُو عِنـدَ لِقَـاءِ العَدُوّ وَذِي السُّلْطَانِ؟

الجَـوَاب: اللهـمَّ إِنَّـا نَجعَلُـكَ فِـي نُحُورِهِم وَنَعُوذُ بِكَ مِن شُرُورِهِم.

28- كَيفَ نَدعُو عَلَى العَدُوّ؟

الجواب: اللَّهُمَّ مُنْزِلَ الكِتَابِ، سَرِيعَ الحِسَـابِ، اهـزِمِ الأَحْـزَابِ اللَّهُـمَّ اهْزِمهُم وَزَلزِلُهم.

29- مَـاذَا يَقُولُ مَن خَافَ قَومًا؟

Answer: It is to say: "Allaahumma Ikfineehum Bima Shi'ta (O Allah, Protect me against them by whatever You Will)."

الجواب: اللَّهُمَّ اكفِنِيهِمْ بِمَا شِئْتَ.

30- What is the Du'aa' to be said for settling a debt?

30- مَا دُعَاءُ قَضَاءِ الدَّيْنِ؟

Answer: It is to say: "Allaahumma Ikfini Bihalaalika 'An Haraamika wa Aghnini Bi Fadhlika 'Amman Siwaaka (O Allah, Make what You Made lawful sufficient for me against what You Made unlawful and Spare me by Your Bounty, the need of others)."

الجواب: اللَّهُمَّ اكفِنِي بِحَلَالِكَ عَنْ حَرَامِكَ وَأَغْنِنِي بِفَضْلِكَ عَمَّنْ سِوَاكَ.

31- What is the Du'aa' for repelling the devil's whispers in prayer and recitation?

31- مَا دُعَاءُ الوَسْوَسَةِ فِي الصَّلَاةِ وَالقِرَاءَةِ؟

Answer: It is to say: "A'oothu Billaahi min Ash-Shaytaan Ar-Rajeem (I seek refuge with Allah from the accursed devil)" then spit on one's left side three times.

الجواب: أَعُوذُ بِاللهِ مِنَ الشَّيْطَانِ الرَّجِيمِ، ثُمَّ أَتفُلْ عَلَى يَسَارِكَ ثَلَاثًا.

32- What is the Du'aa' to be said by one whose affairs became difficult?

32- مَاذَا يَدعُو مَنِ استَصعَبَ أَمرًا؟

Answer: It is to say: "Allaahumma la Sahla Illa ma Ja'altahu Sahlan wa Anta

الجواب: اللَّهُمَّ لَا سَهلَ إِلَّا مَا جَعَلتَهُ سَهلاً وَأَنتَ تَجعَلُ الحَزنَ إِذَا شِئتَ

سَهلاً.

Taj'alu Al-Hazna Itha Shi'ta Sahlan (O Allah, there is nothing easy except that which You Have Made easy, and You Make what is difficult, if You Will, easy)."

33- What should one say when something that he dislikes happens to him and he is overcome with it?

33- مَـاذَا يَقُـولُ إِذَا لَقِـيَ مَـا لا يَرضَـاهُ وغُلِبَ أَمرُه؟

Answer: He should say: "Qadarullaahi wa ma Shaa'a Fa'ala (It is the Decree of Allah and He Does what He Wills)."

الجواب: قَدَرُ اللهِ وَمَا شَاءَ فَعَلَ.

34- What is to be said in congratulation on the newborn?

34- مَا تَهنِئَةَ المَولُودِ لَهُ؟

Answer: It is said: "Baarak Allaahu laka Fi Al-Mawhoob wa Shakarta Al-Waahib wa Balagha Ashuddahu wa Ruzikta Birrahu (May Allah Bless for you what He Has Given to you (this child) and may you be grateful to The One Who Has Given him to you. May he (this child) come to maturity and May Allah Make him dutiful to you)."

الجـواب: بَـارَكَ الله لَـكَ فِـي المَوهُوبِ، وَشَكَرْتَ الوَاهِبِ، وَبَلَغَ أَشُدَّهُ، وَرُزِقتَ بِرَّه.

35- What is to be said in reply of the congratulation?

35- بِمَ يَرُدُّ المُهَنَّأُ عَلَيْه؟

Answer: It is said: "Baarak

الجـواب: بَـارَكَ الله لَـكَ وَبَـارَكَ

Allaahu Laka wa Baaraka 'alayka wa Jazaaka Allaahu Khayran wa Razaqaka Allaahu Mithlahu wa Ajzala laka Thawaabak (May Allah Bless for you and upon You, May Allah Reward you, Provide you with the same and Make abundant your reward)."

36- What is the Du‘aa’ to be said when visiting a sick person?

Answer: It is to say: "La Ba’sa Tahoorun in Shaa’ Allah. As’alu Allaahu Al-‘Atheem Rabba Al-‘Arshi Al-‘Atheemi An Yashfiyaka (There is no harm, may it (the sickness) be purification to you, by the Will of Allah. I ask Allah, The Most Great, Lord of The Mighty Throne to Heal you)" This is to be said seven times.

37- What is the Du‘aa’ to be said by the one who is afflicted by a calamity?

Answer: It is to say: "Inna lillahi wa inna ilayhi Raaji‘oon. Allaahumma U’jorni Fi Museebati wa Ukhluf li Khayran minha (Indeed to Allah we belong

عَلَيْكَ، وَجَزَاكَ اللهُ خَيْرًا، وَرَزَقَكَ اللهُ مِثْلَهُ، وَأَجْزَلَ ثَوَابَكَ.

36- مَا الدُّعَاءُ الَّذِي يُقَالُ عِنْدَ عِيَادَةِ المَرِيضِ؟

الجَوَاب: لَا بَأْسَ طَهُورٌ إِنْ شَاءَ اللهُ.
أَسْأَلُ اللهَ العَظِيمَ رَبَّ العَرْشِ العَظِيمِ أَنْ يَشْفِيَكَ. 7 مرات.

37- مَا دُعَاءُ مَنْ أَصَابَتْهُ مُصِيبَةً؟

الجَوَاب: إِنَّا للهِ وَإِنَّا إِلَيْهِ رَاجِعُونَ: اللَّهُمَّ أَجِرْنِي فِي مُصِيبَتِي، وَاخْلُفْ لِي خَيْرًا مِنْهَا.

and to Him we shall return. O Allah, Reward me for my affliction and Replace it for me with something better).”

38- What is the Du‘aa’ to be said when offering condolence?

Answer: It is to say: “A‘thama Allaahu Ajraka wa Ahsana ‘Azaa‘aka wa Ghafara Li Mayyitik, (May Allah Make Great your reward, Make better your solace and Forgive your deceased).”

39- What should be said when placing the dead in the grave?

Answer: It should be said: “Bismillaah wa ‘Ala Sunnati Rasoolillaah (In the Name of Allah and by the Sunnah of the Messenger of Allah).”

40- What should we say in supplication for the deceased after being buried?

Answer: We should say: “Allaahumma Ighfir lahu, Allaahumma Thabbithuh (O Allah, Forgive him and Grant him firmness).”

41- What is the Du‘aa’ of visiting the graves?

38- مَا دُعاءُ التَّعْزِيَةِ؟

الجواب: أَعظَمَ اللهُ أجرَكَ، وَأَحسَنَ عَزَاءَكَ وَغَفَرَ لِمَيِّتِكَ.

39- مَا يُقَالُ عِندَ إِدخَالِ المَيِّتِ القَبرَ؟

الجواب: بِسْمِ اللهِ وَعَلَى سُنَّةِ رَسُولِ اللهِ.

40- بِمَاذَا نَدعُو لِلمَيِّتِ بَعدَ الدَّفنِ؟

الجواب: اللّهمَّ اغفِر لَهُ اللّهمَّ ثَبِّتَهُ.

41- مَا دُعاءُ زيارَةِ القُبُورِ؟

Answer: It is to say: "As-Salaamu 'alaykom Ahl-ad-Diyaari min Al-Mu'mineena wal Mu'minaati wa Al-Muslimeena wa Al-Muslimaat, wa inna In Shaa' Allaahu bikom Laahikoon, As'alu Allaha lana wa Lakom Al-'Aafiyah (Peace be upon you all, O inhabitants of the graves, from amongst the believers and the Muslims. Verily, we will, Allah willing, join you. We ask Allah for well-being for us and you)."

الجواب: السَّلَامُ عَلَيكُم أَهلَ الدِّيَارِ مِـــنَ الْمُـــؤمِنِينَ وَالمُؤمِنَـــاتِ وَالمُسـلِمِينَ وَالمُسـلِمَاتِ وَإِنَّـا إِن شَـاءَ اللهُ بِكُم لَاحِقُون أَسألُ اللهَ لَنَا وَلَكُم العَافِية.

42- What is the Du'aa' to be said in wind storms?

Answer: It is to say: "Allaahumma Inni As'aluka Khayraha wa A'oothu Bika min Sharriha (O Allah, I ask You for its good and seek refuge with You from its evil).

42- مَا دُعَاءُ الرِّيحِ؟

الجواب: اللَّهُمَّ إِنِّي أَسْأَلُكَ خَيْرَهَا وَأَعُوذُ بك مِنْ شَرِّهَا.

43- What is the Du'aa' to be said upon hearing the thunder?

Answer: It is to say: "Subhaana Al-Lathi Yusabbihu Ar-Ra'du Bihamdihi wal Malaa'ikatu min Kheefatihi (Exalted Is He Whom the thunder exalts with praise and so do the

43- مَا دُعَاءُ الرَّعد؟

الجواب: سُبحَانَ الَّذِي يُسَبِّحُ الرَّعدُ بِحَمدِهِ وَالمَلَائِكَةَ مِن خِيفَتِه.

angels because of His Awe).”

44- What is the Du‘aa’ to be said in asking for rain?

Answer: It is to say: “Allaahumma Aghithna, Allaahumma Aghithna, Allaahumma Aghithna (O Allah Relieve us with rain, O Allah Relieve us with rain, O Allah Relieve us with rain).”

45- What is the Du‘aa’ to be said on rainfall?

Answer: It is to say: “Allaahumma Sayyiban Naafi‘a (O Allah, may it be a beneficial rainy cloud).”

46- What should we say after rainfall?

Answer: We should say: “Mutirna Bifadhl-i-llaahi wa Birahmatih (We were granted rain by the Bounty and Mercy of Allah).”

47- What is the Du‘aa’ for asking for clear skies?

Answer: It is to say: “Allaahumma Hawaalayna wa la ‘alayna, Allaahumma ‘ala Al-Aakaami wal Thiraabi wa Butooni-l-Awdiyah wa Manaabit Ash-Shajar (O Allah, Let the rain fall around us not on us, O

٤٤- مَا دُعَاءُ الاِسْتِسْقَاءِ؟

الجواب: اللّهمَّ أَغِثْنَا، اللّهمَّ أَغِثْنَا، اللّهمَّ أَغِثْنَا.

٤٥- مَا دُعَاءُ نُزُولِ المَطَرِ؟

الجواب: اللّهمَّ صَيِّبًا نَافِعًا.

٤٦- مَاذَا نقول بَعدَ نُزُولِ المَطَرِ؟

الجواب: مُطِرنَا بِفَضلِ اللهِ وَرَحمَتِهِ.

٤٧- مَا دُعَاءُ الاِسْتِصْحَاءِ؟

الجواب: اللّهمَّ حَوَالَينَا وَلَا عَلَينَا اللّهمَّ عَلَى الآكَامِ وَالظِّرَابِ وَبُطُونِ الأَودِيَةِ وَمَنَابِتِ الشَّجَرِ.

Allah, Let it fall on hillocks, hills, valleys and the places where trees grow)."

48- What is the Du‘aa' on seeing the crescent?

Answer: It is to say: "Allaahumma Ahillahu ‘alayna Bil Amni wal Amaani was Salaamati wal Islammi wat Tawfeeqi lima Tuhibbu wa Tardha, Rabbuna wa Rabbuka Allah (O Allah, Let the crescent come to us in safety, faith, peace, and Islam, and in agreement with all that You Love and Is Pleased with. Our Lord and your Lord Is Allah)."

49- What is the Du‘aa' of breaking the fast?

Answer: It is to say: "Thahaba Ath-Thama'u wa Ibtallatil ‘Urooqu wa Thabata Al-Ajru in Shaa'Allah (The thirst has gone and the veins are quenched (moistened), and the reward is confirmed, Allah willing)."

50- What should be said before eating?

Answer: It should be said: "Bismillaah, Allaahumma Baarik lana Feehi wa

٤٨- مَا دُعَاءُ رُوْيَةِ الهِلالِ؟

الجواب: اللّهمَّ أَهِلّهُ عَلَيْنَا بِالأَمنِ وَالإِيمَــانِ وَالسَّــلَامَةِ وَالإِسْــلَامِ وَالتَّوفِيقِ لِمَا تُحِبُّ رَبَّنَا وَتَرضَى رَبَّنَا وَرَبُّكَ اللهُ.

٤٩- مَا دُعَاءُ الصَّائِم عِندَ إفطَارِهِ؟

الجــواب: ذَهَــبَ الظَّمَــأُ وَابتَلَّــتِ العُرُوقُ وَثَبَتَ الأَجرُ إن شَاءَ اللهُ.

٥٠- مَا يُقَالُ قَبْلَ الطَّعَامِ؟

الجواب: بِسْم اللهِ، اللّهمَّ بَارِك لَنَا فِيهِ وَأَطعِمنَا خَيرًا مِنهُ.

At'imna Khayran Minhu (In the Name of Allah, O Allah, Bless it for us and Feed us what is better)."

51- What is the Du'aa' on drinking milk?

Answer: It is to say: "Allaahumma Baarik lana Feehi wa Zidna Minhu (O Allah, Bless it for us and Give us more of it)."

52- What is the Du'aa' to be said after having a meal?

Answer: It is to say: "Al-Hamdu lillaahi Al-Lathi At'amani Haatha wa Razaqaneehi min Ghayri Hawlin Minni wa la Quwwah (Praise be to Allah Who Fed me this and Provided me with it without neither Power nor strength on my part)."

53- What is the Du'aa' of the guest for his host?

Answer: It is to say: "Allaahumma Baarik Lahum Feema Razaqtahum wa Ighfir lahum wa Irhamhum (O Allah, Bless for them what you Provided them with, Forgive them and Have mercy upon them)."

54- What is the Du'aa' of

51- مَا دُعَاءُ مَن شَرِبَ لَبَنَا؟

الجواب: اللّهمَّ بَارِك لَنَا فِيهِ وَزِدنَا مِنهُ.

52- مَا الدُّعَاءُ بَعْدَ الفَرَاغِ مِنَ الطَّعَامِ؟

الجواب: الحَمدُ للهِ الّذِي أطعَمَني هَذَا وَرَزَقَنِيهِ مِن غَيرِ حَولٍ مِنّي وَلَا قُوَّة.

53- مَا دُعَاءُ الضَّيفِ لِلمُضِيفِ؟

الجواب: اللّهمَّ بَارِك لَهُم فِيمَا رَزَقتَهُم وَاغفِر لَهُم وَارحَمهُم.

54- مَاذَا يَقُولُ المُسقِي عَلَيهِ لِمَن سَقَاه؟

the one who is offered a drink for the one who offered it to him?

Answer: It is to say: "Allaahumma At'im Man At'amani wa Isqi man Saqaani (O Allah, Feed him who fed me, and Provide with drink him who provided me with drink)."

55- What is the Du'aa' of the one who breaks his fast in someone's home?

Answer: It is to say: "Aftara 'Indakumu As-Saa'imoona, wa Akala Ta'aamakumu-l-Abraaru, wa Sallat 'alaykumu-l-Malaa'ikah (May the fasting break their fast in your home, and may the righteous eat your food, and may the angels send prayers upon you)."

56- What should the fasting person say when someone insults him?

Answer: He should say: "Inni Saa'im, Inni Saa'im (I am on a fast, I am on a fast)."

57- What should the Muslim say after sneezing?

Answer: He should say: "Al-Hamdulillaah (Praise be to

الجواب: اللَّهُمَّ أَطْعِم مَن أَطْعَمَنِي وَاسقِ مَن سَقَانِي.

55- مَا دُعَاءُ المُفْطِرِ لِمَن أَفطَرَ فِي بَيْتِه؟

الجواب: أَفطَرَ عِندَكُم الصَّائِمُونَ وَأَكَلَ طَعَامَكُم الأَبرَارُ وَصَلَّت عَلَيكُم المَلائِكَةُ.

56- مَاذَا يَقُولُ الصَّائِمُ إِذَا سَابَّهُ أَحَد؟

الجواب: إِنِّي صَائِم، إِنِّي صَائِم.

57- مَاذَا يَقُولُ العَاطِسُ عِندَ العَطسِ؟

الجواب: الحَمدُ لله.

Allah)."

58- How should his fellow Muslim answer him?

Answer: He says to him: "Yarhamuka Allah (May Allah Have mercy upon you)."

58- مَا يَرُدُّ لَهُ صَاحِبه؟

الجواب: يَرحَمُكَ الله.

59- How should the former reply to the latter?

Answer: He says to him: "Yahdeekum Allaahu wa Yuslihu Baalakum (May Allah Guide you and Rectify your affairs)."

59- مَاذَا يَقُولُ العَاطِسُ للرَدُّ عَليه؟

الجواب: يَهدِيكُمُ اللهُ وَيُصلِحُ بَالَكم.

60- What should be said to the non-Muslim if he says 'Al-Hamdulillaah' after sneezing?

Answer: It should be said: "Yahdeekum Allaahu wa Yuslihu Baalakum (May Allah Guide you and Rectify your affairs)."

60- مَاذَا يُقَالُ للكَافِرِ إِذَا عَطَسَ فَحَمِدَ الله؟

الجواب: يَهدِيكُمُ اللهُ وَيُصلِحُ بَالَكم.

61- What is the Du'aa' to be said upon concluding a marriage contract?

Answer: It is to say: "Baarak Allaahu Lakuma wa Baaraka 'alaykuma wa Jama'a Baynakuma Fi Khayr (May Allah Bless it for you and Bless you, and May He Gather you in goodness)."

61- مَا دُعاءُ انْتِهَاءِ عَقدِ الزَّوَاجِ؟

الجواب: بَارَكَ اللهُ لَكَ وَبَارَكَ عَلَيكَ وَجَمَعَ بَينكُمَا فِي خَيرٍ.

62- What is the Du'aa' of

62- مَا دُعاءُ الزَّوج لِنَفسِهِ وَدُعَاءُ شِرَاءِ

الدَّابَّةِ؟

the husband for himself or upon buying a mounting animal?

Answer: He should say: "Allaahumma inni As'aluka khayraha, wa Khayra ma Jabaltaha 'alayhi, wa A'oothu Bika min Sharriha wa Sharri ma Jabaltaha 'alayhi. (O Allah, I ask You for the goodness within her and the goodness that You Have Made her inclined to, and I take refuge with You from the evil within her and the evil that you Have Made her inclined to)."

الجواب: اللّهمَّ إِنِّي أَسْأَلُكَ خَيْرَهَا وَخَيرَ مَا جَبَلْتَهَا عَلَيهِ وَأَعُوذُ بِكَ مِنْ شَرِّهَا وَشَرِّ مَا جَبَلْتَهَا عَلَيهِ.

* * *

آخِرُ المَطَاف

الأذكَارُ بَعدَ الصَّلاَةِ المَفرُوضَة

Athkaar after
the Obligatory Prayers

Athkaar after the Obligatory Prayers

آخِرُ المَطَاف

الأَذكَـارُ بَعــدَ الصَّـلاةِ المَفرُوضَة

1- «Astaghfirullaah, Astaghfirullaah, Astaghfirullaah (I ask Allah for forgiveness)» [Three times].

2- «Allaahumma Anta As-Salaamu wa Minka As-Salaamu, Tabaarakta Ya Tha Al-Jalaali wal Ikraam (O Allah, You are As-Salaam (The Perfection) and from You is peace, Blessed Is You, O Possessor of Majesty and Honor)».

3- «Laa ilaaha illa Allah, Wahdahu la Shareeka lah, Lahul Mulku wa Lahul Hamdu wa Huwa 'Ala Kulli Shay'in Qadeer (There is no deity except Allah Alone; He Has no partner, His are the praise and the dominion and He Is over all things Competent)».

4- «La Hawla wa la Quw-wata Illa Billaah, La Ilaaha Illa Allah wa la Na'budu Illa Iyyaah, Lahu An-Ni'mah wa Lahu Al-Fadhlu wa Lahu Ath-Thanaa'u

1- أَسْـــتَغْفِرُ اللهَ، أَسْـــتَغْفِرُ اللهَ، أَسْتَغْفِرُ اللهَ.

2- اللَّهُـــمَّ أَنـــتَ السَّـلامُ، ومِنْـكَ السَّـلامُ، تَبارَكْـتَ يـاذَا الجـلالِ والإكْرامِ.

3- لا إِلَـهَ إِلاّ اللهُ وَحْـدَهُ لاَ شَرِيكَ لَهُ، لَهُ المُلْكُ وَلَهُ الحَمْدُ وَهُوَ عَلَى كُلِّ شَيءٍ قَدِيرٌ.

4- ولا حَوْلَ ولا قُـوةَ إِلاَّ بِـاللهِ، لا إلَـهَ إلاَّ اللهُ وَلاَ نَعبُـدُ إلَّا إِيَّـاهُ لَـهُ النِّعمَـةُ وَلَـهُ الفَضـلُ وَلَـهُ الثَّنَـاءُ الحَسَـنُ لَا إلـهَ إلَّا اللهُ مُخلِصِينَ لَهُ الدِّينَ وَلَو كَرِهَ الكَافِرُونَ.

Al-Hasan, La Ilaaha Illa Allah Mukhliseena Lahu Ad-Deena wa law Kariha Al-Kaafiroon (There is neither might nor power save with Allah, there is no deity except Allah, we worship none but Him. His is the Blessing and His is the Bounty and to Him is the good praise. There is no deity except Allah, we are sincere to Him in religion even though the disbelievers dislike it)».

5- Allaahumma La Maani'a Lima A'tayta wa la Mu'tiya lima Mana'ta wa la Yanfa'u Tha Al-Jaddi Minka Al-Jaddu (O Allah, none can withhold that which You Give and none can give that which You Withhold, and never will the possessions of an owner avail him before You)».

6- To say: «Subhaan Allah», [33 times], «Al-Hamdulillah», [33 times] and «Allaahu Akbar», [33 times].

7- Having said that, to complete a set of one hundred, he should say: «Laa ilaaha illa Allah, Wahdahu la Shareeka lah, Lahul Mulku wa Lahul Hamdu wa Huwa 'Ala Kulli Shay'in Qadeer (There is no

5- اللَّهُمَّ لَا مَانِعَ لِمَا أَعطَيْتَ، وَلا مُعْطِـيَ لِمَــا مَنَعْـتَ، ولا يَنْفَـعُ ذَا الجَدِّ مِنْكَ الجَدّ.

6- سُبحَانَ الله (33 مَرَّة)، الحَمـدُ للهِ (33 مَـرَّة)، الله أَكبَـــرُ (33 مَرَّة).

7- ثُمَّ يُكَمّـلُ المائَـة: لا إلَـهَ إلاَّ اللَّه وَحْدَهُ لاَ شَرِيكَ لَهُ، لَهُ المُلْكُ وَلَهُ الحَمدُ وَهُوَ عَلَى كُلّ شَيءٍ قَدِيرٌ.

deity except Allah Alone, He Has no partner, His are the praise and the dominion and He Is over all things Competent)».

8- «Laa ilaaha illa Allah, Wahdahu la Shareeka lah, Lahul Mulku wa Lahul Hamdu Yuhyi wa Yumeetu wa Huwa 'Ala Kulli Shay'in Qadeer (There is no deity except Allah Alone, He Has no partner, His are the praise and the dominion He Gives Life and Causes death and He Is over all things Competent)». [To be said 10 times after Maghrib and Fajr prayer]

To recite The Verse of Al-Kursi (which means): *[Allah – there is no deity except Him, the Ever-Living, the Sustainer of [all] existence. Neither drowsiness overtakes Him nor sleep. To Him belongs whatever is in the heavens and whatever is on the earth. Who is it that can intercede with Him except by His permission? He knows what is [presently] before them and what will be after them, and they encompass not a thing of His knowledge except for what He wills. His Kursi extends*

8- لا إِلَـهَ إلاَّ اللهُ وَحْـدَهُ لاَ شَـرِيكَ لَـهُ، لَـهُ المُلْـك وَلَـهُ الحَمـدُ يُحِيِي وَيُمِيتُ وَهُوَ عَلَى كُلِّ شَيءٍ قَدِيرٌ (بَعـدَ صَـلَاةِ المَغـرِبِ وَالصُّـبح 10مَرَّات).

* قِرَاءَةُ آيَةِ الكُرسِيِّ: [الله ...]

over the heavens and the earth, and their preservation tires Him not. And He is the Most High, the Most Great.] [Al-Baqarah: 255]

[البقرة: 255].

To recite the Chapters of Al-Ikhlaas, Al-Falaq and An-Naas, once after each prayer and three times after the Maghrib and Fajr Prayers.

Allah, The Almighty, Says (what means):
[1. Say, "He is Allœh, [who is] One, 2. Allah, the Eternal Refuge. 3. He neither begets nor is born, 4. Nor is there to Him any equivalent."] [Al-Ikhlaas]

[الإخلاص].

Allah, The Almighty, Says (what means):

[1. Say, "I seek refuge in the Lord of daybreak 2. From the evil of that which He created 3. And from the evil of darkness when it settles 4. And from the evil of the blowers in knots 5. And from the evil of an envier when he envies."] [Al-Falaq]

Allah, The Almighty, Says (what means):

[1. Say, "I seek refuge in the Lord of mankind, 2. The Sovereign of mankind, 3. The God of mankind, 4. From the evil of the retreating whisperer. 5. Who whispers [evil] into the breasts of mankind. 6. From among the jinn and mankind."] [An-Naas]

مَرَّةً وَاحِدَةً بَعدَ كُلِّ صَلَاةٍ إِلَّا بَعدَ

صَلَاةُ المَغْرِبِ وَ الصُّبْح فَثَلاثٌ

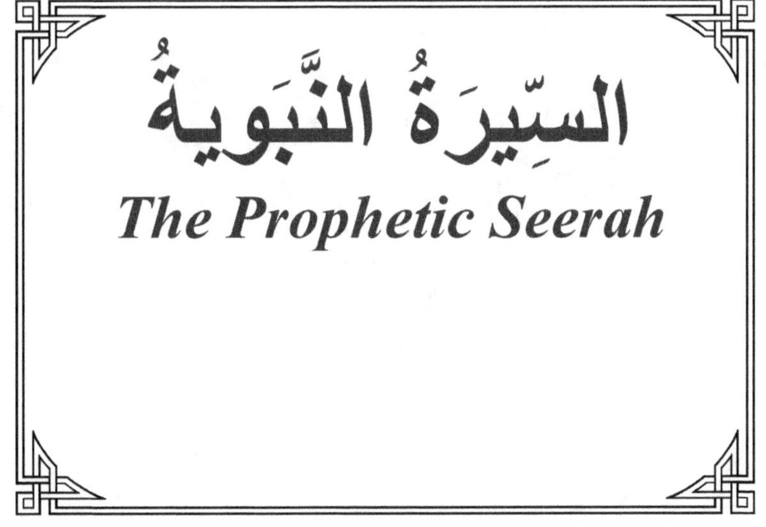

السِّيرَةُ النَّبَوية

The Prophetic Seerah

The Prophetic Seerah Questions and Answers About The Prophetic Seerah during the Makkan Stage

السِّيرَةُ النَّبويَّة
أَسئلَةٌ وَأَجوبةٌ
فِي السِّيرَةِ النَّبويَّة
فِي العَهدِ المَكِّيَّ

1- When and where was the Prophet, sallallaahu 'alayhi wa sallam, born?

Answer: He was born in Makkah, in the month of Rabee' Al-Awwal, in the Year of the Elephant.

١- مَتَى وُلِدَ النَّبِيُّ ﷺ؟وَأَيْنَ؟

الجواب: وُلِدَ فِي رَبِيعِ الأَوَّلِ مِن عَامِ الفِيْلِ، فِي مَكَّةَ المُكَرَّمَةِ.

2- What was his lineage?

Answer: Muhammad ibn 'Abdullaah ibn 'Abd Al-Muttalib ibn Haashim ibn 'Abd Manaaf ibn Qusayy ibn Kilaab ibn Murrah.

٢- مَا نَسَبُهُ ﷺ؟

هُوَ مُحَمَّدُ بنُ عَبْدِ اللهِ بنِ عَبْدِ المُطَّلِبِ بنِ هَاشِمٍ، بنِ عَبدِ مَنَافٍ بنِ قُصَيِّ بنِ كِلَابٍ بنِ مُرَّةَ.

3- What was his father's name? When did he die?

Answer: His father's name was 'Abdullaah ibn 'Abd Al-Muttalib. He died when the Messenger of Allah, sallallaahu 'alayhi wa sallam, was still a fetus in his mother's womb.

٣- مَا اسمُ وَالِدِه وَمَتَى تُوُفِّي؟

الجواب: اسمُهُ عَبْدُ اللهِ بنِ عَبْدِ المُطَّلِبِ. تُوُفِّي وَرَسُولُ اللهِ فِي بَطْنِ أُمِّهِ.

4- Mention some of the names of the Messenger of Allah, sallallaahu 'alayhi wa sallam. What were the most famous of them?

Answer: Muhammad, Ahmad,

٤- اذكُر بَعضَ أَسمَاءِ الرَّسُولِ وَمَا أَشهَرُهَا؟

الجواب: مُحَمَّد، أَحمَد، المَاحِي،

Al-Maahi, Al-Haashir, Al-'Aaqib. The most famous of them were Muhammad and Ahmad.

5- How many times is the name of Muhammad, sallallaahu 'alayhi wa sallam, mentioned in the Quran?

Answer: It is mentioned four times.

6- Who were his uncles who embraced Islam? Which of his uncles remained as disbelievers after he had become a prophet?

Answer: His uncles Hamzah and Al-'Abbaas embraced Islam. Abu Taalib and Abu Lahab remained on their disbelief.

7- Who were his wet nurses?

Answer: Thuwaybah and Haleemah As-Sa'diyyah.

8- Where was the Messenger of Allah, sallallaahu 'alayhi wa sallam, sent to be nursed?

Answer: He was sent to the Banu Sa'd wilderness to be nursed there.

9- What happened to him when he was at the Banu Sa'd wilderness?

Answer: He underwent the 'chest splitting' incident.

الْحَاشِر، الْعَاقِب. وَأَشْهَرُهَا (أَحْمَد، وَمُحَمَّد).

5ـ كَمْ مَرَّةٍ وَرَدَ اسْمُ مُحَمَّدٍ ﷺ فِي الْقُرْآنِ الْكَرِيمِ؟

الْجَوَاب: وَرَدَ فِيهِ أَرْبَعَ مَرَّاتٍ.

6ـ مَنْ أَعْمَامُه ﷺ الَّذِينَ أَسْلَمُوا وَمَنْ بَقِي مِنْهُم فِي الْكُفْرِ بَعْدَ نُبُوَّتِه ﷺ؟

الْجَوَاب: أَسْلَمَ مِنْهُم حَمْزَةُ وَالْعَبَّاس، وَبَقِي فِي الْكُفْرِ أَبُو طَالِب، وَأَبُو لَهَب.

7ـ مَنْ أُمَّهاتِ إِرْضَاعِه ﷺ؟ ثُوَيْبَةُ، وَحَلِيمَةُ السَّعْدِيَّةُ.

8ـ أَيْنَ اسْتُرْضِعَ رَسُولُ الله ﷺ؟

الْجَوَاب: اسْتُرْضِعَ فِي بَادِيَةِ بَنِي سَعْدٍ.

9ـ مَاذَا حَدَثَ لَهُ وَهُوَ فِي بَادِيَةِ بَنِي سَعْدٍ؟

الْجَوَاب: وَقَعَتْ لَهُ حَادِثَةُ شَقِّ

الصَّدْرِ.

10- **What did Haleemah As-Sa‘diyyah do after this incident had taken place?**

Answer: She returned him to his mother as she feared for his safety.

11- **What was the name of the mother of the Prophet, sallallaahu ‘alayhi wa sallam? Where did she die?**

Answer: Her name was Aaminah bint Wahb. She died in Al-Abwaa’.

12- **Who took care of the Prophet, sallallaahu ‘alayhi wa sallam, after his mother’s death?**

Answer: His grandfather ‘Abd Al-Muttalib did.

13- **How old was the Prophet, sallallaahu ‘alayhi wa sallam, when his grandfather ‘Abd Al-Muttalib died?**

Answer: He was eight years old.

14- **When the Messenger of Allah, sallallaahu ‘alayhi wa sallam, was twelve years old, he traveled to Ash-Shaam with his uncle. Whom did he see in this journey?**

Answer: He saw a monk called

10- مَاذَا فَعَلَت حَلِيمَةَ السَّعدِيَّة بَعْدَ هَذِه الحَادِثَةَ؟

الجواب: رَدَّتْهُ إِلَى أُمِّهِ بَعْدَ أَنْ خَشِيَت عَلَيه.

11- مَا اسمُ أُمَّ النَّبِيِّ ﷺ وَأَينَ مَاتَت؟

الجواب: اسمُهَا آمِنَةُ بِنت وَهْبٍ. وَمَاتَتْ بِالأَبْوَاءِ.

12- مَن كَفَلَ النَّبِيّ ﷺ بعد وفاة أمه؟

الجواب: كَفَلَهُ جَدُّهُ عَبدُ المُطَّلِب.

13- كَم كَانَ عُمرُ النَّبِيِّ ﷺ عِندَ وَفَاة جَدِّهِ عَبدِ المُطَّلِب؟

الجواب: كَانَ عُمرُهُ ثَمَانِي سَنَوَات.

14- سَافَرَ الرَّسُولُ ﷺ مَعَ عَمِّهِ إِلَى الشَّام وَعُمرُه اثْنَا عَشرَة سَنَة، فَمَاذَا رَأَى فِي هَذِه الرِّحْلَةِ؟

الجواب: رَأَى رَاهِبًا يُسَمَّى بُحَيرَا.

Baheera.

15- What was the job of the Messenger of Allah, sallallaahu 'alayhi wa sallam, when he was young?

Answer: He was a shepherd.

16- Who was the woman whom the Prophet, sallallaahu 'alayhi wa sallam, married first?

Answer: She was Khadeejah bint Khuwaylid.

17- How old was the Prophet, sallallaahu 'alayhi wa sallam, when he married her?

Answer: He was twenty-five years old.

18- How old was Khadeejah when the Messenger of Allah, sallallaahu 'alayhi wa sallam, married her?

Answer: She was forty years old.

19- Mention some of the virtues of Khadeejah.

Answer:

1- She was known to her people as (The pure and the chaste).

2- The Prophet, sallallaahu 'alayhi wa sallam, did not marry another wife until she

١٥- مَـاذَا عَمِـلَ رَسُـولُ اللهِ ﷺ فِي صِغَرِهِ؟

الجواب: عَمِلَ بِرَعْيِ الغَنَم.

١٦- مَن أَوَّلُ امرأةٍ تَزَوَّجَهَا النَّبِيُّ ﷺ؟

الجواب: خَدِيجَةُ بِنْتُ خُوَيْلِد.

١٧- كَـمْ كَـانَ عُمـرُ النَّبِـيِّ ﷺ حِـينَ تَزَوَّجَهَا؟

الجـواب: كَـانَ عُمـرُهُ خَمسًـا وَعِشْرِينَ سَنَة.

١٨- كَم كَانَ عُمرُ خَدِيجَةَ حِين تَزَوَّجَهَا الرَّسُولُ ﷺ؟

الجواب: كَانَ عُمرُهَا أربعينَ سَنَة.

١٩- اذكُر بَعْضَ فَضَائِلِ خَدِيجَةَ؟

الجواب: مِن فَضَائِلِهَا:

١- عُرِفَتْ عِنْدَ قَومِهَا (بِالطَّاهِرَةِ العَفِيفَة).

٢- لَم يَنكِح زَوْجَةً غَيرَهَا حَتَّى مَاتَتْ.

died.

3- The Prophet, sallallaahu 'alayhi wa sallam, was commanded to convey to her the Greeting of her Lord.

4- She was the first woman to believe in him.

5-The Prophet, sallallaahu 'alayhi wa sallam, had all his children with her apart from his son Ibraaheem whose mother was Maariyah Al-Qibtiyyah.

20- Who were the children of the Prophet, sallallaahu 'alayhi wa sallam?

Answer:

His sons were: Al-Qaasim, 'Abdullaah and Ibraaheem.

His daughters were: Zaynab, Ruqayyah, Umm Kulthoom and Faatimah.

21- Which day was it when the Revelation was first sent down unto the Messenger of Allah, sallallaahu 'alayhi wa sallam?

Answer: It was Monday.

22- What were the first verses of the Quran that were revealed to the Prophet, sallallaahu 'alayhi wa sallam?

Answer: The first verses of the Quran that were revealed were:

[*Recite in the Name of your*

3- وَأُمِرَ النَّبِيُّ ﷺ أَنْ يُبَلِّغَهَا التَّحِيَّةَ مِن رَبِّهَا.

4- أَوَّلُ مُؤْمِنَةٍ آمَنَتْ بِهِ.

5- جَمِيعُ أَوْلَادِهِ مِنْهَا مَا عَدَا إِبْرَاهِيمَ، فَإِنَّهُ مِن مَارِيَةَ القِبْطِيَّةِ.

20- مَن أَوْلَادُ النَّبِيّ ﷺ؟

الجواب: أَوْلَادُ النَّبِيّ ﷺ:
الذُّكُورُ: القَاسِمُ، وَعَبْدُ اللهِ، وَإِبْرَاهِيمُ.
الإِنَاثُ: زَيْنَبُ، وَرُقَيَّةُ، وَأُمُّ كُلْثُومٍ، وَفَاطِمَةُ.

21- أَيَّ يَوْمٍ نَزَلَ الوَحْيُ عَلَى رَسُولِ اللهِ ﷺ؟

الجواب: يَوْمَ الاثْنَيْنِ.

22- مَا أَوَّلُ مَا أُنْزِلَ مِنَ القُرْآنِ؟

أَوَّلُ مَا أُنْزِلَ مِنَ القُرْآنِ قَوْلُهُ تَعَالَى: ﴿اقْرَأْ بِاسْمِ﴾

Lord Who Created Created man from a clinging substance]* [Al-'Alaq:1-2]

[العلق: 1 - 5].

23- What were the stages of Revelation?

Answer:

1- The true vision.

2- The angel invisibly casts Revelation in the Prophet's heart.

3- The angel assumes the shape of a man (i.e., appear in a human form).

4- The angel comes to him in a state that resembles the clanking of bells.

23- اذْكُر مَرَاتِبَ الوَحْيِ؟

الجواب:

1- الرُّؤْيَا الصَّادِقَة.

2- مَا يُلْقِيهِ المَلَكُ فِي قَلْبِهِ مِن غَيْرِ أَن يَرَاه.

3- تَمَثُّلُ المَلَكِ لَهُ رَجُلًا.

4- إِتْيَانُه لَهُ ﷺ فِي مِثْلِ صَلْصَلَةِ الجَرَسِ.

24- What were the phases of Da'wah in the life of the Prophet, sallallaahu 'alayhi wa sallam?

Answer: There were two phases:

The first phase: Da'wah in secret; it lasted for three years.

The second phase: Da'wah in public; it lasted until the end of his life.

24- مَا مَرَاحِلُ الدَّعوَةِ فِي حَيَاتِهِ ﷺ؟

الجواب: لِدَعْوَتِهِ مَرْحَلَتَانِ:

المَرحَلَةُ الأُولَى: دَعوَتُهُ سِرًّا، وَقد استَمَرَّت ثَلَاثَ سَنَوَاتٍ.

المَرحَلَةُ الثَّانِيَة: دَعوَتُهُ جَهرًا، وَدَامَتْ مَا بَقِيَ مِنْ حَيَاتِهِ ﷺ.

25- Who were the first pioneers in accepting Islam?

25- مَنِ السَّابِقُونَ فِي دُخُولِ الإِسْلام؟

Answer: The first pioneers in accepting Islam were:

From women: Khadeejah bint Khuwaylid.

From men: Abu Bakr As-Siddeeq.

From youth: 'Ali ibn Abi Taalib.

From freed slaves: Zayd ibn Haarithah.

26- Was Waraqah ibn Nawfal one of the first pioneers of Islam?

Answer: Yes, he was one of the first pioneers of Islam (i.e., the earliest Muslims).

27- Mention the names of some of those who accepted Islam on the hands of Abu Bakr As-Siddeeq?

Answer: Some of them were:

'Uthmaan ibn 'Affaan, Az-Zubayr ibn Al-'Awwaam, 'Abdul-Rahmaan ibn 'Awf, Sa'd ibn Abi Waqqaas and Talhah ibn 'Ubaydillaah.

28- When did the phase of making public Da'wah begin?

Answer: It began by the revelation of the verse in which Allah, The Almighty, Says (what means):

[And warn, [O Muhammad],

الجواب: السَّابِقُونَ مِنْهُم مَا يَأْتِي:

مِنَ النِّسَاءِ: خَدِيجَةُ بِنْتُ خُوَيْلِدٍ.

مِنَ الرِّجَالِ: أَبُو بَكْرٍ الصِّدِّيقِ.

مِنَ الصِّبْيَانِ: عَلِيِّ بنُ أَبِي طَالِبٍ.

مِنَ المَوَالِي: زَيْدُ بن حَارِثَةَ.

26- هَل وَرَقَةُ بن نَوْفَل مِنَ السَّابِقِين؟

الجواب: نَعَم، هُوَ مِنَ السَّابِقِينَ الأَوَّلِينَ.

27- اذكُر بَعْضَ مَن أَسْلَمَ عَلَى يَدِ أَبِي بَكْرٍ الصِّدِّيقِ؟

الجواب: مِنْ هَؤُلَاءِ:

عُثْمَانُ بِن عَفَّانَ، وَالزُّبَيرُ بِنُ العَوَّام، وَعَبْدُ الرَّحَمنِ بنُ عَوْفٍ، وَسَعدُ بن أَبِي وَقَّاص، وَطَلَحَةُ بنُ عُبَيْدِ الله.

28- مَتَى بَدَأَتِ الدَّعوَةُ الجَهْرِيَّةُ؟

الجواب: بَدَأَت بِنُزُولِ قُولِ اللهِ تَعَالَى:

your closest kindred] [As-Shu'araa': 214]

29- Where did the Prophet sallallaahu 'alayhi wa sallam, used to meet his Companions at the beginning of Da'wah?

Answer: In the house of Al-Arqam ibn Abi Al-Arqam.

30- What was the destination of the first immigration?

Answer: It was Ethiopia.

31-When was it?

Answer: It took place in the fifth year of the Ba'thah (beginning of the Prophet's divine mission).

32- What was the reason for that immigration?

Answer: It was to protect their religion and flee from the land of oppression and temptation to the land of safety.

33- How many were the immigrants during that immigration?

Answer: They were twelve men and four women.

34- Mention the names of some of them.

Answer: Some of them were:

'Uthmaan ibn 'Affaan, his wife Ruqayyah; daughter of the Messenger of Allah, sallallaahu

[الشعراء: 214].

29- أَيْنَ المَقَرُّ الَّذِي كَانَ يَجْتَمِعُ فِيهِ النَّبِيُّ ﷺ بِأَصْحَابِهِ فِي بِدَايَةِ الدَّعْوَةِ؟

الجواب: دَارُ الأَرْقَمِ بْنِ أَبِي الأَرْقَمِ.

30- أَيْنَ كَانَت الهِجْرَةُ الأُولَى؟

الجواب: كَانَت إِلَى الحَبَشَةِ.

31- مَتَى كَانَت هَذِهِ الهِجْرَةُ؟

الجواب: كَانَت فِي السَّنَةِ الخَامِسَةِ مِنَ البِعْثَةِ.

32- مَا السَّبَبُ الَّذِي أَدَّى إِلَى هَذِهِ الهِجْرَةِ؟

الجواب: حِفَاظًا عَلَى دِينِهِم وَفِرَارًا مِن بِلَاد الفِتنَةِ إِلَى بِلَادِ الأَمَانِ.

33- كَم عَدَدُ المُهَاجِرِينَ فِي هَذِهِ الهِجْرَةِ؟

الجواب: كَانُوا اثنَي عَشَرَ رَجُلًا وَأَربَعَ نِسوَةٍ.

34- عَيِّنْ بَعضَ الأَسْمَاءِ مِن هَؤُلَاءِ؟

الجواب: مِنهُم: عُثمَانُ بنُ عَفَّان وَزَوجَتُهُ رُقَيَّةُ بِنتُ رَسُولِ الله ﷺ، وَأَبُو سَلَمَةَ

'alayhi wa sallam, Abu Salamah, his wife Umm Salamah, 'Uthmaan ibn Math'oon and Mus'ab ibn 'Umayr.

35- How long did they stay in Ethiopia?

Answer: They stayed there for the months of Sha'baan and Ramadhaan of the fifth year after the Ba'thah and returned to Makkah in Shawwaal of the same year.

36- What do we deduce from the permission given by the Prophet, sallallaahu 'alayhi wa sallam, to his Companions to immigrate to Ethiopia?

Answer: We deduce the permissibility of emigrating from the land of polytheism to the land of Islam.

37- What was the main reason behind the immigrants' return from Ethiopia?

Answer: It was the rumor of the Quraysh accepting Islam.

38- What was the advice of the Messenger of Allah, sallallaahu 'alayhi wa sallam, to his Companions after they had returned and learnt about the false report and after the torment had intensified?

وَزَوجَتُـهُ أَمُّ سَـلَمَة، وَعُثَمَـانُ بـنُ مَظْعُون، وَمُصعَبُ بنُ عُمَير.

٣٥- مَا مُدَّةُ إِقَامَتِهم فِي الحَبَشَةِ؟

الجَوَاب: أَقَامُوا بِالحَبَشَـةِ شَـهرَي شَـعبَانَ وَرَمَضَـانَ مِـنَ السَّـنَةِ الخَامِسَـةِ مِـنَ البِعثَـةِ، وَعَـادُوا إِلَـى مَكَّةَ فِي شَوَّال مِنْ نَفسِ السَّنَةِ.

٣٦- مَـاذَا نَسـتَنتِج مِـنْ إِذْنِ النَّبِـيِّ ﷺ صَحَابَتَهُ بِالهِجرَةِ إِلَى الحَبَشَةِ؟

الجَوَاب: مَشـرُوعِيَّةُ الهِجـرَةِ مِـن دَارِ الشِّـركِ إِلَى دَارِ الإِسلَام.

٣٧- مَا السَّبَبُ الرَّئِيس لِعَودَةِ المُهَاجِرِينَ مِنَ الحَبَشَةِ؟

الجَوَاب: هُـوَ الإِشَـاعَةُ بِإِسـلَام قُرَيْش.

٣٨- بِمَ أَرْشَدَ الرَّسُولُ ﷺ الصَّحَابَةَ لَـمَّا عَـادُوا وَرَأَوا بِـأَنَّ الـبَلَاغَ كَـاذِبٌ وَأَنَّ التَّعذِيبَ أَسوأُ مِمَّا سَبَقَ؟

Answer: He advised them to immigrate to Ethiopia once more.

الجواب: أَرْشَدَهم بِأَنْ أَذِنَ لَهُم ﷺ بِهِجْرَةٍ ثَانِيَةٍ لِلْحَبَشَةِ.

39- What was the number of the immigrants in the second immigration to Ethiopia?

39- كَمْ عَدَدُ المُهَاجِرِينَ فِي الهِجْرَةِ الثَّانِيَةِ؟

Answer: The number was estimated at one hundred and one immigrants in total, eighty-three men and eighteen women.

الجواب: قُدِّرَ العَدَدُ بِمائَةٍ وَوَاحِدٍ عُمُومًا. ثَلَاثَةٌ وَثَمَانُونَ رَجُلًا وَثَمَانِي عَشْرَةَ أمرَأةً.

40- What did the Quraysh do after the return of the immigrants to Ethiopia?

40- مَاذَا فَعَلَت قُرَيشٌ بَعْدَ عَودَةِ المُهَاجِرِينَ لِلْحَبَشَةِ؟

Answer: They sent an official delegation to Negus to incite him to hand the immigrants over to them.

الجواب: بَعَثَتْ وَفْدًا رَسْمِيًا إِلَى النَّجَاشِيِّ يُحَرِّضُونَهُ بِالرَّدِّ وَالتَّسْلِيمِ إِلَيهِم.

41- Who were the members of the delegation?

41- مِمَّ يَتَكَوَّنُ هَذَا الوَفْدُ؟

The delegation included two members:

الجواب: يَتَكَوَّنُ مِن عُضْوَيْنِ بَارِزَيْنِ هُمَا:

1- 'Amr ibn Al-'Aas.

1- عَمرُو بنُ العَاصِ.

2- 'Abdullaah ibn Abi Umayyah.

2- عَبدُ اللهِ بنُ أَبِي أَمَيَّة.

42- Who answred the Quraysh's delegation on behalf of the Muslims?

42- مَنِ الَّذِي تَوَلَّى الرَّدَّ لِوَفدِ قُرَيشٍ نِيَابَةً عَنِ المُسْلِمِين؟

Answer: Ja'far ibn Abi Taalib.

الجواب: جَعْفَر بن أَبِي طَالِب.

43- What did Negus say when he heard the speech of Ja'far ibn Abi Taalib?

43- مَاذَا قَالَ النَّجَاشِيُّ لَـمَا سَمِعَ كَلَامَ جَعْفَر بن أَبِي طَالِب؟

Answer: He said, «Indeed, this religion and what Jesus came with emerge from the same

الجواب: قَالَ: (إنَّ هَذَا وَالَّذِي جَاءَ بِهِ عِيسَى يَخْرُجُ مِنْ مِشْكَاةٍ

lantern. Go, for, by Allah, never shall I hand them over to you».

44- What do we deduce from this situation?

Answer: We deduce that truth is dominant and falsehood is perishable, that fearing Allah is a cause for relief of distress and that belief overcomes hypocrisy and disbelief.

This comes in confirmation of the Statement of Allah, The Almighty (which means): [*And whoever fears Allah - He Will Make for him a way out*] [At-Talaaq: 2]

45- Did Negus believe in the prophethood of Muhammad, sallallaahu 'alayhi wa sallam?

Answer: Yes, he believed in what Muhammad, sallallaahu 'alayhi wa sallam, came with and had faith in him.

46- What was the attitude of the Quraysh when the number of the Muslims increased?

Answer: They gathered and agreed on entirely boycotting the Banu Haashim and the Banu Al-Muttalib. They wrote the boycott's terms on a scroll which they hung inside the Ka'bah.

وَاحِـدَةٍ، انْطَلِقَـا وَاللهِ لَا أَسَـلِمُهُم إِلَيْكُمَا أَبَدًا).

44- مَاذَا نَسْتَنْتِجُ مِنْ هَذَا المَوقِفِ؟

الجواب: نَسْتَنْتِجُ أَنَّ الحقَّ غَالِبٌ وَأَنَّ البَاطِـلَ زَاهِـقٌ وَأَنَّ تَقْـوَى اللهِ سَبَبُ الخُـرُوج مِـن المَـآزِقِ وَأَنَّ الإيمَانَ يَغْلِبُ النِّفَاقَ وَالكُفْرَ.

وَهَـذَا مِصْـدَاقٌ لِقَولِـهِ تَعَـالَى: ﴿وَمَن يَتَّقِ ٱللَّهَ يَجْعَل لَّهُۥ مَخْرَجًا﴾ [الطلاق:2].

45- هَلْ آمَنَ النَّجَاشِيُّ بِنُبُوَّةِ مُحَمَّدٍ ﷺ؟

الجواب: نَعَم، آمَنَ بِمَا جَاءَ بِـه مُحَمَّدٌ ﷺ وَصَدَّقَهُ.

46- مَـا موقِـفُ قُرَيشٍ عِنـدَمَا ازدَادَ الدَّاخِلونَ فِي الإسلامِ؟

الجواب: اجْتَمَعُوا وَاتَّفَقُـوا عَلَـى مُقَاطَعَـةِ بَنِـي هَاشِـمٍ وَبَنِـي عَبـدِ المُطَّلَـبِ بِالكُلِّيَّـةِ وَكَتَبُـوا تِلْـكَ المُقَاطَعَةَ فِي صَحِيفَةٍ وَعَلَّقُوها فِي جَوفِ الكَعْبَةِ.

47- Who wrote the boycott scroll?

Answer: It was Bagheedh ibn 'Aamir ibn Haashim. The Messenger of Allah, sallallaahu 'alayhi wa sallam, supplicated against him, which caused his hand to be paralyzed.

48- For how long did the boycott last?

Answer: It lasted for about three years.

49- A noble Companion was born during the time of the boycott; who was he?

Answer: He was 'Abdullaah ibn 'Abbaas.

50- Who was the one who (destroyed the scroll) anulled the boycott?

Answer: Hishaam ibn 'Amr ibn 'Aamir ibn Lu'ayy.

51- What do we conclude from what the Quraysh did?

Answer: We conclude the following:

1-The harm and persecution that was inflicted on the Messenger of Allah, sallallaahu 'alayhi wa sallam, and the believers by the disbelievers of the Quraysh.

2- The trial that afflicted the Messenger of Allah, sallallaahu

47- مَنْ تَوَلَّى كِتَابَةَ الصَّحِيفَةِ؟

الجواب: تَوَلَّى كِتَابَتَهَا بَغِيضُ بنُ عَامِرِ بنِ هَاشِمٍ فَدَعَا عَلَيهِ رَسُولُ اللهِ ﷺ فَشُلَّتْ يَدُه.

48- كَمْ كَانَتْ مُدَّةُ المُقَاطَعَةِ؟

الجواب: زُهَاءَ ثَلَاثِ سِنِين.

49- فِي فَتْرَةِ المُقَاطَعَةِ وُلِدَ صَحَابِيٌّ جَلِيلٌ فَمَنْ هُوَ؟

الجواب: عَبْدُ اللهِ بنِ عَبَّاس.

50- مَنْ قَامَ بِنَقْضِ الصَّحِيفَةِ؟

الجواب: قَامَ بِنَقْضِهَا هِشَامُ بنُ عَمْرِو بنِ عَامِرِ بنِ لُؤَي.

51- مَاذَا نَسْتَنْتِجُ مِمَّا قَامَتْ قُرَيْشٌ بِفِعْلِه؟

الجواب: نَسْتَنْتِجُ مَا يَأتِي:

1- مَا تَعَرَّضَ لَهُ الرَّسُولُ ﷺ وَالمُؤمِنُونَ مِنَ الأَذَى وَالاضْطِهَادِ مِن قِبَلِ كُفَّارِ قُرَيْش.

2- مَا أَصَابَ رَسُولَ اللهِ ﷺ مِنْ

‘alayhi wa sallam, is a consolation for every believer who may suffer in his life.

3- It was the believers' firm belief deep within their hearts that helped them to survive the trial and to be patient with it.

4-They had their goal realized, which was the protection of the Religion and the soundness of their belief without concern for worldly ambitions or physical safety.

52- When did Abu Taalib die?

Answer: He died in the tenth year after the Ba‘thah, shortly after he had gotten out of the defile where the Banu Haashim was besieged.

53- Did he die while adering to disbelief?

Answer: Yes, even though he was the protecting right arm of the Messenger of Allah, sallallaahu ‘alayhi wa sallam.

54- Why was the Prophet, sallallaahu ‘alayhi wa sallam, sad when his uncle Abu Taalib died?

Answer: Because he was his defender, protector and supporter.

55- When did Khadeejah die?

ابْتِلَاءٍ عَزَاءٌ لِكُلِّ مَا يُصِيبُ المُؤْمِنَ فِي حَيَاتِهِ.

3- مَا أَدَّى إِلَى صَبْرِهِم وَثَبَاتِهِم عَلَى هَذَا الابْتِلَاءِ، هُوَ تَمَسُّكُهُم بِعَقِيدَتِهِم الَّتِي تَعَلَّقَت وَامْتَزَجَت بِهَا قُلُوبُهُم.

4- تَحْقِيقُ هَدَفِهِم: هُوَ أَمْنُ الدِّينِ وَسَلَامَةُ العَقِيدَةِ لَا تَحْقِيقُ مَطَامِعِ الدُّنْيَا وَسَلَامَةُ الجَسَدِ.

52- مَتَى مَاتَ أَبُو طَالِبٍ؟

الجواب: مَاتَ فِي السَّنَةِ العَاشِرَةِ مِنَ البِعْثَةِ، بُعَيْدَ خُرُوجِهِ مِنَ الشِّعْبِ.

53- هَل مَاتَ عَلَى الكُفْرِ؟

الجواب: نَعَم، مَعَ كَوْنِهِ السَّاعِدَ الأَيمَنَ لِلرَّسُولِ ﷺ.

54- لِمَاذَا حَزِنَ النَّبِيُّ ﷺ لَمَّا مَاتَ عَمُّهُ أَبُو طَالِبٍ؟

الجواب: لأَنَّهُ كَانَ ذَائِدَهُ وَحَافَّهُ وَنَاصِرَهُ.

55- مَتَى تُوُفِّيَت خَدِيجَةُ؟

Answer: She died in the tenth year after the Ba'thah, shortly before the Hijrah

الجواب: تُوُفِّيَتْ فِي السَّنَةِ الْعَاشِرَةِ مِنَ الْبَعْثَةِ، وَقُبَيْلَ الْهِجْرَةِ.

56- What was the attitude of the Quraysh after the death of the Prophet's uncle and wife?

56- مَاذَا كَانَ مَوْقِفُ قُرَيْشٍ بَعْدَ مَوْتِ عَمِّهِ وَزَوْجِهِ؟

Answer: They grew more undutiful and oppressive, their animosity increased and their harm intensified.

الجواب: كَانَ مَوْقِفُهَا أَعَقَّ وَأَظْلَمَ إِذِ ازْدَادَتْ عَدَاوَتُهَا وَأَذِيَّتُهَا.

57- What was the attitude of the Prophet, sallallaahu 'alayhi wa sallam, toward such erroneous bigotry?

57- مَا مَوْقِفُ النَّبِيِّ ﷺ مِنْ هَذِهِ الْعَصَبِيَّةِ الْبَاطِلَةِ؟

Answer: He decided to go to At-Taa'if and he actually headed to it.

الجواب: عَزَمَ الْخُرُوجَ إِلَى الطَّائِفِ وَسَارَ إِلَيْهَا.

58- Did someone accompany him on this journey?

58- هَلْ رَافَقَهُ أَحَدٌ فِي هَذِهِ الرِّحْلَةِ؟

Answer: Yes, his freed-slave Zayd ibn Haarithah accompanied him.

الجواب: نَعَم رَافَقَهُ مَوْلَاهُ زَيْدُ بِن حَارِثَةَ.

59- Was he welcomed by the people of At-Taa'if?

59- هَلْ رَحَّبَ بِهِ أَهْلُ الطَّائِفِ؟

Answer: No, on the contrary, they disappointed him, hurt him and expelled him.

الجواب: لَا، بَلْ خَيَّبُوا آمَالَهُ وَآذَوهُ وَأَخْرَجُوهُ.

60- How long did he stay in At-Taa'if?

60- مَا مُدَّةُ إِقَامَتِهِ بَالطَّائِفِ؟

Answer: He stayed there for a month or ten days.

الجواب: كَانَتْ شَهْرًا أَوْ عَشَرَةَ أَيَّامٍ.

61- Did the Messenger of Allah, sallallaahu 'alayhi wa sallam, meet someone on his

61- هَلْ لَقِيَ الرَّسُولُ ﷺ أَحَدًا فِي طَرِيقِ عَوْدَتِهِ؟

way back?

Answer: Yes, he met 'Addaas the Christian who believed him and had faith in him.

62- How did the Messenger of Allah, sallallaahu 'alayhi wa sallam, return from At-Taa'if?

Answer: He returned sad and depressed, but Allah Sent for him the angel of mountains to carry out whatever order he might receive from the Prophet, sallallaahu 'alayhi wa sallam.

63- Deduce some beneficial lessons from this tiresome journey.

Answer:

1-The steadfastness of the Messenger of Allah, sallallaahu 'alayhi wa sallam, and his persistence, no matter how events and calamities aggravated.

2- The ill treatment he received from the people of At-Taa'if.

3-He did not pay back their ill treatment with its like, but he supplicated for them with his famous supplication: «O Allah, Guide the Thaqeef and Bring them (as Muslims)».

4-The compassion of the Prophet, sallallaahu 'alayhi wa sallam, to his people, his

الجَوَاب: نَعَمْ لَقِيَ عَدَّاسًا النَّصْرَانِيَّ فَآمَنَ بِهِ وَصَدَّقَه.

62- كَيْفَ عَادَ ﷺ مِنَ الطَّائِفِ؟

الجَوَاب: عَادَ مَهْمُومًا مَغْمُومًا وَلَكِنَّ اللهَ أَرْسَلَ إِلَيْهِ مَلَكَ الجِبَالِ لِيَكُونَ مُنَفِّذًا أَوَامِرَه إِنْ أَمَرَ.

63- اسْتَخْرِجْ مِنْ هَذِهِ الرِّحْلَةِ الشَّاقَّةِ بَعْضَ العِبَرِ الَّتِي نَسْتَفِيدُ مِنْها.

الجواب:

1- ثَبَاتُ الرَّسُولِ ﷺ وَعَدَمُ يَأْسِهِ مَهْمَا عَظُمَتِ الأَحْدَاثُ وَالمَصَائِبُ.

2- سُوءُ مُعَامَلَةِ أَهْلِ الطَّائِفِ.

3- لَمْ يُجَازِ مُعَامَلَتَهم السَّيِّئَة بِمِثْلِه بَلْ دَعَا لَهُم بِدُعَائِهِ المَشْهُورِ: «اللَّهُمَّ اهْدِ ثَقِيفًا وَأْتِ بِهِم».

4- شَفَقَةُ النَّبِيِّ ﷺ عَلَى قَوْمِهِ، وتَحَمُّلِهِ وصَبْرِهِ عَلَى ظُلْمِهِم.

tolerance and endurance of their injustice.

64- When did the Israa' and Mi'raaj take place?

Answer: It took place before the Hijrah and after the Ba'thah.

65- Did the Israa' and Mi'raaj occur more than once?

Answer: No, it occurred only once.

66- Mention some of the events that the Prophet, sallallaahu 'alayhi wa sallam, went through during the night of Israa' and Mi'raaj.

Answer: He did not pass by a group of angels except that they advised him of cupping by saying, «O Muhammad, order your Ummah to undergo cupping therapy ».

He saw a man sitting, on whose right and left sides there were multitudes of people. When he looked at his right side he smiled and when he looked at his left side he cried. He said, «Welcome to the righteous prophet and the righteous son», the Prophet, sallallaahu 'alayhi wa sallam, then asked Jibreel, «Who is that man?» He said, "He is your father Aadam».

64- مَتَى كَانَ الإِسْرَاءُ وَالمِعْرَاجُ؟

الجواب: كَانَ قَبْلَ الهِجْرَةِ وَبَعْدَ البعثةِ.

65- هَل تَكَرَّرَ الإِسْرَاءُ وَالمِعْرَاجُ؟

الجواب: لا، بَلْ كَانَ مَرَّةً وَاحِدَة.

66- اذكُر بَعضَ مَا رَآهُ النَّبِيُّ ﷺ لَيلَةَ الإِسْرَاءُ وَالمِعْرَاجُ؟

الجواب: مَا مَرَّ بِمَلأٍ مِنَ المَلَائِكَة إِلَّا أَمَرُوهُ بِالحِجَامَةِ، وَقَالُوا: يَا مُحَمَّدُ مُر أُمَّتَكَ بِالحِجَامَةِ.

رَأى رَجُلًا قَاعِدًا عَلَى يَمِينِه أَسوِدَةٌ وَعَلَى يَسَارِهِ أَسوِدَةٌ إِذَا نَظَرَ قِبَلَ يَمِينِه ضَحِكَ، وَإِذَا نَظَرَ قِبَلَ يَسَارِهِ بَكَى فَقَالَ: مَرحَبًا بِالنَّبِيّ الصَّالِح وَالابن الصَّالِح قُلتُ لِجبرِيلَ: «مَن هَذَا»؟ قَالَ: هَذَا أَبُوكَ آدَم.

The Prophet, sallallaahu 'alayhi wa sallam, said, «During the journey of Mi'raaj, I passed by people who had nails of copper with which they scratched their faces and chests, I asked Jibreel who were they and he said: «They are those who eat people's flesh and vilify their honor».

The Prophet, sallallaahu 'alayhi wa sallam, said, «On the Night of Israa', I met Ibraaheem and he said to me, 'Convey my greeting of peace to your Ummah and tell them that the soil of Paradise is good and its water is fresh. Its lands are leveled and to plant in it is to say Subhaan Allah, Al-Hamdu lillaah, laa illaaha illa Allah, Allaahu Akbar and la Hawla wa la Quwwata illa billaah».

67- What was the stance of the Quraysh regarding the incident of the Israa' and Mi'raaj?

Answer: They denied and belied it.

68- Did the call of the Prophet, sallallaahu 'alayhi wa sallam, cease after this incident?

Answer: No, he continued to call people in different

وَقَالَ ﷺ: «لَمَّا عُرِجَ بِي مَرَرْتُ بِقَوْمٍ لَهُمْ أَظْفَارٌ مِنْ نُحَاسٍ يَخْمُشُونَ وُجُوهَهُمْ وَصُدُورَهُمْ فَقُلْتُ: مَنْ هَؤُلَاءِ يَا جِبْرِيلُ؟ قَالَ: هَؤُلَاءِ الَّذِينَ يَأْكُلُونَ لُحُومَ النَّاسِ وَيَقَعُونَ فِي أَعْرَاضِهِمْ».

وَقَالَ ﷺ: «لَقِيتُ إِبْرَاهِيمَ عَلَيْهِ السَّلَام لَيْلَةَ أُسْرِيَ بِي، فَقَالَ: يَا مُحَمَّدُ، أَقْرِئْ أُمَّتَكَ مِنِّي السَّلَامَ، وَأَخْبِرْهُمْ أَنَّ الْجَنَّةَ طَيِّبَةُ التُّرْبَةِ، عَذْبَةُ الْمَاءِ، وَأَنَّهَا قِيعَانٌ، وَأَنَّ غِرَاسَهَا: سُبْحَانَ الله وَالْحَمْدُ لله وَلَا إِلَهَ إِلَّا الله، وَالله أَكْبَرُ وَلَا حَوْلَ وَلَا قُوَّةَ إِلَّا بِالله».

٦٧- مَاذَا كَانَ مَوْقِفُ قُرَيْشٍ مِنْ حَادِثَةِ الإِسْرَاءُ وَالمِعْرَاجُ؟

الجَوَاب: كَانَ مُوقِفُهَا إِنْكَارًا وَتَكْذِيبًا.

٦٨- هَلْ تَوَقَّفَتْ دَعْوَتُهُ ﷺ بَعْدَ ذَلِكَ؟

الجَوَاب: لَا، بَلِ استَمَرَّ فِي دَعوَاهُ

(spiritual) seasons as well as in other times.

69- Did anyone respond to him during his Da‘wah effort on those seasons?

Answer: Yes, few people, no more than nine, of the Khazraj tribe responded to him at Al-‘Aqabah.

70- What urged them to respond to his call?

Answer: Among the reasons that urged them to do so was that the Jews threatened them with the imminent emergence of a prophet whom they would follow and support and with whom they would fight them. Hence, when they knew about the Ba‘thah of the Prophet, sallallaahu ‘alayhi wa sallam, they responded to his call and followed him.

71- How many Muslims from the Ansaar came from Al-Madeenah in the twelfth year of the Ba‘thah?

Answer: Twelve Muslim men came from Al-Madeenah that year.

72- Did the Messenger of Allah, sallallaahu ‘alayhi wa sallam, meet them?

Answer: Yes, he met them in

لِلنَّاسِ فِي المَوَاسِمِ وَغَيرِهَا.

69- هَلِ اسْتَجَابَ لَهُ أَحَدٌ فِي تَجْوَالِهِ فِي المَوَاسِمِ؟

الجَوَاب: نَعَمْ أَجَابَهُ رَهْطٌ مِنَ الخَزرَجِ عِندَ العَقَبَةِ.

70- مَا الَّذِي دَعَاهُم لِلإِجَابَةِ بِدَعْوَتِهِ؟

الجَوَاب: مِن ذَلِكَ أَنَّ اليَهُودَ كَانُوا يُهَدِّدُونَهُم بِقُرْبِ مَبْعَثِ نَبِيٍّ يَتَّبِعُونَهُ وَيَقِفُونَ بِجَانِبِهِ وَيُقَاتِلُونَ مَعَهُ ضِدَّهُم فَلَمَّا عَلِمُوا بَعْثَهُ ﷺ أَجَابُوا دَعْوَتَهُ وَاتَّبَعُوه.

71- كَمْ رَجُلًا مِنْ مُسْلِمِي الأَنْصَارِ قَدِمَ مِنَ المَدِيْنَةِ فِي العَامِ الثَّانِي عَشَرَ مِنَ البِعْثَةِ؟

الجَوَاب: قَدِمَ مِنَ المَدِيْنَةِ اثْنَا عَشَرَ رَجُلًا مِنَ المُسلِمِين.

72- هَلْ لَقِيَهُمُ الرَّسُولُ ﷺ؟

الجَوَاب: نَعَمْ التَقَى بِهِم مَعَ جَمَاعَةٍ

the presence of a group of his Companions wherein they gave him the pledge of allegiance that is known as the Pledge of Women.

73- Did the Messenger of Allah, sallallaahu 'alayhi wa sallam, send someone with them on their return home?

Answer: Yes, he sent Mus'ab ibn 'Umayr with them.

74- Who was his host in Al-Madeenah?

Answer: As'ad ibn Zuraarah was his host in Al-Madeenah.

75- What was the mission of Mus'ab which he undertook by the aid of As'ad ibn Zuraarah?

Answer: His mission was to spread awareness about Islam and call people to it.

76- What was the result of that call?

Answer: The result was that many people accepted Islam; among whom was Usayd ibn Hudhayr and Sa'd ibn Mu'aath.

77- When did Mus'ab ibn 'Umayr return from Al-Madeenah?

Answer: He returned a short while before the season of Hajj

مِــنْ أَصْــحَابِهِ حَتَّــى بَــايَعُوهُ بَيعَــةَ النِّسَاءِ.

73- هَلْ بَعَثَ مَعَهُم رَسُولُ اللهِ ﷺ أَحَدًا عِنْدَ عَوْدَتِهِم؟

الجَــوَاب: نَعَــمْ، أَرْسَــلَ مَعَهـــم مُصعَبَ بنَ عُمَيرٍ.

74- مِنْ صَارَ ضَيْفًا عِنْدَه فِي المَدِيْنَةِ؟

الجَوَاب: صَــارَ عِنْـدَ أَسْـعَدَ بـنِ زُرَارَةَ.

75- كَيْفَ قَامَ مُصعَبٌ بِمُسَاعَدَةِ أَسْعَدَ بنِ زُرَارَةَ؟

الجَوَاب: قَــامَ بِالتَّوعِيـةِ وَالـدَّعوةِ لِلإِسْلَامِ.

76- مَاذَا كَانَتْ نَتِيجَةَ هَذِه الدَّعْوَةِ؟

الجواب: كَانَــت النَّتِيجَــةُ أَنْ دَخَــلَ خَلْقٌ كَثِيرٌ فِي الإِسْلَامِ، مِنْهُم أُسَيدُ بن حُضَيرٍ، وَسَعدُ بن مُعَاذٍ.

77- مَتَـى عَادَ مُصعَبُ بن عُمَيرٍ مِن المَدِينَةِ؟

الجواب: عَادَ قُبيلَ مَوسِمِ الحَجِّ فِي السَّنَةِ الثَّالِثَةَ عَشْرةَ مِـن البَعْثَـةِ

in the thirteenth year of the Ba'thah. He gave the Messenger of Allah, sallallaahu 'alayhi wa sallam, the good news of the success of his call in Al-Madeenah.

مُبَشِّرًا الرَّسُولَ ﷺ بِنَجَاحِ مُهِمَّتِـهِ الدَّعَوِيَّةِ.

78- When was the second Bay'ah (pledge of allegiance) of Al-'Aqabah?

78- مَتى كَانَتْ بَيْعَةُ العَقَبَةِ الثَّانِيَةِ؟

Answer: It was in the season of Hajj in the thirteenth year of the Ba'thah.

الجَوَاب: كَانَت فِي مَوسِمِ الحَجِّ مِن العَامِ الثَّالِثَ عَشَرَ مِنَ البِعْثَةِ.

79- What was the reason behind it?

79- مَا سَبَبُهَا؟

Answer: The reason behind it was to present to the Messenger of Allah, sallallaahu 'alayhi wa sallam, the idea of Hijrah to Al-Madeenah after Islam had found therein a land to settle.

الجَوَاب: كَانَ سَبَبُهَا عَرضَ مَوضُوعِ هِجْرةِ الرَّسُولِ ﷺ إِلَى المَدِينَةِ وَبَعْدَ أَنِ اسْتَقَرَّ الإِسْلَام فِي المَدِينَةِ.

80- What was their number in total?

80- كم كَانَ عَدَدُهُم إِجْمَالاً؟

Answer: They were seventy-two people; two women and seventy men.

الجَوَاب: كَانَ العَدَدُ اثْنَيْنِ وَسَبْعِينَ نَفَرًا، امْرَأَتَينِ وَسَبْعِينَ رَجُلًا

81- Was the Prophet, sallallaahu 'alayhi wa sallam, accompanied by any of his relatives at the time of this Bay'ah?

81- هَلْ كَانَ مَعَه أَحَدٌ مِن أَقْرِبَائِه ﷺ فِي هَذِه البَيعَةِ؟

Answer: Yes, he was accompanied by his uncle Al-'Abbaas ibn 'Abd Al-Muttalib.

الجَوَاب: نَعَـمْ كَـانَ مَعَـهُ عَمُّـهُ العَبَّاسُ بن عَبدِ المُطَّلِبِ.

82- Was Al-'Abbaas a Muslim at that time?

Answer: No, he was not a Muslim but he attended to take care of his nephew's affairs and verify the matter for him.

83- What were the terms of 'Aqabah Pledge of Allegiance?

Answer: It was narrated on the authority of Jaabir, May Allah Be Pleased with him, that he said, «We said, 'O Messenger of Allah, on what do we give you our pledge of allegiance?' He said, 'On obedience in both activity and rest, to spend (in the Cause of Allah) in both adversity and prosperity, to enjoin good and forbid evil, to strive in the Cause of Allah paying no attention to people's criticism, to support me when I come to you and to protect me from what you protect your selves, your wives and your children from. And Paradise will be your reward». [Ahmad]. The Quraysh grew furious when they heard of this pledge and pursued those who joined the Ansaar from among its people. They managed to catch only S'ad ibn 'Ubaadah whom

٨٢- هَلْ كَانَ العَبَّاسُ آنَذَاكَ مُسْلِمًا؟

الجواب: لَا، لَمْ يَكُنْ مُسْلِمًا وَلَكِنَّه حَضَرَ لِيَنْظُرَ أَمْرَ ابْنِ أَخِيهِ وَيَسْتَوْثِقَ لَه.

٨٣- مَا بُنُودُ هَذِهِ البَيْعَةِ؟

الجواب: قَالَ جَابِرٌ: قُلْنَا: يَا رَسُولَ الله، عَلَامَ نُبَايِعُكَ؟ قَالَ: «عَلَى السَّمْعِ وَالطَّاعَةِ فِي النَّشَاطِ وَالْكَسَلِ، وَعَلَى النَّفَقَةِ فِي الْعُسْرِ وَالْيُسْرِ، وَعَلَى الأَمْرِ بِالْمَعْرُوفِ وَالنَّهْيِ عَنِ الْمُنْكَرِ، وَعَلَى أَنْ تَقُومُوا فِي اللهِ وَلَا تَأْخُذَكُمْ فِي اللهِ لَوْمَةُ لَائِمٍ، وَعَلَى أَنْ تَنْصُرُونِي إِذَا قَدِمْتُ إِلَيكِم، وَتَمْنَعُونِي مِمَّا تَمْنَعُونَ مِنْهُ أَنْفُسَكُمْ وَأَزْوَاجَكُمْ وَأَبْنَاءَكُمْ، وَلَكُمُ الْجَنَّةُ». رواه أحمد.

فَلَمَّا سَمِعَتْ قُرَيْشٌ بِهَذِهِ البَيْعَةِ الْمُبَارَكَةِ اشْتَدَّ غَضَبُها وَتَتَبَّعَتْ مَا لَحِقَ مِن أَهْلِهَا، فَلَم تَظْفَر إِلَا بِسَعدِ بنِ عُبَادَةَ فَعَذَّبَتْهُ، ثُمَ نَجَّاهُ الله تَعَالَى، فَلَحِقَ بِالمَدِينَةِ، وَأَمَرَ النَّبِيُّ

 المُؤمِنينَ بِالهِجرَةِ إِلى المَدِينَةِ.

they tortured, but Allah The Almighty Saved him later and then he went to Al-Madeenah. Afterwards, the Prophet, sallallaahu 'alayhi wa sallam, ordered all the believers to migrate to Al-Madeenah.

* * *

فِقهِ العِبَادَات

Fiqh of the Acts of Worship

Fiqh of the Acts of Worship
Questions and Answers In the Fiqh of the Acts of Worship

1- What is Fiqh?

Answer: It is to infer the rulings of Sharee‘ah from their detailed evidence by way of reasoning.

2- What are the rulings of Fiqh?

Answer: There are five rulings: the Fardh (obligatory act), the Sunnah (voluntary act that was practiced by the Prophet, sallallaahu ‘alayhi wa sallam), the Mubaah (permissible act), the Haraam (prohibited act) and the Makrooh (disliked act).

3- What is purification?

Answer: It is to get purified from the Hadath (minor or major ritual impurity) and remove filth.

4- What are the methods of purification?

Answer: Water, earth, stone and tanning (for animals' skins).

5- How can we purify impurities?

فقه العِبَادَات
أَسْئِلَةٌ وَأَجْوِبَةٌ
فِي فِقْهِ العِبَادَات

1- مَا الفِقْهُ؟

الجواب: هُوَ العِلْمُ بِالأَحْكَامِ الشَّرْعِيَّةِ عَنْ أَدِلَّتِهَا التَّفْصِيلِيَّةِ بِالاسْتِدْلَالِ.

2- مَا أَحْكَامُ الفِقْهِ؟

الجواب: أَحْكَامُهُ خَمَسَةٌ: الفَرْضُ وَالسُّنَّةُ وَالمُبَاحُ وَالحَرَامُ وَالمَكْرُوه.

3- مَا الطَّهَارَةُ؟

الجواب: هِيَ رَفْعُ الحَدَثِ وَإِزَالَةُ الخَبَثِ.

4- مَا وَسَائِلُ الطَّهَارَةِ؟

الجواب: هِيَ المَاءُ أَوِ التُّرَابُ أَوِ الحَجَرُ أَوِ الدَّبْغُ.

5- كَيْفَ نُطَهِّرُ النَّجَاسَات؟

Answer: By removing the impurity and washing it off with water.

الجواب: بِإِزَالَتِهَا وَغَسلِهَا بِالمَاءِ.

6- How can purity from the Hadath be attained?

6- بِمَاذا تَكُونُ طَهَارَةُ الحَدَثِ؟

Answer: By performing Wudhoo' (ablution), Ghusl (ritual bath) or Tayammum (dry ablution).

الجواب: بِالوُضُوءِ أَوِ الغُسْلِ أَوِ التَّيَمُّمِ.

7- What are the types of water?

7- ما أَقسَامُ المِيَاهِ؟

Answer: There are four types of water:

1- Absolute water.

2- Used water.

3- Water that is mixed with a pure substance.

4- Water that is contaminated with an impure substance.

الجواب: أَقسَامُهَا أَرْبَعَةٌ وَهِيَ:
1- المَاءُ المُطلَقُ.
2- المَاءُ المُستَعمَلُ.
3- المَاءُ الَّذِي خَالَطَهُ طَاهِرٌ.
4- المَاءُ الَّذِي وَقَعَتْه النَّجَاسَةُ.

8- What is the type of water that is valid for purification?

8- مَا المَاءُ الَّذِي يُتَطَهَّرُ بِهِ؟

Answer: It is the water that comes down from the sky or springs from the earth as long as its color, taste or smell has not changed.

الجواب: هُوَ كُلُّ مَا نَزَلَ مِنَ السَّمَاءِ أَوْ نَبَعَ مِنَ الأرضِ مَا لَم يَتَغَيَّر لُونُهُ أَو طَعمُهُ أَو رِيحُهُ.

9- What is impurity?

9- ما النَّجَاسَةُ؟

Answer: It is the repulsive filth that should be removed from what it affects.

الجواب: النَّجَاسَةُ هِيَ القَذَارَةُ الَّتِي يُتَنَزَّهُ عَنها وَيَغسِلُ مَا أَصَابَته.

10- What is Istinjaa'?

10- مَا الاستِنجَاءُ؟

Answer: It is to wash the eliminatory outlets of the body with water in order to remove

الجواب: هُوَ غَسْلُ السَّبِيلَيْنِ بِالمَاءِ لإزَالَةِ الخَارِجِ مِنهُمَا.

all traces of impurities which have come out of them.

11- What is Istijmaar?

Answer: It is to remove the traces of urine or stool by stones, wood pieces or pure paper.

12- What are the materials valid for making Istijmaar?

Answer: Stones and pure papers.

13- What is Wudhoo'?

Answer: It is purification performed by water for specific body parts.

14- What are the conditions of the validity of Wudhoo'?

1- Islam.

2- Sanity.

3- Discernment.

4- Having performed Istinjaa' or Istijmar.

5- The used water should be pure and permissible to use.

6- Intention.

7- Removing whatever hinders water from reaching the skin.

8- Absence of any of the Wudoo' nullifiers.

9- The time when the prayer becomes due for the person who has an incessant type of

١١- مَا الاستِجمَار؟

الجواب: الاسْتِجمَارُ: إِزالَـةُ أَثَرِ البَــوْلِ أَوِ الغَــائِطِ بِالأَحْجَــارِ أَوِ الحَطَبِ أَوِ الأورَاقِ الطَّاهِرَة.

١٢- مَــا هِــيَ الأَشـيَاءُ الَّتِـي يَجُـوزُ الاستِجمَارُ بِهَا؟

الجــوَاب: الأَحْجَــار - الأورَاقُ الطَّاهِرَة.

١٣- مَا الوُضُوء؟

الجواب: الوُضُــوء هُـوَ طَهَــارَةٌ مَائِيَّةٌ لأَعْضَاءٍ مَخصُوصَةٍ.

١٤- مَا شُرُوطُ صِحَّةِ الوُضُوء؟

١- الإِسْلَامُ.

٢- العَقلُ.

٣- التَّميِيزُ.

٤- استِنْجَاءٌ أَو استِجمَار.

٥- طَهُورِيَّةُ المَاءِ وَإِبَاحتُهُ.

٦- النِّيَّة.

٧- إِزَالَـة مَا يَمنَـعُ وُصُـولَ المَـاءِ إِلَى البَشرَةِ.

٨- أَنْ لَا يَطرَأَ مَا يُبطِلُ الوُضُوءَ.

٩- دُخُــولُ وَقتِ الصَّـلاةِ فِي حَقِّ مَن حَدَثُهُ دَائِمٌ.

أَسَاسِيَّاتٌ فِت التَّرْبِيَةِ الإِسْلَامِيَّةِ

Hadath.

15- What are the obligatory acts in Wudhoo'?

Answer: There are six obligatory acts in Wudhoo':

1- Washing the face including rinsing the mouth and sniffing water.

2- Washing the hands up to and including the elbows.

3- Wiping the whole head including the ears with water.

4- Washing the feet with the ankles included.

5- Observing the prescribed sequence of these acts.

6- Performing the acts successively without interruption.

16- What are the nullifiers of Wudhoo'?

1- Having something passed out of any of the two outlets of the body.

2- Obscurity of reason owing to sleeping or another reason.

3- Touching a private part with the inner part of the hand.

4- Apostasy, May Allah Protect us and the Muslims from that.

17- What is Tayammum?

Answer: It is to wipe the face and the hands with pure earth

15- مَا فُرُوضُ الوُضُوءِ؟

الجواب: فُرُوضُ الوُضُوءِ سِتَّةٌ، وَهِيَ:

1- غَسْلُ الوَجهِ وَمِنهُ المَضْمَضَةُ وَالإِستِنشَاقُ.

2- غِسْلُ اليَدَينِ إِلَى المِرْفَقَينِ.

3- مَسْحُ جَمِيعِ الرَّأسِ وَمِنهُ الأُذُنَانِ.

4- غَسْلُ الرِّجْلَينِ إِلَى الكَعْبَينِ.

5- التَّرْتِيبُ.

6- المُوَالَاةُ.

16- مَا نَوَاقِضُ الوُضُوءِ؟

1- الخَارِجُ مِنَ السَّبِيلَينِ.

2- زَوَالُ العَقلِ بِنَومٍ أَو غَيرِه.

3- مَسُّ الفَرجِ بِبَاطِنِ الكَفِّ.

4- الرِّدَّةُ عَنِ الإِسلَامِ، أَعَاذَنَا الله وَالمُسلِمِينَ مِن ذَلِكَ.

17- مَا التَّيَمُّمُ؟

الجواب: هُوَ مَسْحُ الوَجهِ وَاليَدَينِ بِتَرَابٍ طَاهِرٍ بَدَلًا مِنَ الوُضُوءِ أَوِ

instead of making Wudhoo' or Ghusl.

18- What are the cases in which Tayammum is permissible?

Answer:

1- Illness.

2- Absence of water either in travel or residence.

3- Excessive coldness of water.

4- Keeping water for saving lives.

19- What are the conditions of the validity of Tayammum?

1- Islam.

2- Sanity.

3- Discernment.

4- Intention.

5- Purity of the used earth.

20- What are the obligatory acts in Tayammum?

1- Wiping the face.

2- Wiping the hands to the wrists.

3- Observing the prescribed sequence.

4- Performing the acts successively without interruption.

21- What are the nullifiers of Tayammum?

الغَسْلِ.

18- مَا الأَسْبَابُ الَّتِي تُبِيحُ التَّيَمُّمَ؟

الجواب:

1- المَرَضُ.

2- فَقْدُ المَاءِ فِي السَّفَرِ أَو فِي الحَضَرِ.

3- شِدَّةُ البُرُودَة فِي الماءِ.

4- إِنْقَاذُ المَاءِ للنَّفْسِ.

19- مَا شُرُوطُ صِحَّةِ التَّيَمُّمِ؟

1- الإِسْلاَمُ.

2- العقلُ.

3- التَّمْيِيزُ.

4- النِّيَّةُ.

5- طَهَارَةُ التُّرَابِ.

20- مَا فُروضُ التَّيَمُّمِ؟

1- مَسْحُ الوَجْهِ.

2- مَسْحُ اليَدَينِ إِلَى الرُّسْغَينِ.

3- التَّرْتِيبُ.

4- المُوَالاَةُ.

21- مَا نَوَاقِضُ التَّيَمُّمِ؟

1- The nullifiers of Wudhoo'.
2- The presence of water.
3- The absence of what first caused its permissibility.

22- What is prayer?

Answer: It is a set of sayings and acts that starts with Takbeer and ends with Tasleem.

23- For whom is prayer obligatory?

Answer: Prayer is obligatory for every sane adult Muslim.

24- What are the conditions of the validity of prayer?

Answer: they are:
1- Islam.
2- Sanity.
3- Discernment.
4- Purity from the Hadath.
5- Removing impurity.
6- Concealing 'Awrah.
7- Knowing that the prayer time has become due.
8- Facing the Qiblah.
9- Intention.

25- How many are the pillars of prayer? What are they?

Answer: They are fourteen pillars:

1- نَوَاقِضُ الوُضُوءِ.
2- وُجُودُ المَاءِ.
3- زَوَالُ المُبِيحِ.

21- مَا الصَّلاةُ؟

الجَوَابُ: أَقْوَالٌ وَأَفْعَالٌ مُبْتَدَأَةٌ بِالتَّكْبِيرِ مُخْتَتَمَةٌ بِالتَّسْلِيمِ.

23- عَلَى مَن تَجِبُ الصَّلاةُ؟

الجَوَابُ: عَلَى كُلِّ مُسْلِمٍ بَالِغٍ عَاقِلٍ.

24- مَا شُرُوطُ الصَّلاةِ؟

الجَوَابُ: شُرُوطُ الصَّلاةِ هِيَ:
1- الإِسْلامُ.
2- العَقْلُ.
3- التَّمْيِيزُ.
4- رَفْعُ الحَدَثِ.
5- إِزَالَةُ النَّجَاسَةِ.
6- سَتْرُ العَورَةِ.
7- دُخُولُ الوَقْتِ.
8- استِقْبَالُ القِبْلَةِ.
9- النِّيَّةُ.

25- مَا أَرْكَانُ الصَّلاةِ؟ وَمَا هِيَ؟

الجَوَابُ: أَرْكَانُ الصَّلاةِ أَرْبَعَةَ عَشَرَ رُكْنًا. وَهِيَ:

1- To stand (in prayer) when one is able.	1- القِيَامُ مَعَ القُدْرَة.
2- Saying Takbeer with an audible voice.	2- تَكْبِيرَةُ الإِحْرَام
3- Reciting Surat Al-Faatihah.	3- قِرَاءَةُ الفَاتِحَة.
4- Bowing (Rukoo').	4- الرُّكُوع.
5- Rising from the bowing position.	5- الرَّفْعُ مِنْه.
6- Standing up straight after rising from the bowing position.	6- الاعْتِدَالُ قَائِمًا.
7- Prostration (Sujood).	7- السُّجُود.
8- Rising from prostration.	8- الرَّفْعُ مِنْه.
9- Sitting between the two prostrations.	9- الجُلُوسُ بَيْنَ السَّجْدَتَين.
10- Performing all acts with tranquility.	10- الطُّمَأْنِينَةُ فِي جَمِيعِ الأَفْعَالِ.
11- Reciting the last Tashahhud.	11- التَّشَهُّدُ الأَخِير.
12- Sitting while reciting Tashahhud.	12- الجُلُوسُ مِنْه.
13- Asking Allah to Confer His blessings on the Prophet, sallallaahu 'alayhi wa sallam.	13- الصَّلَاةُ عَلَى النَّبِيِّ ﷺ.
14- Making Tasleem on one's right and left sides.	14- التَّسْلِيمَتَان.

26- How many are the obligatory acts in prayer? What are they?

26- مَا وَاجَبَاتُ الصَّلَاةِ؟ وَمَا هِيَ؟

Answer: The obligatory acts in prayer are eight, they are:

الجواب: وَاجَبَاتُ الصَّلَاةِ ثَمَانِيَةٌ، وَهِيَ:

1- To recite Takbeer while shifting from one position to

1- تَكْبِيرَاتُ الانْتِقَال.

another.

2- Saying, «Sami'a Allaahu liman Hamidah (Allah Listens to him who praises Him)».

2- سَمِعَ اللهُ لِمَن حَمَدَه.

3- Saying, «Rabbana wa lak-al-Hamd (Our Lord, all praise be to You)».

3- رَبَّنَا وَلَكَ الحَمد.

4- Saying, «Subhaana Rabbiya Al-'Atheem (Exalted Is my Lord, The Most Great)».

4- سُبحَانَ رَبِّيَ العَظِيم.

5- Saying, «Subhaana Rabbiya Al-A'ala (Exalted Is my Lord, The Most High)».

5- سُبحَانَ رَبِّيَ الأَعلَى.

6- Saying, «Rabbi Ighfir li (O my Lord, Forgive me)», between the two prostrations.

6- رَبِّ اغفِر لِي – بَينَ السَّجدَتَين.

7- Reciting the first Tashahhud.

7- التَّشَهُّدُ الأَوسَطُ.

8- Sitting while reciting it.

8- الجُلُوسُ لَه.

27- What are the nullifiers of the prayer?

27- مَا مُبطِلاتُ الصَّلاةِ؟

Answer:

الجواب:

1- Leaving a condition or a pillar deliberately and without an excuse.

1- تَركُ شَرطٍ أَو رُكِن عَمْدًا بِلَا عُذْرٍ.

2- Eating or drinking.

2- الأَكلُ وَالشُّرب.

3- To speak on purpose.

3- الكَلَامُ عَمْدًا.

4- Laughter.

4- الضَّحِكُ.

5- Making useless movements excessively.

5- العَبَثُ الكَثِيرُ المُتَوَالِي فِي الصَّلَاة.

6- To noticeably drift from the direction of Qiblah.

6- الانحِرَافُ الكَثِيرُ عَن جِهَةِ القِبلَة.

7- Having the 'Awrah exposed.

7- انكِشَافُ العَورَة.

8- To exit the state of ritual purity.

8- انْتِقَاضُ الطَّهَارَةِ.

28- What is Zakaah (obligatory charity)?

28- مَا الزَّكَاةُ؟

Answer: It is a specific amount taken from a specific property owned by a specific class of Muslims.

الجواب: هِيَ مِقدَارٌ مَخصُوصٌ مِــنْ مَــالٍ مَخصُــوصٍ لِطَائِفَــةٍ مَخصُوصَةٍ.

29- What are the conditions of the obligation of Zakaah?

29- مَا شُرُوطُ وجوبِ الزكاةِ؟

1- Islam.

1- الإِسلَامُ.

2- Freedom.

2- الحُرِّيَةُ.

3- Reaching the Nisaab.

3- بُلُوغُ النِّصَابِ.

4- Absolute ownership (of the property).

4- المِلكُ التَّامُ.

5- Having a Hawl (a Hijri year) elapsed since the person first owned the Nisaab.

5- تَمَــامُ الحَــولِ فِــي بَعــضِ الأَموَالِ.

30- For whom is Zakaah obligatory?

30- عَلَى مَنْ تَجِبُ الزَّكَاةُ؟

Answer: Zakaah is obligatory for every free Muslim who owns the Nisaab.

الجواب: تَجِبُ عَلَى المُسلِمِ الحُرِّ المَالِكِ لِلنِّصَابِ.

31- What is the Nisaab?

31- ما النِّصَابُ؟

Answer: It is a certain amount of money on which Zakaah becomes due.

الجواب: هُوَ القَدْرُ المُعَيَّنُ الَّذِي تَجِبُ عَلَيهِ الزَّكَاةُ.

32- What is the Nisaab of the Zakaah on gold?

32- مَا نِصَابُ زَكَاةِ الذَّهَبِ؟

Answer: It is 20 Dinars, (85 grams of gold approximately).

الجواب: عِشــرُونَ دِينَــارًا (85 جرَام تَقرِيبًا).

33- What is the Nisaab of the Zakaah on silver?

33- مَا نِصَابُ زَكَاةِ الفِضَّةِ؟

Answer: 200 Dirhams (624 grams approximately).

الجواب: مِــــائَتَي دِرهَــم (624 جِرَام تَقْرِيبًا).

34- *What is the Nisaab of the Zakaah on agricultural produce?*

Answer: It is five Wasqs (the Wasq is 60 Saa's).

34- مَا نِصَابُ زَكَاةِ الزُّرُوعِ؟

الجواب: خَمْسَةُ أَوْسُقٍ (الوَسْقُ 60 صَاعًا).

35- *What is the Nisaab of the Zakaah on camels?*

Answer: It is five camels.

35- مَا نِصَابُ زَكَاةِ الإِبِلِ؟

الجواب: خَمْسَةٌ مِنَ الإِبِلِ.

36- *What is the Nisaab of the Zakaah on cows?*

Answer: It is thirty cows.

36- مَا نِصَابُ زَكَاةِ البَقَرِ؟

الجواب: ثَلَاثُونَ بَقَرَة.

37- *What is the Nisaab of the Zakaah on sheep?*

Answer: It is forty sheep.

37- مَا نِصَابُ زَكَاةِ الغَنَمِ؟

الجواب: أَرْبَعُونَ شَاة.

38- *To whom is the Zakaah given?*

Answer: Zakaah is given to the following categories of people:

1- The poor.
2- The needy.
3- The Zakaah collectors.
4- To attract the hearts of those inclined to Islam.

38- لِمَن تُصْرَفُ الزَّكَاةُ؟

الجواب: تُصْــــرَفُ الزَّكَــاةُ إِلــى الأَصْنَافِ التَّالِيَةِ:

1- الفُقَرَاءُ.
2- المَسَاكِين.
3- العَامِلُونَ عَلَيهَا.
4- المُؤَلَّفَةُ قُلُوبُهُم.

5- Freeing captives or slaves	5- فَكَّ الرِّقَابِ.
6- (Insolvent) debtors.	6- الغَارِمُونَ.
7- Those who strive in the Cause of Allah.	7- السَّاعُونَ فِي سَبِيلِ اللهِ.
8- The travelers.	8- المُسَافِرُونَ.

39- Who are not allowed to receive it?

39- مَنِ المَمْنُوعُ بِدَفْعِها؟

1- The disbelievers.

1- الكَافِرُ.

2- The slaves.

2- الرَّقِيقُ.

3- The rich.

3- الغَنِيُّ.

4- Those of whom the Muslim is ordered to provide for.

4- مَن تَلْزَمُكَ نَفَقَتُهُ.

5- The Banu Haashim.

5- بَنُو هَاشِمٍ.

40- What are the kinds of property on which Zakaah is due?

40- مَا الأَجْنَاسُ المَفْرُوضَةُ عَلَيْهَا الزَّكَاةُ؟

1- Agricultural produce.

1- الحَرثُ.

2- Livestock.

2- المَاشِيَةُ.

3- Gold and silver.

3- النَّقدَانِ (الذَّهَبُ وَالفِضَّة).

41- What are the kinds of livestock on which Zakaah is due?

41- مَا المَوَاشِي الَّتِي تَجِبُ الزَّكَاةُ فِيهَا؟

1- Camels.

1- الإِبِلُ.

2- Cows.

2- البَقَرُ.

3- Sheep.

3- الغَنَمُ.

42- What are the conditions of the Zakaah of livestock?

42- مَا شُرُوطُ زَكَاةِ المَوَاشِي؟

1- Reaching the Nisaab.

1- النِّصَابُ.

2- Having a Hawl (Hijri year) elapsed since their owner

2- اكْتِمَالُ الحَوْلِ.

possessed the Nisaab.

3- The animals being Saa'imah (animals that graze in fields and do not live on fodder).

43- What is the Hawl?

Answer: It is a complete set of twelve Hijri months.

44- When was Zakaah ordained?

Answer: It was ordained in the second year after Hijrah.

45- What are the kinds of property on which Zakaah is due?

1- Grains and fruits.

2- The Saa'imah from among the cattle.

3- Gold and silver.

4- Commercial commodities.

5- Metal and Rikaaz (every thing that is mined from the earth).

46- On whom is the Zakkah of Fitr due?

Answer: It is due on every free Muslim who owns what exceeds his need and that of those whom he maintains in a whole day.

47- What are the channels of paying the Zakaah of Fitr?

Answer: They are the same pertaining to the obligatory

٣- كَوْنُهَا سَائِمَة.

٤٣- مَا الحَوْلُ؟

الجَوَابُ: الْحَوْلُ اكْتِمَالُ اثْنَيْ عَشَرَ شَهْرًا.

٤٤- مَتَى فُرِضَتِ الزَّكَاة؟

الجواب: فِي العَامِ الثَّانِي لِلهِجرَةِ.

٤٥- مَا الأصْنَاف الَّتِي تَجِبُ فِيهَا الزَّكَاة.

١- الحبُوبُ وَالثِّمَار.

٢- السَّائِمَةُ مِنَ الأنعَام.

٣- الذَّهَبُ وَالفِضَّة.

٤- عُرُوضُ التِّجَارَة.

٥- المَعدِنُ وَالرِّكَاز.

٤٦- عَلَى مَن تَجِبُ زَكَاةُ الفِطر؟

الجواب: عَلَى كُلِّ مُسلِمٍ حُرٍّ مَالِكٍ مَا يَزِيدُ عَن قُوتِهِ وَقُوتِ مَن يَعُولُهُ فِي اليومِ وَاللَّيْلَةِ.

٤٧- مَا مَصَارِفُ زَكَاةِ الفِطرِ؟

الجواب: هِيَ المَصَارِفُ الثَّمَانِيَةُ الَّتِي تُخرَجُ لَهَا الزَّكَاة.

Zakaah.

48- What is the amount of the Zakaah of Fitr?

Answer: It is one Saa' of the kind of food that is commonly eaten.

49- When was the Zakaah of Fitr ordained?

Answer: It was ordained in the same year that the obligatory Zakaah was ordained.

50- What is Sawm (fasting)?

Answer: It is the abstention from everything that breaks fasting from dawn time to sunset. This is to be associated with an intention to fast.

51- What is the ruling on fasting Ramadhaan?

Answer: It is obligatory.

52- When was fasting ordained?

Answer: In the second year after Hijrah.

53- What are the pillars of fasting?

Answer: There are two pillars of fasting:

1- Intention.

2-Abstention from whatever breaks fasting.

54- How is the start of Ramadhaan verified?

48- مَا مِقدَارُ زَكَاةِ الفِطرِ؟

الجواب: صَاعٌ مِمَّا يُعْتَادُ مِنَ الْقُوتِ الْغَالِبِ.

49- مَتَى شُرِعَت زَكَاةُ الفِطرِ؟

الجواب: فِي نَفسِ العَـامِ الَّـذِي فُرِضَت فِيهِ الزَّكَاةُ.

50- مَا الصّومُ؟

الجواب: الإمسَـاكُ عَـن جَمِيـعِ المُفطِرَاتِ مِن طُلُـوعِ الفَجرِ إِلَـى غُرُوبِ الشَّمسِ مَعَ النِّيَّةِ.

51- مَا حُكمُ صِيَامِ رَمَضَانَ؟

الجواب: حُكْمُهُ وَاجِبٌ.

52- مَتَى فُرِضَ الصِّيَامُ؟

الجواب: فِي العَامِ الثَّانِي للهِجرَةِ.

53- مَا أَركَانُ الصِّيَامِ؟

الجواب: للصِّيَامِ رُكنَانِ، هُمَا:

1- النِّيَّةُ.

2- الإمسَاكُ عَنِ المُفطِرَاتِ.

54- بِمَ يَثْبُتُ شَهرُ رَمَضَانَ؟

Answer: By sighting the Hilaal (crescent) of Ramadhaan or by the completion of the thirty days of Sha'baan.

55- *What are the days in which fasting is prohibited?*

Answer: The Day of 'Eed Al-Fitr, The Day of 'Eed Al-Adh-ha, the Days of Tashreeq and the Day of doubt (the day that is doubted to be the last of Sha'abaan or the first of Ramadhaan).

56- *What are the Days of Tashreeq?*

Answer: The three days that follow the Day of 'Eed Al-Adh-ha.

57- *What is the voluntary fasting?*

Answer: It is to fast days other than the obligatory days under Sharee'ah.

58- *What is the best fasting apart from Ramadhaan?*

Answer: Fasting the Month of Al-Muharram.

59- *What is the reward for fasting the Day of 'Arafah?*

Answer: The atonement of the sins committed in the previous and coming years.

60- *What is the reward for fasting the Day of 'Aashooraa'*

الجواب: بِرُؤْيَةِ الهِلَالِ أَوْ تَمَامِ شَهْرِ شَعْبَانَ (ثَلَاثُونَ يَوْمًا).

55- مَا الأَيَّامُ الَّتِي يَحرُمُ فِيهَا الصَّومُ؟

الجواب: يَومَا العِيدِ وَأَيَّامُ التَّشْرِيقِ وَيَومُ الشَّكِّ.

56- مَا أَيَّامُ التَّشْرِيقِ؟

الجواب: ثَلَاثَةُ أَيَّامٍ تَلِي عِيدَ الأَضْحَى.

57- مَا التَّطَوُّعُ مِنَ الصِّيَامِ؟

الجواب: صُوْمُ غَيْرِ الْوَاجِبِ.

58- مَا أَفْضَلُ صَوْمٍ فِي غَيْرِ رَمَضَانَ؟

الجواب: صَوْمُ شَهْرِ الْمُحَرَّمِ.

59- مَا جَزَاءُ صَوْمِ يَومِ عَرَفَةَ؟

الجواب: تَكْفِيرُ الخَطَايَا بِسَنَةٍ قَبْلَهَا وَسَنَةٍ بَعْدَهَا.

60- مَا جَزَاءُ صَوْمِ يَومِ عَاشُورَاءَ؟

(10th of Al-Muharram)?

Answer: The atonement of the sins committed in the previous year.

الجَوَاب: تَكْفِيرُ الخَطَايَا بِسَنَةٍ قَبْلَهَا.

61- What are the White Days?

61- مَا الأَيَّامُ البِيض؟

Answer: They are the thirteenth, the fourteenth and the fifteenth days of every lunar month.

الجَوَاب: ثَلَاثَةَ عَشَرَ، وَأَرْبَعَةَ عَشَرَ، وَخَمْسَةَ عَشَرَ مِنْ كُلِّ شَهْرٍ قَمَرِي.

62- Mention five of the manners of fasting.

62- اذْكُرْ خَمْسًا مِن آدَابِ الصِّيَام؟

Answer:

الجَوَاب:

1- Having the Suhoor meal.

1- السُّحُور.

2- Hastening to break the fast.

2- تعجِيلُ الفِطر.

3- Reciting the Quran.

3- قِرَاءَةُ القُرآن.

4- Showing diligence in worship.

4- الجِدُّ فِي العِبَادَة.

5- Supplicating Allah on breaking the fast.

5- الدُّعَاءُ عِندَ الإفطَار.

63- What is Hajj?

63- مَا الحَجُّ؟

Answer: It is to set out for the Sacred House of Allah to perform the rites.

الجَوَاب: هُوَ قَصْدُ بَيتِ اللهِ الحَرَامِ للنُّسُك.

64- What are the rites?

64- مَا النُّسُكُ؟

Answer: They are the specific actions performed in Hajj including its pillars and obligatory actions.

الجَوَاب: النُّسُكُ مَا يُؤَدَّى مِن أَعمَالِ الحَجِّ مِن أركَانِهِ وَوَاجِبَاتِه.

65- What are the types of Hajj?

65- مَا أَضْرُبُ الحَجِّ؟

Answer:

الجَوَاب:

1- Qiraan Hajj.

1- حَجُّ القِرَان.

2- Ifraad Hajj.

3- Tamattu' Hajj.

66- What are the pillars of Hajj?

Answer:

1- Ihraam, which is the intention to start the rites.

2- Standing at 'Arafah.

3- Tawaaf Al-Ifaadhah.

4- Performing Sa'y.

67- What are the obligatory actions of Hajj?

Answer:

1- Assuming Ihraam from the Meeqaat.

2- Staying at 'Arafah until sunset.

3- Spending the night in Muzdalifah.

4- Spending the nights of the eleventh and twelfth days of Thul Hijjah in Mina.

5- Throwing the pebbles.

6- Shaving or shortening the hair.

7- Tawaaf Al-Wadaa' (Farewell Tawaaf).

68- What are the forbidden acts in Ihraam?

Answer:

1- Cutting the hair.

٢- حَجُّ الإِفْرَادِ.

٣- حَجُّ التَّمَتُّعِ.

٦٦- مَا أَرْكَانُ الحَجِّ؟

الجواب:

١- الإِحْرَامُ: وَهُوَ نِيَّةُ الدُّخُولِ فِي النُّسُكِ.

٢- الوُقُوفُ بِعَرَفَةَ.

٣- طَوَافُ الإِفَاضَةِ.

٤- السَّعْيُ.

٦٧- مَا وَاجِبَاتُ الحَجِّ؟

الجواب:

١- الإِحْرَامُ مِنَ المِيقَاتِ.

٢- الوُقُوفُ بِعَرَفَةَ إِلَى غُرُوبِ الشَّمْسِ.

٣- المَبِيتُ بِمُزْدَلِفَةَ.

٤- المَبِيتُ بِمِنًى لَيْلَتَي الحَادِي عَشَرَ وَالثَّانِي عَشَرَ.

٥- رَمْيُ الجِمَارِ.

٦- الحَلْقُ أَوِ التَّقْصِيرُ.

٧- طَوَافُ الوَدَاعِ.

٦٨- مَا محظورات الإحرام؟

الجواب:

١- حَلْقُ الشَّعْرِ.

2- Trimming the nails

3- Using perfume.

4- Killing land game.

5- Concluding marriage contract.

6- Wearing Khuffs[1] and form fitting clothes[2].

7- Covering the head. (Women are excluded).

8- Satisfying the sexual desire.

9- Engaging in non-penetrative sexual contact.

٢- تَقْلِيمُ الأَظَافِرِ.

٣- مَسُّ الطِّيبِ.

٤- قَتْلُ صَيدِ البَرِّ.

٥- عَقْدُ النِّكَاحِ.

٦- لُبْسُ المَخِيطِ وَالخُفَّينِ لِغَيرِ المَرأَةِ.

٧- تَغْطِيَةُ الرَّأسِ لِلرَّجُلِ.

٨- تَأْدِيَةُ الْغَرِيزَةِ الجِنْسِيَّةِ.

٩- المُبَاشَرَةُ دُونَ الفَرجِ.

---

(1) Or any footwear that covers the ankles.

(2) Women can wear their regular clothing as long as it fulfills normal Islamic standards.

قَصَصُ الأَنبِيَاء
بِطَريقَةِ سُؤَالٍ وَجَوَاب
Stories of the Prophets
Questions and Answers

قَصَصُ الأَنْبِيَاءِ بِطَرِيقَةِ سُؤَالٍ وَجَوَاب

Stories of The Prophets Questions and Answers

1- Who is a Messenger?

Answer: A Messenger is a man to whom a new Sharee'ah is revealed and is ordered to convey it to those to whom he is sent.

For example, the prophets of the Children of Israel who came after Moosa were sent to convey the Sharee'ah of Moosa. Allah, The Almighty, Did not Order them to convey a new revelation or a new Sharee'ah. For this reason, they were prophets but not messengers.

2- Who is a prophet?

Answer: A prophet is a man who is sent to confirm the Sharee'ah of the messengers who came before him.

3- What are the characteristics that distinguish prophets from ordinary people?

1- Receiving Revelation.

2- They are to be interred in the

1- مَنِ الرَّسُولُ؟

الجواب: الرَّسُولُ: هُوَ مَنْ أُوحِيَ إِلَيْهِ بِشَرعٍ جَدِيدٍ وَإِبْلَاغٍ مَنْ أُرْسِلَ إِلَيهم.

فَمَثَلاً: أَنَّ مَا بَعدَ مُوسَى مِنْ أَنْبِيَاءِ بَنِي إِسْرَائِيلَ مَبْعوثُون بِشَرِيعَةِ مُوسَى وَلَمْ يُكَلِّف الله لَهَم بِاِبْلَاغِ وَحيٍّ جَدِيدٍ وَشَرِيْعَةٍ جَدِيْدَةٍ، فَهُم إِذًا أَنْبِيَاءُ وَلَيْسُو بِرُسُلٍ.

2- مَنِ النَّبِيُّ؟

الجواب: النَّبَيُّ: هُوَ المَبْعُوثُ لِتَقرِيرِ شَرعِ مَن سَبَقَهُ.

3- مَا الخَصَائِصُ الَّتِي تُمَيِّزُ الأَنْبِيَاءَ عَنْ غَيْرِهِم؟

الجواب: أَوَّلاً: الوَحيُ.

ثَانِيًا: مُوَارَاتُهُم حَيْثُ فَارَقَت

same place they died.

3- They are granted choice whether to leave the Worldly life or remain alive.

4- Their eyes sleep but their hearts are ever awake.

5- The earth does not consume their bodies after their death.

4- Does the call of all the prophets preach the same thing?

Answer: Yes, the call of all the prophets is the call for monotheism and abandoning polytheism and paganism.

The Story of Aadam:

5- From what Did Allah Create Aadam?

Answer: Allah Created Aadam from earth.

6- On which day was Aadam created?

Answer: Allah Created Aadam on Friday.

7- What are the general characteristics that distinguish Aadam from others?

1- He is the father of mankind.

2- Allah, The Almighty, Created him with His Hand.

3- Allah Breathed from His

رُوْحُهُم.

ثَالِثًا: التَّخْيِيُر بَيْنَ مُفَارَقَةِ الدُّنْيَا أَوِ البَقَاءِ فِيهَا.

رَابِعًا: تَنَامُ أَعْيُنُهُم وَتَسْهَرُ قُلُوبُهُم.

خَامِسًا: لَا تَأْكُلُ الأَرْضُ أَجْسَادَهُم.

٤- هَل دَعوَةُ الأَنبِيَاءِ وَاحِدَةٌ؟

الجَوَاب: نَعَم، كَانَت دَعْوتُهم وَاحِدَةً وَهِي الدَّعوةُ إِلَى التَّوحِيد وَنَبذِ الشِّركِ وَالوَثَنِيَّة.

قِصَّةُ آدَم عليه السلام:

٥- مِمَّ خَلَقَ اللهُ آدَم؟

الجَوَاب: خَلَقَهُ مِن تُرَابٍ.

٦- أَيَّ يَومٍ خُلِقَ آدَم؟

الجَوَاب: خَلَقَه اللهُ يَومَ الجُمُعَة.

٧- مَا الخَصَائِصُ العَامَةُ التي تَمَيَّزَ بِهَا آدَمُ عَن غَيرِه؟

الجَوَاب: أَوَّلاً: أَنَّهُ أَبُو البَشَر.

ثَانِيًا: أَنَّ اللهَ خَلَقَهُ بِيَدِه.

ثَالِثًا: أَنَّ اللهَ نَفَخَ فِيهِ مِن رُوحه.

Soul into him.

4- Allah Ordered the angels to prostrate themselves to him.

رَابِعًا: أَمَرَ اللهُ الْمَلَائِكَةَ بِالسُّجُودِ لَهُ.

8- In which heaven is Aadam?

Answer: He is in the first heaven (the nearest to the earth).

8- فِي أَيِّ سَمَاءٍ هُوَ؟

الجواب: هُوَ فِي السَّمَاءِ الأُولَى.

9- Who were the angels who were ordered to prostrate themselves to Aadam?

Answer: The order included all the angels in the heaven and the earth. This is supported by the Saying of Allah, The Almighty (which means): [*So the angels prostrated - all of them entirely*] [Al-Hijr: 30]

9ـ مَا الْمَلَائِكَةُ الَّذِينَ أُمِرُوا بِالسُّجُودِ لآدَمَ؟

الجواب: جَمِيعُ الْمَلَائِكَةِ فِي السَّمَاءِ وَالأَرْضِ؛ لِقَوْلِهِ تَعَالَى:

﴿فَسَجَدَ الْمَلَائِكَةُ كُلُّهُمْ أَجْمَعُونَ﴾

[الحجر: 30].

10- Who refused to prostrate himself to Aadam?

Answer: Satan refused.

10- مَنْ رَفَضَ السُّجُودَ لآدَمَ؟

الجواب: إبليس.

11- What caused him not to prostrate?

Answer: Arrogance and claiming superiority.

11- مَا سَبَبُ امتِنَاعِه مِنَ السُّجُودِ؟

الجواب: سَبَبُ امتِنَاعِهِ مِنَ السُّجُودِ الكِبُرُ وادِّعَاءُ الأَفْضَلِيَّةِ.

12- Is Satan an angel?

Answer: No, he is not an angel.

12- هَل هُوَ مِنَ الملَائِكَةِ؟

الجواب: لاَ، لَيسَ مِنَ الْمَلَائِكَةِ.

13- What was the paradise in which Aadam lived?

Answer: It was the Paradise of Eternity.

13- مَا الجَنَّةُ الَّتِي كَانَ فِيهَا آدَم؟

الجواب: هِيَ جَنَّةُ الخُلدِ.

14- What was the reason

14- مَا سَبَبُ خُرُوجِ آدَمَ مِنَ الجَنَّةِ؟

behind Aadam's getting out of Paradise?

Answer: He did what he was forbidden from doing, i.e., eating from the Tree.

15- What made Aadam and Hawwaa' eat what they were forbidden from eating in Paradise?

Answer: The devil's adorning the deed for them and his whispering to them.

16- What do we conclude from the story of Aadam?

1- Envy is one of the most evil morals and the most fatal ailments that destroy the slave. Therefore, it is incumbent upon the Muslim to avoid this bad moral and fatal ailment. Moreover, arrogance was the cause that led Satan to his doom of being cursed and expelled.

2- When a slave commits a sin, he should hasten to repent and admit his guilt.

3- The danger of sins, being a cause of the deprivation of blessings.

4- One always reaps what he sows. Satan was punished in a way that went against the pride

الجواب: سَبَبُ خُرُوجِهِ مِنَ الجَنَّةِ وقُوعُهُ فِيمَا نُهِيَ عَنهُ وَهُوَ أَكلُهُ مِنَ الشَّجَرَةِ.

15- مَا الَّذِي دَعَا آدَمَ وحَوَّاءَ إِلَى أَكلِ مَا نُهِيَا عَنْهُ فِي الجَنَّةِ؟

الجواب: دَعاهُمَا تَزيينُ الشيطانِ وَوَسْوستُهُ وَإِغرَاؤهُ فِي ذَلِكَ.

16- مَاذَا نَسْتنتِجُ مِن قِصَّةِ آدَم؟

الجواب: أَوَّلاً: أَنَّ الحَسَدَ مِن أَسْوأ الأَخْـلَاقِ الذميمةِ وَأَخْطَـرِ الأَمْرَاضِ الفَتَّاكَةِ عَلَى العَبدِ؛ لِذَا يَنْبَغِي عَلَى المُسْلِمِ أَنْ يَتَجَنَّبَ هَذَا الخُلُقَ وَهَذَا الَمرَضَ. وَأن الكِبرَ هُوَ الَّذِي أَدَّى بِـإِبْلِيسَ إِلَى مَا آلَ إِلَيهِ مِن اللَّعْنَةِ وَالطَّردِ.

ثانِيًا: يَنْبَغِي لِلعَبدِ إِذَا وَقَعَ فِي ذَنبٍ أَن يُبَادِرَ إِلَى التَّوبَةِ وَالاعتِرَافِ.

ثالِثًا: خَطَرُ المَعَاصِي وَأَنَّهَا سَبَبٌ لِزَوَالِ النِّعَمِ.

رَابِعًا: الجَزَاءُ مِن جِنسِ العَمَـلِ، فَاللهُ عَامَلَ إِبلِيسَ بِنَقِيضِ قَصدِهِ.

he intended for himself.

5- Caution should be taken from the animosity of the devil as he is an enemy of man.

خامسًا: الحَذَرُ مِن عَدَاوَةِ الشَّيطَانِ وَأَنَّهُ عَدُوٌّ لِلإنسَانِ. وَقَد أَخبَرَنَا الله بِعَدَاوَتِهِ لَنَا.

Allah, The Almighty, Informed us about his enmity as He Says (what means): **[*[Iblees] said, "My Lord, because You Have Put me in error, I will surely make [disobedience] attractive to them on earth, and I will mislead them all*]** [Al-Hijr: 39]

قَالَ تَعَالَى عَنهُ: ﴿◆✌ا•🔔 ر◆بِّ
◆□ﺗ③◆□ﻏ□أ ⑥ ✎□▦ﺑ
❀ﺯ⊡③☪◆♊ ☠♑•⑦ ⑦
ا﴿❀☛رْضِ
□◆❀♉ﻏ□③◆✵♣☠
أ□ﺟ◆✓×◆﴾
[الحجر: 39]

6- Aadam's repentance was accepted and his supplication was answered.

سادسًا: قَبُولُ التَّوبَةِ مِنهُ وَإِجَابَةُ دَعْوَتِه.

17- What is the remedy of the hearts that have been stained with sins?

17- مَا عِلاجُ القُلُوبِ التِي كَدَّرَتْهَا الذُّنُوبُ؟

Answer: Its remedy lies in repentance, for it treats the heart and washes it in the same way as water washes dirt out of a dress.

الجواب: عِلَاجُها التَّوبَةُ؛ لِأَنَّهَا تُعَالِجُ القَلبَ وَتَغْسِلُهُ كَمَا يَغْسِلُ المَاءُ الوسخَ مِنَ الثَّوبِ.

18- What are the conditions of repentance?

19- مَا شُرُوطُ التَّوبَة ؟

Answer:

الجواب:

1- To give up committing the sin.

1- أَنْ يقلِعَ عَنِ المَعصِيةِ.

2- To feel remorse for having committed it.

3- To be determined not to return to it again.

19- Did Hawwaa' eat with Aadam from the Tree?

Answer: Yes, she ate with him from the Tree.

20- What was the result of their eating from the Tree after they had been forbidden from it?

Answer: They were made to descend to earth.

21- What were the words that Aadam received from His Lord thereby He Accepted his repentance?

Answer: They are mentioned in the Saying of Allah, The Almighty (which means):

[«*Our Lord, we have wronged ourselves, and if You Do not Forgive us and Have mercy upon us, we will surely be among the losers.*] [Al-A'raaf: 23].

2- أَنْ يَنْدَمَ عَلَى فِعْلِهَا.

3- أَنْ يَعْزِمَ أَنْ لَا يَعُودَ إِلَيْهَا أَبَدًا.

19- هَلْ شَارَكَت حَوَّاءُ مَعَ آدَمَ بِالأَكْلِ؟

الجواب: نَعَمْ، شَارَكَت حَوَّاءُ مَعَ آدَمَ بِالأَكْلِ؟

20 - مَاذَا كَانَت نَتِيجَةَ أَكْلِهِمَا بَعْدَ أَنْ نُهِيَا عَنْهَا؟

الجواب: كَانَتْ النَّتِيجَةَ إِنزَالَهُمَا إِلَى الأَرْضِ.

21- مَا الكَلِمَاتُ الَّتِي تَلَقَّاهَ آدَمُ مِن رَبِّهِ فَتَابَ عَلَيه؟

الجواب: هِيَ مَا ذَكَرَهَا سبحانه فِي قَوْلِهِ: ﴿رَبَّنَا ظَلَمْنَا أَنفُسَنَا وَإِن لَّمْ تَغْفِرْ لَنَا وَتَرْحَمْنَا لَنَكُونَنَّ مِنَ الْخَاسِرِينَ﴾

[الأعراف: 23].

The story of the two sons of Aadam

قِصَّةَ ابْنِي آدَمَ:

22- What is the story of the two sons of Aadam?

22- مَا قِصَّةَ ابْنِي آدَمَ؟

Answer: Their story is that Allah, The Exalted, Asked them to present an offering to draw closer to Him. They did what He Asked them to do. Allah, The Almighty, Accepted the offering of one of them and Rejected the offering of the other. The one whose offering was rejected transgressed against the one whose offering was accepted. He ultimately killed him out of envy and aggression.

الجَوَابُ: قِصَّتُهُمَا أَنَ اللهَ طَلَبَ مِنْهُمَا قُرْبَانًا يَتَوَاصَلَانِ بِهِ إِلَيْهِ فَفَعَلَا مَا طُلِبَ مِنْهُما فَتُقُبِّلَ مِنْ أَحَدِهِمَا وَلَمْ يُتَقَبَّلْ مِنَ الآخَرِ، فَاعْتَدَى الَّذِي لَمْ يُتَقَبَّلْ مِنْهُ عَلَي الَّذِي قُبِلَ مِنْهُ فَقَتَلَهُ حَسَدًا وَبَغْيًا.

23- Who are the two sons of Aadam whom Allah, The Almighty, Mentions in the relevant noble verse?

23- مَنِ ابْنَا آدَمَ اللَّذَانِ ذَكَرَهُمَا اللهُ تَعَالَى فِي الآيَةِ الْكَرِيمَةِ؟

Answer: They are Qaabeel and Haabeel (Cain and Abel).

الجواب: هُمَا قَابِيلُ وَهَابِيلُ.

24- Why did they present the offering?

Answer: They presented the offering because Allah Ordered both of them to do so, and this was in order to Instruct them that this would be one type of charity enjoined on the coming generations.

25- What was the offering that they presented?

Answer: Each of them presented two rams. Haabeel presented the best rams he had and that is why they were accepted from him. As for Qaabeel, he presented the worst rams he had so they were rejected.

26- What was the sign by which they knew that their charity was accepted?

Answer: The sign was that a fire would come down from the sky and devour the accepted offering.

27- Why Did Allah, The Almighty, Accept the offering of one of them and rejected the other's?

Answer: Allah Accepted the offering of the one who presented it seeking the

24- لِمَاذَا قَرَّبَا القُرْبَانَ؟

الجواب: قَرَّبَا القُرْبَانَ؛ لِأَنَّ اللهَ أَذِنهما لِيُعلِّمَهُمَا أنه بمَثَابةِ الصَّدقَةِ الَّتِي سَتَجْري فِيمَا بَعْدَه مِنَ البَشَرِيَّة.

25- مَا نوعُ القُربانِ الَّذِي قَدَّماهُ؟

الجواب: قَدَّمَا كَبْشَيْنِ، لَكِنَّ هابِيْل قَدَّمَ أَحْسَنَ كِبَاشِه فتُقبِّل مِنْهُ أَمَّا قَابِيْل فَقَدَّمَ أَسْوَأً كِبَاشِه فرُدَّ قُربَانُه وَلَمْ يُتقَبَّل مِنْهُ.

26- مَا العَلَامَةُ الَّتِي عَرَفَا بِهَا قَبُولَ الصَّدَقَةِ؟

الجواب: كَانَتِ العَلَامَةُ نَارًا تَنزِلُ مِنَ السَّمَاءِ فتَأْكُلُ القُربَانَ المُتَقَبَّلَ.

27- لَمَاذَا تَقَبَّلَ اللهُ قُربَانَ أَحَدِهِمَا وَلَم يَتَقَبَّلْ مِنَ الآخَرِ؟

الجواب: تَقَبَّلَ اللهُ أَحَدَ القُربَانَينِ؛ لِأَنَّ صَاحِبَه قَدم هَذَا القُرْبَانَ لوجهِ الله، وَأَمَّا الآخَرُ فَلَمْ يَكُنْ مُتَقَبَّلاً

أَسَاسِيَّاتٌ فِي التَّرْبِيَةِ الإِسْلامِيَّةِ

Pleasure of His Lord. The other, however, was rejected since the one who presented it did not seek thereby the Pleasure of His Lord.

28- Why did Qaabeel kill his brother?

Answer: Qaabeel killed his brother out of envy because of the reward with which Allah Honored him, namely, that Allah Accepted his brother's offering and Rejected his. For this reason, he succumbed to committing such a heinous act and earned the title of «the First Perpetrator of murder on Earth».

29- Did he invent a way to bury his brother or did he find something that guided him how to bury him?

Answer: He did not invent a way to bury his brother; rather, he found a crow searching in the ground. Thereupon, he returned and buried his brother. In this respect, Allah, The Almighty, Says (what means):

[*Then Allah Sent a crow searching in the ground to show him how to hide the disgrace of his brother*]

[Al-Maa'idah: 31]

مِنْـهُ؛ لِأَنَّ صَـاحِبَهُ لَـمْ يُقَـدِّمْ هَـذَا القُرْبَانَ لِوَجْهِ اللهِ.

٢٨- لِمَاذَا قَتَلَ قَابِيلُ أَخَاهُ؟

الجواب: قَتَلَ قَابِيلُ أَخَاهُ حَسَدًا فِي مَثُوبَـةٍ أَكْرَمَهَـا اللهُ تَعَـالَى لِأَخِيْـهِ حَيْثُ قَبِلَ قُرْبَانَهُ وَلَمْ يَقْبَلْ قُرْبَانَ قَابِيلَ؛ لِذَا انْقَادَتْ نَفْسُهُ إِلَى تَنْفِيْذِ هَـذِهِ العَمَلِيَّـةِ الشَّـنِيعَةِ الَّتِـي صَـارَ إِمَامَهَا فَوْقَ هَذِهِ اليَابِسَةِ.

٢٩- هَلِ اخْتَـرَعَ لِدَفْنِ أَخِيـهِ أَمْ وجدَ مَا يُرْشِدُ لِدَفْنِهِ؟

الجواب: لَمْ يَخْتَرِعْ لِدَفْنِهِ بَلْ وجَدَ غُرَابًـا يَبَحـثُ فِـي الأرضِ فَعَـادَ فَدَفَنَ أَخَاهُ.

كَمَـا قَـالَ تَعَـالَى: ﴿فَبَعَثَ اللهُ غُرَابًا يَبْحَثُ فِي الأرضِ﴾

[المائدة: 31].

30- مَاذَا نَسْتَنْتِجُ مِن هَذِهِ القِصَّةِ؟

الجواب: نَسْتَنْتِجُ مَا يَأْتِي:

1- خُطُورَةَ الحَسَدِ؛ لِأَنَّ مَا حَمَلَ قَابِيْلَ عَلَى قَتْلِ هَابِيْلَ هُوَ الحَسَدُ وَالشُّعُورُ بِالنَّقْصِ.

2- جَرَأَةَ الإِنْسَانِ عَلَى مَحَارِمِ اللهِ وَعَدَمِ اسْتِحْيَائِهِ مِنَ اللهِ.

3- قُوَّةَ الإِيْمَانِ وَهُوَ مَا مَنَعَ أَنْ يُبْسُطَ هَابِيْلُ يَدَه لِأَخِيْهِ.

4- قَبُولَ القُرْبَانِ نَتِيْجَةَ العَمَلِ الصَّالِحِ.

5- إحْدَاثَ سُنَّةٍ سَيِّئَةٍ يَتَحَمَّلُ وِزرَهَا مُشرِّعُها.

30- What do we deduce from this story?

Answer:

1- The danger of envy; since it was the envy of Qaabeel and his feeling of inferiority that urged him to kill Haabeel.

2- Man's boldness to violate the Sanctities of Allah and his failure to be bashful of his Lord.

3- The firm faith of Haabeel was the reason behind his abstention from raising his hand against his brother to kill him.

4- The acceptance of the

offering was the result of the good deeds.

5- The sin of every bad deed is borne by the one who had first introduced it.

* * *

قصة نوح عليه السلام:

The Story of Nooh (Noah):

31- كَيْفَ كَانَتْ حَالَةُ الْبَشَرِ قَبْلَ نُوح؟

31- How was the state of mankind before the advent of Nooh (Noah)?

الجواب: عَاشَ الْبَشَرُ بعد أبينا آدَمَ عِيشَةً آمِنَةً هَادِئَةً مُطْمَئِنَّةً وَمُسْتَقِرَّةً؛ لِأَنَّهُمْ كَانُوا قِلَّةً مُتَحَابِّينَ وَمُهْتَدِينَ، مَنْهَجُهُمْ وَشَرْعُهُمْ وَاحِدٌ، وَكَانُوا مُتَمَتِّعِينَ بِالرَّفَاهِيَةِ وَرَغْدِ الْعَيْشِ فَبَطِرُوا، وَبَدَأَ الشَّرُّ يَدُبُّ فِيمَا بَيْنَهُم وَانْتَشَرَ الْخِلَافُ، وَنَتِيجَةً لِهَذَا بَعَثَ الله النَّبِيِّينَ مُبَشِّرِينَ وَمُنْذِرِينَ.

Answer: Mankind lived in security, stability and prosperity after the time of our father Aadam because they were few in number, guided and loving each other. They had a single method and a single Sharee'ah. They enjoyed a prosperous flourishing life but they denied the Bounty of Allah and evil began to creep in between them and discord started to spread. Hence, Allah Sent the prophets as bearers of glad tidings and warners of punishment.

32- مَنِ الْمُرْسَلُ إِلَى الْبَشَرِيَّةِ أَوَّلاً؟

32- Who was the first Messenger sent by Allah to mankind?

الجواب: كَان الْمُرْسَلُ إِلَى الْبَشَرِيةِ أَوَّلاً نُوحًا عليه السلام.

Answer: Nooh (Noah) was the first Messenger sent by Allah to mankind.

33- هَلْ كَانَ مِن أُولِي الْعَزمِ مِنَ الرُّسُلِ؟

33- Was he one of the resolute Messengers?

الجواب: نَعَم، كَانَ مِنْ أُولِي الْعَزمِ.

Answer: Yes, he was one of the resolute Messengers.

34- مَاذَا كَان سَبَبُ شِركِ قَومِهِ؟

34- What was the reason of his people's polytheism?

Answer: It was their extremism in venerating the righteous people among them and their false belief in them.

الجواب: كَانَ السَّبَبُ فِي شِرِكِهِم الغُلُوَّ وَالاعْتِقَادَ البَاطِلَ فِي الصَّالِحِين.

35- What was the call of Nooh (Noah) to his people?

35- مَا دَعْوَةُ نُوحٍ عليه السلام إِلَى قَومِه؟

Answer: He called them to monotheism and to dedicate worship exclusively to Allah.

الجواب: دَعَاهَم إِلَى التَّوحِيدِ وَنَبْذِ الشِّركِ وَإِخلاصِ العِبَادَةِ لله.

36- For how long did his call last?

36- كَم سَنَة كَانَتْ دَعْوتُه؟

Answer: It lasted for a thousand years minus fifty years (950 years).

الجواب: كَانَتْ دَعْوتُه أَلفَ سَنَةٍ إِلَّا خَمسِينَ عَامًا.

37- Did he suffer and face hardship through his call to his people?

37- هَلْ كَابَدَ وَعَانَى فِي دَعوةِ قَومِه؟

Answer: Yes, he suffered, faced hardships, and strived greatly in his call.

الجواب: نَعَم، كَابَدَ وَعَانَى وَاجْتَهَدَ اجْتِهَادًا عَظِيمًا فِي هذه الدَّعوةِ.

38- What was the result of his call?

38- مَاذَا كَانَت نَتِيجَةَ دَعوتِه؟

Answer: His call did not give the fruits that he expected since only few of his people believed in him.

الجواب: لَمْ تُثْمِرْ دَعْوَتُهُ كَمَا كَانَ يَتَوَقَّعُ حَيْثُ لَمْ يُؤْمِنْ بِهِ إِلَّا القَلِيْلُ مِنْهُمْ.

39- Mention some of the accusations that the people of Nooh (Noah) leveled at him.

39- اذكُر بَعضَ الاتِّهَامَاتِ الَّتِي لَقِيَهَا نُوحٌ مِن قِبَلِ قَومِه؟

1- They accused him of madness.

2- They accused him of excessive arguing.

3- They accused him of error.

الجواب: 1- اتَّهَمُوهُ بِالجُنُونِ.
2- اتَّهَمُوهُ بِكَثرَةِ الجِدَالِ.
3- اتَّهَمُوهُ بِالضَّلَال.

40- Was any of his household influenced by the attitude of his people?

Answer: Yes, his son and his wife followed the religion of their people.

41- Did they ask him to make punishment descend upon them?

Answer: Yes, they did.

42- Did Nooh (Noah) supplicate against his people?

Answer: Yes, he supplicated against them.

43- Did Allah Answer the supplication of His Prophet Nooh (Noah)?

Answer: Yes, Allah Answered the supplication of His Prophet Nooh (Noah).

44- How did Nooh (Noah) know that they would not be get but a wicked?

Answer: Allah, The Almighty, Informed him of that as He Says (what means): [*And it was revealed to Nooh (Noah): "None of your people will believe except those who have believed already. So be not sad because of what they used to do*]. [Hood: 36]

40- هَلْ تَأَثَّرَ أَحَدٌ مِنْ أَهْلِ بَيْتِهِ بِقَوْمِهِ؟

الجواب: نَعَم، تَأَثَّرَ ابنُهُ وزوجَتُه حَيْثُ كَانَا يَعْتَنِقَانِ دِينَ قَوْمِهِم.

41- هَل طَلَبوا مِنْه إِنْزَالَ العَذَابِ؟

الجواب: نَعَم، طَلَبُوا منه.

42- هَل دَعَا نُوحٌ عَلَى قَومِهِ؟

الجواب: نَعَم، دَعَا عَلَيهِم.

43- هَل اسْتَجَابَ الله دُعَاءَ نَبِيِّهِ نُوحٍ عليه السلام؟

الجواب: نَعَم، اسْتَجَابَ اللهُ دُعَاءَ نَبِيِّهِ نُوحٍ عليه السلام.

44- كَيفَ عَرَفَ نُوحٌ أَنَّهم لا يَلِدُونَ إِلاَّ فَاجِرًا؟

الجواب: أَخبَرَهُ اللهُ بِذَلِكَ. كما قال تعالى: ﴿...﴾

He also knew that through observing their morals and how their hearts were blocked against believing in Allah, The Almighty.

45- What caused Nooh (Noah) to supplicate against his people?

Answer: There were two causes for that:

1- The fact that Allah, The Almighty, Revealed to him that none of his people would believe except those who had already believed. Allah, The Almighty, Says (what means):

[And it was revealed to Nooh (Noah): «None of your people will believe except those who have believed already. So be not sad because of what they used to do]. [Hood: 36]

2- He feared that they would cause others to deviate.

46- When did Nooh (Noah) know that Allah Would

⟨ ... ⟩ [هود: 36].

وَعَرَفَ ذَلِكَ أَيْضًا بِاسْتِقْرَاءِ أَحْوَالِهِم وَسَدِّ قُلُوبِهِم مِنَ الإِيمَانِ بِاللَّهِ تَعَالَى.

45- مَا حَمَلَ نُوحًا أَن يَدعوَ عَلَى قَوْمِهِ؟

الجواب: حَمَلَهُ عَلَى ذَلِكَ أَمْرَانِ: الأول: أَوْحَى اللهُ تَعَالَى إِلَيه أَنَّه لَنْ يُؤْمِنَ مِنْ قَوْمِهِ إِلَّا مَنْ قَدْ آمَنَ كَمَا قَالَ تَعَالَى: ⟨ ... ⟩ [هود: 36].

الثَّانِي: خَافَ أَنَّهَمْ يُضِلُّون غَيرَهم.

46- مَتَى عَرَفَ نُوحٌ أَنَّ اللهَ سَيُهْلِكُ قَوْمَهُ؟

Destroy his people?

Answer: When Allah Ordered him to build a ship on which He Would Save him along with those who believed with him.

47- What Did Allah Order him to load upon the ship?

Answer: Allah Ordered him to load the following:

1- Of every creature two mates.

2- Those who believed from among his family.

3- Those who believed from among his people.

48- How Did Allah Destroy the people of Nooh (Noah)?

Answer: Allah Destroyed them by drowning.

49- What do we learn from this story?

Answer: We learn the following:

1- Patience in calling to Allah and tolerating hardship for its sake just as Nooh (Noah) was patient and tolerant.

2- Following various methods of calling to Allah. Encouragement and intimidation should be used interchangeably.

3- Destruction is the end of injustice.

الجواب: عِندَمَا أَمَرَه اللهُ بِصِنَاعَةِ السَّفِينَةِ لِيَنجُوَ بِهَا هُوَ وَمَن مَعَهُ.

47- مَاذَا كلَّفه اللهُ أَنْ يَحمِلَ فِي السَّفِينَةِ؟

الجواب: كلَّفهُ مَا يَأْتِي:

1- أَنْ يَحْمِلَ مِن كُلِّ صِنفينِ ذَكَرًا وَأُنثَى.

2- أَنْ يَحْمِلَ مَعَـهُ مَـنَ آمَـنَ مِـنْ أَهْلِهِ.

3- أَنْ يَحْمِلَ مَنْ آمَنَ بِهِ مِن قَومِهِ.

48- بِمَاذَا أَهْلَكَ اللهُ قَومَ نُوحٍ؟

الجواب: أَهْلَكَهُمُ اللَّهُ بِالغَرَقِ.

49- مَاذَا نَستَنْتِجُ مِنْ هَذِهِ القِصَّةِ؟

الجواب: نَسْتَنْتِجُ مَا يَأْتِي:

1- الصَّبَرَ عَلَـى الـدَّعوَةِ إِلَـى اللهِ وَتَحَمُّـلَ مَشَـاقِّهَا، كَمَـا صَبَرَ نُوحٌ وَتحمَّلَ.

2- تَنويـعَ أساليب الـدَّعوَةِ: مَـرَّةً بِالتَّرغِيبِ، وَمَرَّةً بِالتَّرهِيبِ.

3- أَنَّ نَتِيجَةَ الظُّلمِ الهَلَاكُ.

4- لَـيسَ الانْتِمَـاءُ لِـذَوِي الفَضْـلِ منجِيًـا لأحـدٍ، وَإِنَّمَـا النَّجَـاةُ فِـي الإِيمَانِ بِاللهِ وَالعَمَلِ الصَّالِحِ.

4- Belonging to virtuous people does not grant one salvation. It is the act of believing in Allah and doing righteous deeds that grant salvation.

* * *

The Story of Hood:

50- To whom, was the Prophet of Allah Hood sent?

Answer: Allah Sent His Prophet Hood to the tribe of 'Aad.

51- When was he sent to them?

Answer: He was sent to them after the time of Nooh (Noah).

52- Where did they dwell?

Answer: They dwelt in a valley called Al-Ahqaaf.

53- What did he call them to?

Answer: He called them to worship Allah Alone, to abandon polytheism and to dedicate their deeds to Him with sincerity.

54- Mention some of the methods that Hood adopted in calling his people.

Answer:

1- Highlighting the danger of polytheism to them and warning them against the evil doom of those who commit it.

قصة هود عليه السلام:

50- إِلَى مَن أُرسِلَ نَبِيُّ اللهِ هُودٌ عليه السلام؟

الجواب: أَرسَلَ اللهُ نبيَّهُ هُودًا عليه السلام إِلَى قَبِيلَةِ عَاد.

51- مَتَى كَانَ إِرسَالُه إِلَى هَؤُلاءِ القَومِ؟

الجواب: كَانَ إِرسَالُه عليه السلام بَعدَ نُوحٍ عليه السلام.

52- أَينَ كَانُوا؟

الجواب: كَانُوا بِوَادٍ يُسمَّى الأَحْقَاف.

53- مَا الَّذِي كَانَ يَدعُوهُمْ إِلَيهِ؟

الجواب: كَانَ يَدعُوهُم إِلَى عِبَادَةِ اللهِ وَحدَهُ وَنَبْذِ الشِّركِ وَإِخْلَاصِ العَمَلِ لَهُ.

54- اذكُر بَعضَ الأَسَالِيبِ الَّتِي استَعْمَلَهَا هُودُ في دَعوَةِ قَومِهِ؟

الجواب:
1- تَبصِيرُهُم بِخُطُورَةِ الشِّركِ، وَبِمَ تَصِيرُ نَتِيجَةُ مَن أَشرَكَ.
2- تذكِيرُهُم بِنِعَمِ اللهِ عَلَيهِم.
3- التَّرغِيبُ وَنَتِيجَتُه.

2- Reminding them of the favors bestowed by Allah on them.

3- Encouraging them to attain the bliss promised to the believers.

4- Intimidating them through warnings of the evil doom upon those who persist in polytheism.

55- Were the people of Hood known for their luxury and extravagance? Support your answer with evidence

Answer: Yes, they were. Allah, The Almighty, Says (what means): [*And the eminent among his people who disbelieved and denied the meeting of the Hereafter while We Had Given them luxury in the worldly life said, "This is not but a man like yourselves. He eats of that from which you eat and drinks of what you drink.*]

[Al-Mu'minoon: 33]

4- التَّخْوِيفُ وَنَتِيجَةُ مَنْ تَمَادَى فِي الشِّرْكِ.

55- كَانَ قَوْمُ هُودٍ أَهْلَ تَرَفٍ وَبَذَخٍ؟ اذْكُر مَا يَدُلُّ عَلَى ذَلِكَ؟

الجَوَابُ: قَالَ تَعَالَى:

﴿ ... ﴾ [المؤمنون: 33].

وَكَانَت دِيَارُهُم مِن أخصَبِ البِلَادِ وَأكثَرِهَا زِرَاعةً وَأنعَامًا؟

Their dwellings were located in one of the most fertile lands and the richest in agricultural produce and livestock.

56- ذكُر مَا يَدُلُّ عَلَى تَكَبُّرٍ وَتَجَبُّرٍ قَومٍ عَادٍ؟

56- Mention a piece of evidence to prove the arrogance and tyranny of the people of 'Aad.

الجَوَاب: قَالَ تَعَالَى: ﴿ ... ﴾ [فصلت: 15]. قَالُوا ذَلِكَ غُرُورًا وَعَجَبًا بِقُوَّتَّهِم.

Answer: Allah, The Almighty, Says (what means): [*As for 'Aad, they were arrogant upon the earth without right and said, "Who is greater than us in strength?"*] [Fussilat: 15]. They said so out of conceit and admiration of their strength.

فَرَدَّ الله عَلَيهِم بِقَولِهِ: ﴿ ... ﴾

Allah, The Almighty, Answered them by Saying (what means): [*Did they not consider that Allah Who Created them Is Greater than them in strength? But they were rejecting Our Signs*]. [Fussilat: 15]

﴿... ﴾ [فصلت: 15].

57- *What was the outcome of the call of Hood to his people?*

Answer: They persisted in their disbelief and their arrogance increased.

58- *What did they ask him to do?*

Answer: They asked him to bring forward the punishment prepared for them if he was truthful.

59- *How were they destroyed?*

Answer: They were destroyed by the violent wind.

Allah, The Almighty, Says (what means) [*And they denied him, so We Destroyed them. Indeed, in that is a sign, but most of them were not to be believers*]

[Ash-Shu‘araa: 139]

57- مَاذَا كَانَت نَتِيجَةَ دَعْوةِ هُودٍ لِقَومِهِ؟

الجواب: كَانَتِ النَّتِيجَةُ اسْتِمْرَارَ الكُفرِ وَازْدِيادَ التَّكبرِ.

58- مَاذَا طَلَبُوا مِنْه؟

الجواب: طَلَبُوا مِنه أَنْ يَأْتِيَ بِمَا يَعِدُ لَهُم مِنَ العَذَابِ إِنْ كَانَ صَادِقًا.

59- كَيفَ كَانَ هَلاكُهُم؟

الجواب: كَانَ هَلاكُهُم بِالرِّيحِ العَاتِيَة. قَالَ تَعَالَى: ﴿... ﴾ [الشعراء: 139].

60- Who was saved from the punishment?

Answer: Hood and those who believed with him were saved.

This was stated in the Saying of Allah, The Almighty (which means): [***And when Our Command came, We Saved Hood and those who believed with him, by mercy from Us; and We Saved them from a harsh punishment.***] [Hood: 58]

60- مَنْ نَجَا مِن هَذا الْعَذَابِ؟

الجواب: نَجَا مِنُه هُودٌ وَالذِين آمَنُوا مَعَه وَهَذا مَا صَرَّحَ بِهِ في قَولِهِ تَعالى:

﴿□◆⌂•☺ا جـ⊠ا✎↗◆

أ□☜✡◆ا ✞⑩□✡ا ⚖□دًا

□◆ا✍✎⍾⇦✖◆

↗◆ا✋◆☪□ا☎ ✋◆⊠⚪⓵

بِر◆☺⊠□ ✋☪ا

□◆✞⑩✡□⓵☹ ♊✋

ع◆ذ⊠ابٍ غ⊠◼⑩ظٍ﴾ [هـــود: 58].

61- What do we learn from this story?

Answer: We learn the following:

1- Calling to Allah and promoting monotheism.

2- Reliance on Allah in all the affairs no matter what they are.

3- Disassociation from

61- مَاذَا نَستَنْتِجُ مِنْ هَذِهِ القِصَّةِ؟

الجواب: نَستَنْتِجُ مَا يَأْتِي:

1- الدَّعْوَةَ إِلَى اللهِ بِالتَّوحِيْدِ.

2- التّوكُّلَ عَلَى اللهِ فِي كُلِّ أمرٍ وَمَهْمَا كَانَ هَذَا الأَمْرُ.

3- التّبرأ مِن الشّرْكِ وَأَهْلِهِ.

4- الصبرَ وَالحِلمَ عَلَى مَا يلقاه الدَّاعيةُ مِنَ الأَذَى.

5- البُعْدَ عَنِ التَّكَبُّرِ وَالطُّغيانِ.

polytheism and its people.

4- The caller to Allah must show patience and forbearance of the harm he faces.

5- Shunning arrogance and tyranny.

6- Eschewing taking pride in the progress, advancement and prosperity that the Ummah achieved.

7- Material and moral strength do not benefit a person if he disbelieves in Allah and His Messenger, sallallaahu 'alayhi wa sallam.

6- البُعدَ عَنِ الافْتِخَارِ بِمَا حَقَّقَتِ الأُمَّةُ مِنَ التَّقَدُّمِ وَالرُّقِيِّ وَالازْدِهَارِ.

7- أَنَّ القُوَّةَ المَادِيَّةَ وَالمَعْنَوِيَّةَ لَا تَنْفَعُ صَاحِبَها إِذَا كَانَ خَالِيًا عَنِ الإِيمَانِ بِاللهِ وَرَسُولِهِ.

* * *

قِصَّة صَالِح عليه السلام:

62 - إِلَى مَن أُرسِلَ نَبِيُّ اللهِ صَالِح عليه السلام؟

الجواب: أَرْسَلَ اللهُ نَبِيَّه صَالِحًا إِلَى قَومِ ثَمُودَ، كَمَا قَالَ تَعَالَى:

﴿وَإِلَىٰ ثَمُودَ أَخَاهُمْ صَالِحًا ۚ قَالَ يَا قَوْمِ اعْبُدُوا اللَّهَ مَا لَكُم مِّنْ إِلَٰهٍ غَيْرُهُ ۖ هُوَ أَنشَأَكُم مِّنَ الْأَرْضِ وَاسْتَعْمَرَكُمْ فِيهَا فَاسْتَغْفِرُوهُ ثُمَّ تُوبُوا إِلَيْهِ ۚ إِنَّ رَبِّي قَرِيبٌ مُّجِيبٌ﴾ [هود: 61].

63- أَينَ كَانَت مَنَازِلُهُم؟

الجواب: كَانَت مَنَازِلُهُم فِي الحِجرِ، وَهِي تَقَعُ بَينَ الحِجَازِ وَالشَّامِ.

The Story of Prophet Saalih:

62- To whom, was the Prophet of Allah Saalih sent?

Answer: Allah Sent His Prophet Saalih to the people of Thamood. Allah, The Almighty, Says (what means):

[*And to Thamood [We Sent] their brother Saalih. He said, "O my people, worship Allah; you have no deity other than Him, He has produced you from the earth and settled you in it, so ask forgiveness of Him and then repent to Him. Indeed, my Lord is near and responsive"*] [Hood: 61]

63- Where were their dwellings?

Answer: Their dwellings were at Al-Hijr region which is located between Al-Hijaaz and Ash-Shaam.

64- What did they worship?

Answer: They worshipped idols just as their ancestors did.

65- What prevented them from believing in what Saalih called them to?

Answer: Arrogance and tyranny prevented them as they believed that none could be better than them.

66- What was the sign that they asked him to bring?

Answer: They wanted a pregnant she-camel to come out of a rock.

67- After he had brought the sign, what did Saalih ask his people to do?

Answer: He asked them to preserve the she-camel, give it special care and not to expose it to the least harm.

68- Why did he forbid them from exposing it to harm?

Answer: He did so because he feared destruction for them should they harm it.

69- Did they follow his

64- مَاذَا كَانُوا يَعبُدُونَ؟

الجَوَاب: كَانُوا يَعبُدُونَ الأَصْنَامَ كَأَسْلَافِهِم.

65- مَا مَنَعَهُم مِنَ الإِيمَانِ بِمَا دَعَاهُم صَالِحٌ عليه السلام؟

الجواب: مَنَعَهم التَّكَبُّرُ والطَّغْيَانُ حَيْثُ إِنَّهم كَانُوا يَرَونَ أَنْ لَا أَحَدَ أَفضَلُ عَلَيهِم.

66- مَا الآيَةَ الَّتِي طَلَبُوهَا مِن نَبِيِّهم صَالِح عليه السلام؟

الجواب: كَانَتِ الآيَةُ نَاقَةً عشرَاء تَخْرُجُ مِن صَخْرَةٍ.

67- مَاذَا طَلَبَ صَالِحٌ مِن قَومِهِ عِنْدَ مَجِيءِ الآيَةِ؟

الجواب: طَلَبَهُم أَن يَحْفَظُوا هَذِهِ النَّاقَةَ وَأَنْ يُعطُوهَا عِنَايَةً خَاصَّةً وَأَن لَا يَمَسُّوهَا بِسُوءٍ.

68- لِمَاذَا نَهَاهُم عَنِ التَّعَرُّض لِلنَّاقَةِ بِالأَذَى والسُّوءِ؟

الجواب: نَهَاهُم لِخَوفِهِ عَلَيهِم بِالهَلَاكِ إِذَا أَذَوهَا.

69- هَل نَفَّذُوا تَوجِيهَاتِه بِمُعَامَلَةِ النَّاقَةِ؟

instructions regarding the treatment of the she-camel?

Answer: No, they did not. Rather, they slaughtered it.

70- Who undertook slaughtering it?

Answer: A man of them called Qudaar ibn Saalif did.

71- Did Saalih warn them of punishment after the slaughter of the she-camel?

Answer: Yes, he warned them of punishment that would befall them after three days.

72- On what did they agree and resolve after they received the warning?

Answer: They resolved on getting rid of him by exterminating him.

73- Did the warning take effect?

Answer: Yes, it took effect and Allah Sent down His Punishment upon them.

74- How were his people destroyed?

Answer: They were destroyed by the punishment that lasted for three days.

Allah, The Almighty, Says (what means): [*But they hamstrung her, so he said,*

الجَوَابُ: لَاَ، لَـمْ يُنَفِّـذوها وَلَكِـنَّـهُم عَقَروا النَّاقةَ.

70- مَنْ تَوَلَّى عَقْرَهَا؟

الجَوَاب: تَوَلَّى عَقْرَهَا رَجُلٌ مِنهم يُسَمَّى قُدَار بن سَالف.

71- هَل أَنذَرَهم صَالحُ بَعدَ العَقْرِ؟

الجَوَاب: نَعَمْ أنذَرَهم بَالعَذابِ بَعدَ ثَلاثَةَ أَيَّام.

72- عَلامَ اجْتَمَعُوا وَعَزَمُوا بَعْدَ الإِنْذَارِ؟

الجَـوَاب: عَزَمُـوا عَلَـى الـتَّخَلُّـصِ مِنْهُ وَقَتْلِهِ نِهَائِيًّا.

73- هَل تَحَقَّقَ الإِنْذَارُ؟

الجَوَاب: نَعَـم تَحَقَّـقَ وَأَنْـزَلَهُمُ اللهُ بِالعَذابِ.

74- كَيْفَ كَانَ هَلاَكُ قَومِهِ؟

الجَوَاب: كَانَ هَلاَكُ قَومِهِ بِالعَذابِ بَعدَ ثَلاَثَةِ أَيَّام.

قَالَ تَعَالَى: ﴿فَعَقَرُوهَا فَقَالَ

"Enjoy yourselves in your homes for three days. That is a promise not to be denied"]
[Hood: 65]

[هود: 65].

75- What did Saalih say to them after the punishment and destruction were carried out?

Answer: He said to them that he had fulfilled his duty, conveyed the Message of his Lord and advised them, but they rejected all what he had said.

75- مَاذَا قَالَ لهم صَالِحٌ عليه السلام بَعْدَ تَحَقُّقِ الْعَذَابِ وَالْهَلَاكِ؟

الجواب: قَالَ لَهُمْ: أَدَّيتُ وَاجِبِي وَأَبْلَغْتُكم رِسَالَةَ رَبِّي وَنَصحتُ لَكُم وَلَكِن رَفَضْتُم كُلَّ مَا قُلْتُ لَكُمْ.

76- What did the Prophet, sallallaahu 'alayhi wa sallam, say when he passed by the dwellings of Thamood?

Answer: He said to his Companions: «Enter not these dwellings unless you are weeping and for the purpose of deriving lessons».

76- مَاذَا قال النَّبِيُّ ﷺ لَمن مَرَّ بِديار ثمودَ؟

الجواب: قَالَ لَهُمْ: لَا تَدْخُلُوا تِلْكَ الدِّيَارَ إِلَّا أَن تكُونُوا بَاكِين لِلِاعْتِبَارِ.

77- What do we learn from this story?

Answer: We learn the following:

1- Calling to monotheism is the profession of all the prophets.

2- Believing in all the Messengers

77- مَاذَا نَسْتَنْتِجُ مِن هَذِه القِصَّةِ؟

الجواب: نَسْتَنْتِجُ مَا يَأْتِي:
1- أَنَّ مِهنَةَ الأَنْبِياءِ هِيَ الدَّعوةُ إِلَى التَّوحيدِ.
2- الإِيمَانَ بالرُّسلِ جَميعًا؛ لأَنَّ

of Allah; because belying one of them is to belie all of them.

3- The caller to Allah should remind those who are called of the Favors of Allah on them.

4- There were nine people from among the disbelievers of Saalih's people who were more evil and wicked than others. Therefore, punishment was hastened for them before their people.

5- Calling to Allah and the existence of signs do not avail those whose hearts are blocked and unable to accept faith and have insight through the Light of Allah.

6- To have faith in the Victory of Allah, even if it does not come at the time when you expect it.

7- To derive lessons and exhortation from what befell the evildoers who were ruined. This is to be done especially when one passes by the dwellings of Thamood, since our Prophet, sallallaahu 'alayhi wa sallam, ordered us to weep when we pass by them.

مـن كَـذبَ وَاحـدًا مِـنْـهُم فَـقَـدْ كـذب جميعَ الرُّسُل.

3- أَنَّ أَيَّ دَاعٍ يُذكِّرُ بِنِعَمِ اللهِ عَلَى من يَدعُو إِلَيهِ.

4- أَنَّ تِسعَةً مِنْ كُفَّارِ قَومِـهِ كَـانُوا أَكْثَرَ شَرًّا وَفَسادًا؛ ولذلكَ عُجِّلَ اللهُ لَهُم العُقُوبَة قبلَ قومِهِم.

5- أَنَّ الـدعوةَ وَالآيَـاتِ لَا تَنْفَعُ إِذا كَانَـتِ القُلـوبُ مُغْلَقَـةً عَـن دُخُـولِ الإِيمَانِ وَالتّبصر بِنُورِ اللهِ.

6- أَنَّ الثِّقَـةَ بِنصرِ اللهِ وَإِن تَـأَخَّرَ وَلَـمْ يَـأتِ فِي الَمـوعِدِ الَّذِي كُنَـتَ تَرجُوه.

7- الاعْتِبَـارَ والاتِّعَـاظَ بِمَا أَصَابَ المجرِمينَ الَّذِينَ أَهلَكُـوا وَخَاصَّـةً عِنْـدَ الُمرُورِ بِديَارِ ثَمُـودَ؛ لِأَنَّ نَبِينَـا ﷺ أَمَرَنَـا بِالبُكَـاءِ عِنْـدَ المـرورِ عَلَيـهَا.

* * *

رِجَالٌ وَنِسَاءٌ حَولَ الرَّسُول

Men and Women around the Messenger of Allah

Men and Women around the Messenger of Allah

1- Who are the rightly guided Caliphs?

Answer: The rightly guided Caliphs are:

1- Abu Bakr As-Siddeeq, May Allah Be Pleased with him.

2- 'Umar ibn Al-Khattaab, May Allah Be Pleased with him.

3- 'Uthmaan ibn 'Affaan, May Allah Be Pleased with him.

4- 'Ali ibn Abi Taalib, May Allah Be Pleased with him.

2- Who are the ten who were given the glad tidings of entering Paradise?

Answer: The ten Companions who were given the glad tidings of entering Paradise are:

1- Abu Bakr As-Siddeeq, May Allah Be Pleased with him.

2- 'Umar ibn Al-Khattaab, May Allah Be Pleased with him.

3- 'Uthmaan ibn 'Affaan, May Allah Be Pleased with him.

4- 'Ali ibn Abi Taalib, May Allah Be Pleased with him.

5- Talhah ibn 'Ubaydillaah, May Allah Be Pleased with him.

6- Sa'd ibn Abi Waqqaas, May Allah Be Pleased with him.

7- Az-Zubayr ibn Al-'Awwaam, May Allah Be Pleased with him.

رِجَالٌ وَنِسَاءٌ حَوْلَ الرَّسُولِ:

1- مَنِ الخُلَفَاءُ الرَّاشِدُونَ؟

الجواب: الخُلَفَاءُ الرَّاشِدُونَ هُم:

1- أَبُو بَكْرٍ الصِّدِّيق رضي الله عنه.

2- عُمَرُ بنُ الخَطَّاب رضي الله عنه.

3- عُثْمَانُ بنُ عَفَّان رضي الله عنه.

4- عَلِيُّ بنُ أَبِي طَالِبٍ رضي الله عنه.

2- مَنِ العَشَرَةُ المُبَشَّرونَ بِالجَنَّةِ؟

الجواب: العَشَرَةُ المُبَشَّرونَ بِالجَنَّةِ هُم:

1- أَبُو بَكْرٍ الصِّدِّيق رضي الله عنه.

2- عُمَرُ بنَ الخَطَّاب رضي الله عنه.

3- عُثْمَانُ بنُ عَفَّان رضي الله عنه.

4- عَلِيُّ بنُ أَبِي طَالِبٍ رضي الله عنه.

5- طَلْحَةُ بنُ عُبَيدِ الله رضي الله عنه.

6- سَعدُ بنُ أَبِي وَقَّاصٍ رضي الله عنه.

7- الزُّبَيرُ بنُ العَوَّام رضي الله عنه.

8- عَبدُ الرَّحمنِ بنُ عَوفٍ رضي الله عنه.

9- أَبُو عُبَيدَةَ بنُ الجَرَّاح رضي الله عنه.

10- سَعيدُ بنُ زَيدٍ رضي الله عنه.

8- 'Abdul-Rahmaan ibn 'Awf, May Allah Be Pleased with him.

9- Abu 'Ubaydah ibn Al-Jarraah, May Allah Be Pleased with him.

10- Sa'eed ibn Zayd, May Allah Be Pleased with him.

3- What is the name of Abu Bakr As-Siddeeq, May Allah Be Pleased with him?

٣- مَا اسْمُ أَبِي بَكْرٍ الصِّدِّيقِ ﷺ؟

Answer: His name is 'Abdullaah ibn Abi Quhaafah. The name of Abu Quhaafah was 'Uthmaan.

الجواب: اسْمُهُ عَبْدُ اللهِ بْنُ أَبِي قُحَافَةَ. وَاسْمُ أَبِي قُحَافَةَ عُثْمَان.

4- Who is the first to accept Islam from among men?

٤- مَنْ أَوَّلُ مَنْ أَسْلَمَ مِنَ الرِّجَالِ؟

Answer: He is Abu Bakr As-Siddeeq, May Allah Be Pleased with him.

الجواب: أَوَّلُ مَنْ أَسْلَمَ مِنْهُم أَبُو بَكْرٍ الصِّدِّيقِ ﷺ.

5- Who accompanied the Messenger of Allah, sallallaahu 'alayhi wa sallam, in his Hijrah from Makkah to Al-Madeenah?

٥- مَنْ مُرَافِقٌ رَسُولِ اللهِ ﷺ فِي هِجْرَتِهِ مِنْ مَكَّةَ إِلَى المَدِينَةِ؟

Answer: It was Abu Bakr As-Sideeq, May Allah Be Pleased with him

الجواب: المُرَافِقُ هُوَ أَبُو بَكْرٍ الصِّدِّيقِ ﷺ.

6- What is the nickname of 'Umar ibn Al-Khattaab?

٦- مَا كُنْيَةُ عُمَرَ بْنِ الخَطَّابِ ﷺ؟

Answer: Abu Hafs.

الجواب: أَبُو حَفْصٍ.

7- Who is Al-Faarooq?

٧- مَنِ الفَارُوقُ؟

Answer: He is 'Umar ibn Al-Khattaab, May Allah Be Pleased with him.

الجواب: هُوَ عُمَرُ بْنُ الخَطَّابِ ﷺ.

8- Who was the one who

٨- مَنِ المُدَوِّنُ لِلتَّارِيخِ الهِجْرِيِّ؟

decided the use of the Hijri calendar?

Answer: He was 'Umar ibn Al-Khattaab, May Allah Be Pleased with him.

9- What did 'Umar, May Allah Be Pleased with him, wish when others expressed their wishes for having great wealth?

Answer: He wished to have many men like Abu 'Ubaydah ibn Al-Jarraah, May Allah Be Pleased with him.

10- Who is Thu-Noorayn (The possessor of the two lights)?

Answer: He is 'Uthmaan ibn 'Affaan, May Allah Be Pleased with him.

11- Why was he called Thu-Noorayn?

Answer: Because he married two of the daughters of the Messenger of Allah, sallallaahu 'alayhi wa sallam.

12- Who was the first to accept Islam from among the youth?

Answer: 'Ali ibn Abi Taalib, May Allah Be Pleased with him.

13- Who slept in the bed of the Messenger of Allah, sallallaahu 'alayhi wa sallam, in the night of Hijrah?

الجواب: الْمُدَوِّنُ هُوَ عُمَرُ بنُ الخَطَّابِ ﷺ.

9- مَاذَا تَمَنَّى عُمَرُ بنُ الخَطَّابِ ﷺ عِندَمَا تَمَنَّى غَيْرُهُ بِالمَالِ؟

الجواب: تَمَنَّى عُمَرُ رِجَالاً مِثْلَ أَبِي عُبَيْدَةَ بنِ الجَرَّاحِ ﷺ.

10- مَنْ ذُو النُّورَيْنِ؟

الجواب: هُوَ عُثْمَانُ بنُ عَفَّانَ ﷺ.

11- لِمَاذَا سُمِّيَ ذُو النُّورَيْنِ؟

الجواب: لِأَنَّهُ تَزَوَّجَ اثْنَتَيْنِ مِن بَنَاتِ الرَّسُولِ ﷺ.

12- مَنْ أَوَّلُ مَن أَسْلَمَ مِنَ الصِّبْيَانِ؟

الجواب: عَلِيُّ بنُ أَبِي طَالِبٍ ﷺ.

13- مَنْ نَامَ فِي فِرَاشِ الرَّسُولِ ﷺ لَيْلَةَ الهِجْرَةِ؟

Answer: It was Ali ibn Abi Taalib, May Allah Be Pleased with him.

14- One of the Companions, May Allah Be Pleased with them, was sent by the Messenger of Allah, sallallaahu 'alayhi wa sallam, to the people of Yemen. He recited the Book of Allah to them, whereupon, the Tribe of the Hamdaan entirely accepted Islam.

He wrote to the Messenger of Allah, sallallaahu 'alayhi wa sallam, a message to that effect and he fell in prostration to Allah. Who was that Companion?

Answer: He is 'Ali ibn Abi Taalib, May Allah Be Pleased with him.

15- An honorable Companion about whom the Messenger of Allah, sallallaahu 'alayhi wa sallam, said, "Tomorrow, I will hand the banner to a man who loves Allah and His Messenger and whom Allah and His Messenger love." Who was he? When did this happen?

Answer: He was 'Ali ibn Abi Taalib and this happened

الجواب: عَلِيُّ بنُ أَبِي طَالِبٍ ﵁.

١٤- أَحَدُ الصَّحَابَةِ — رِضوَانُ اللهِ عَلَيهِم — بَعَثَهُ رَسُولُ اللهِ ﷺ إِلَى أَهلِ اليَمَنِ فَقَرَأَ عَلَيهِم كِتَابَ اللهِ فَأَسلَمَت هَمَدَانُ جَمِيعًا، وَكَتَبَ بِذَلِكَ إِلَى رَسُولِ اللهِ ﷺ فَخَرَّ سَاجِدًا. مَن هَذَا الصَّحَابِيُّ؟

الجواب: عَلَيُّ بنُ أَبِي طَالِبٍ ﵁.

١٥- صَحَابِيٌّ جَلِيلٌ قَالَ عَنهُ النَّبِيُّ ﷺ: «لَأُعطِيَنَّ الرَّايَةَ غَدًا رَجُلاً يُحِبُّ اللهَ وَرَسُولَهُ وَيُحِبُّهُ اللهُ وَرَسُولُهُ». مَن هُوَ؟ وَمَتَى كَانَ ذَلِكَ؟

الجواب: هُوَ عَلِيُّ بنُ أَبِي طَالِبٍ ﵁، وَكَانَ ذَلِكَ فِي فَتحِ خَيبَرَ سَنَة

during the Conquest of Khaybar.

16- Mention three titles which the Messenger of Allah, sallallaahu 'alayhi wa sallam, gave to Talhah ibn 'Ubaydillaah.

Answer:

1- The living martyr.

2- Talhah Al-Khayr (of goodness).

3- Talhah Al-Jood (of generosity).

17- What was the age of Sa'd ibn Abi Waqqaas when he accepted Islam?

Answer: He was seventeen years old.

18- Was there a kinship relation between the Messenger of Allah, sallallaahu 'alayhi wa sallam, and Sa'd ibn Abi Waqqaas?

Answer: Yes, he was a maternal uncle of the Messenger of Allah, sallallaahu 'alayhi wa sallam.

19- Who was the first one to shoot an arrow in the Cause of Allah?

Answer: He was Sa'd ibn Abi Waqqaas, May Allah Be Pleased with him.

20- Who was the sole

7هـ.

16- اذكر ثَلَاثَةَ أَلْقَابٍ لَقَّبَهَا الرَّسُولُ ﷺ طَلْحَةَ بْنَ عُبَيْدِ الله؟

الجواب:

1- الشَّهِيدُ الحَيّ.

2- طَلْحَةُ الخَيْرِ.

3- طَلْحَةُ الجُودِ.

17- كَمْ كَانَ سِنُّ سَعْدِ بْنِ أَبِي وَقَّاصٍ ﷺ عِنْدَمَا أَسْلَمَ؟

الجواب: كَانَ سِنُّهُ سَبْعَ عَشْرَةَ سَنَةً.

18- هَلْ كَانَ بَيْنَ الرَّسُولِ ﷺ وَبَيْنَ سَعْدِ بْنِ أَبِي وَقَّاصٍ صِلَةُ رَحِمٍ؟

الجواب: نَعَمْ كَانَ سَعْدٌ خَالَ الرَّسُولِ ﷺ.

19- مَنْ أَوَّلُ مَنْ رَمَى سَهْمًا فِي سَبِيلِ الله؟

الجواب: سَعْدُ بْنُ أَبِي وَقَّاصٍ ﷺ.

20- مَنِ الوَحِيدُ مِنَ الصَّحَابَةِ الَّذِي قَالَ

Companion to whom the Messenger of Allah, sallallaahu ‘alayhi wa sallam, said, "May my father and mother be sacrificed for you"?

لَهُ الرَّسُولُ ﷺ «فِدَاكَ أَبِي وَأُمِّي»؟

Answer: He was Sa‘d ibn Abi Waqqaas, May Allah Be Pleased with him.

الجواب: سَعْدُ بنُ أَبِي وَقَّاصٍ ﵁.

21- Concerning whom was the verse in which Allah, The Almighty, Says (what means): [But if they endeavor to make you associate with Me that of which you have no knowledge, do not obey them but accompany them in [this] worldly life with appropriate kindness and follow the way of those who turn back to Me [in repentance]. Then to Me will be your return, and I Will Inform you about what you used to do] [Luqmaan: 15] revealed?

21- فِيمَنْ نَزَلَ قَوْلُهُ تَعَالَى: ﴿وَإِن جَٰهَدَاكَ عَلَىٰٓ أَن تُشۡرِكَ بِي مَا لَيۡسَ لَكَ بِهِۦ عِلۡمٌ فَلَا تُطِعۡهُمَاۖ وَصَاحِبۡهُمَا فِي ٱلدُّنۡيَا مَعۡرُوفٗاۖ وَٱتَّبِعۡ سَبِيلَ مَنۡ أَنَابَ إِلَيَّۚ ثُمَّ إِلَيَّ مَرۡجِعُكُمۡ فَأُنَبِّئُكُم بِمَا كُنتُمۡ تَعۡمَلُونَ ١٥﴾ [لقمان: 15].

Answer: It was revealed concerning Sa‘d ibn Abi Waqqaas, May Allah Be Pleased with him.

الجواب: في سَعْدِ بنِ أَبِي وَقَّاصٍ ﵁.

22- What was the title given by the Messenger of Allah, sallallaahu ‘alayhi wa sallam, to Az-Zubayr ibn Al-

22- مَا اللَّقَبُ الَّذِي لَقَّبَهُ الرَّسُولُ ﷺ للزُّبَيْرِ بنِ العَوَّامِ؟

'Awwaam?

Answer: It was 'The disciple of the Messenger of Allah'.

الجواب: حَوَارِيُّ رَسُولِ الله.

23- Who was the first one to unsheathe a sword in the Cause of Allah?

٢٣- مَن أَوَّلُ مَن سَلَّ سَيْفًا فِي سَبِيلِ الله؟

Answer: He was Az-Zubayr ibn Al-'Awwaam.

الجواب: الزُّبَيْرُ بنُ العَوَّام.

24- Who were the two Companions whom the Messenger of Allah, sallallaahu 'alayhi wa sallam, sent to retrieve the message of Haatib ibn Abi Balta'ah?

٢٤- مَن بَعَثَهُمَا الرَّسُولُ ﷺ بِرَدِّ كِتَابِ حَاطِبِ بنِ أَبِي بَلْتَعَة؟

Answer: They were 'Ali ibn Abi Taalib and Az-Zubayr ibn Al-'Awwaam, May Allah Be Pleased with them.

الجواب: عَلِيُّ بنُ أَبِي طَالِبٍ وَالزُّبَيْرُ بنُ العَوَّام.

25- In what battle was Az-Zubayr martyred? How old was he then?

٢٥- مَا المَوقِعَةُ التِي اسْتُشْهِدَ بِهَا الزُّبَيْرُ؟ وَكَم كَانَ عُمْرُه؟

Answer: He was martyred in the Battle of Al-Jamal. He was seventy-five years old.

الجواب: اسْتُشْهِدَ يَومَ وَقعَةِ الجَمَل، وَكَانَ عُمْرُهُ خَمْسًا وَسَبعِينَ عَامًا.

26- What was the nickname of Az-Zubayr ibn Al-'Awwaam, May Allah Be Pleased with him?

٢٦- مَا كُنْيَةُ الزُّبَيرِ بنِ العَوَّام ﷺ؟

Answer: It was Abu 'Abdullaah.

الجواب: أَبُو عَبدِ الله.

27- What was the name of 'Abdul-Rahmaan ibn 'Awf before he embraced Islam?

٢٧- مَا اسمُ عَبدِ الرَّحمَنِ بنِ عَوفٍ ﷺ قَبلَ الإسلام؟

Answer: His name was 'Abd

الجواب: كَانَ اسمُهُ عَبدُ عَمرو.

'Amr.

28- By whom was the Prophet, sallallaahu 'alayhi wa sallam, led in prayer during the Battle of Tabook?

28- مَنْ الَّذِي صَلَّى رَسُولُ اللهِ ﷺ خَلْفَهُ فِي غَزْوَةِ تَبُوكَ؟

Answer: The Prophet, sallallaahu 'alayhi wa sallam, was led in prayer by 'Abdul-Rahmaan ibn 'Awf during the Battle of Tabook.

الجواب: عَبْدُ الرَّحَمَنِ بنُ عَوفٍ رضي الله عنه.

29- Who was the Companion whom the Prophet, sallallaahu 'alayhi wa sallam, set a bond of brotherhood between him and 'Abdul-Rahmaan ibn 'Awf?

29- مَنِ الَّذِي آخَاهُ الرَّسُولُ ﷺ بِعَبْدِ الرَّحْمَنِ بنِ عَوفٍ ﷺ؟

Answer: He was Sa'd ibn Ar-Rabee', May Allah Be Pleased with him.

الجواب: سَعدُ بنُ الرَّبِيعِ رضي الله عنه.

30- Who was the one who said to his brother in Islam (Abdul-Rahman ibn 'Awf), "Here is my wealth, my house and my two wives; so, take whatever you like of them."

30- مَنِ القَائِلُ لِأَخِيهِ فِي الإِسْلَامِ: هَذَا مَالِي، وَدَارِي، وَزُوجَتَاي فَخُذْ مَا تَشَاءُ؟

Answer: He was Sa'd ibn Ar-Rabee', May Allah Be Pleased with him.

الجواب: سَعدُ بنُ الرَّبِيعِ رضي الله عنه.

31- At what age did 'Abdul-Rahmaan ibn 'Awf die? Where was he buried?

31- كَمْ كَانَ سِنُّ عَبْدِ الرَّحْمَنِ بنِ عَوفٍ ﷺ عِندَمَا تُوُفِّيَ وَأَينَ دُفِنَ؟

Answer: He died at the age of seventy-five and was buried in Al-Baqee' cemetery.

الجواب: كَـــانَ عُمـرُهُ خَمْسًـا وَسَبعِينَ سَنَةً، وَدُفِنَ بِالبَقِيعِ.

32- Who is the Trustworthy of this Ummah?

Answer: He is Abu 'Ubaydah ibn Al-Jarraah, May Allah Be Pleased with him.

32- مَنْ أَمِينُ هَذِهِ الأُمَّةِ؟

الجواب: أَبُو عُبَيْدَةَ بنُ الجَرَّاحِ ﷺ.

33- What was the name of Abu 'Ubaydah, May Allah Be Pleased with him?

Answer: His name was 'Aamir ibn 'Abdullaah ibn Al-Jarraah, May Allah Be Pleased with him.

33- مَا اسمُ أَبِي عُبَيْدَةَ ﷺ؟

الجواب: عَامِرُ بنُ عَبدِ اللهِ بنِ الجَرَّاحِ ﷺ.

34- Who was the Companion whom the Prophet, sallallaahu 'alayhi wa sallam, set a bond of brotherhood between him and Abu 'Ubaydah ibn Al-Jarraah, May Allah Be Pleased with him?

Answer: He was Sa'd ibn Mu'aath, May Allah Be Pleased with him.

34- مَنْ آخَاهُ الرَّسُولُ ﷺ بِأَبِي عُبَيْدَةَ ﷺ؟

الجواب: سَعدُ بنُ مُعَاذٍ ﷺ.

35- Who was the noble Companion whose death caused the Mighty Throne of Allah to shake?

Answer: He was Sa'd ibn Mu'aath, May Allah Be Pleased with him.

35- مَنِ الصَّحَابِيُّ الجَلِيلُ الَّذِي اهتَزَّ لِمَوتِهِ عَرشُ الرَّحمَنِ؟

الجواب: هُوَ سَعدُ بنُ مُعَاذٍ ﷺ.

36- At what age did Abu 'Ubaydah ibn Al-Jarraah, May Allah Be Pleased with him, die?

Answer: He died at the age of

36- كَمْ كَانَ سِنُّ أَبِي عُبَيْدَةَ بنِ الجَرَّاحِ ﷺ عِندَمَا مَاتَ؟

الجواب: كَانَ سِنُّهُ ثَمَانِيَ وَخَمسِينَ

fifty-eight.	سَنَةً.

37- What was the relation between Sa‘eed ibn Zayd and ‘Umar ibn Al-Khattaab, May Allah Be pleased with them?

37- مَا الصِّلَةُ الَّتِي بَيْنَ سَعِيدِ بنِ زَيْدٍ وعُمَرَ بنِ الخَطَّابِ ﷺ؟

Answer: They were paternal cousins. Sa‘eed was also the husband of Faatimah bint Al-Khattaab, the sister of ‘Umar.

الجَوَابُ: هُمَا ابْنَا عُمُومَةٍ، وَزَوْجُ أُخْتِهِ فَاطِمَةَ بِنتِ الخَطَّابِ.

38- Many were those who accepted Islam from among the family of Sa‘eed ibn Zayd, May Allah Be Pleased with him. Mention three of them.

38- أَسْلَمَ كَثِيرٌ مِن عَائِلَةِ سَعِيدِ بنِ زَيْدٍ ﷺ أذكُرْ ثَلَاثَةً مِنهُم؟

Answer:

الجَوَابُ:

1- Zayd ibn ‘Amr ibn Nufayl.
2- Faatimah bint Al-Khattaab.
3- Zayd ibn Al-Khattaab.

1- زَيدُ بنُ عَمرِو بنِ نُفَيلٍ.
2- فَاطِمَةُ بِنتُ الخَطَّابِ.
3- زَيدُ بنُ الخَطَّابِ.

39- Where did Sa‘eed ibn Zayd die? Where was he buried?

39- أَينَ مَاتَ سَعِيدُ بنُ زَيْدٍ ﷺ وَأَينَ دُفِنَ؟

Answer: He died in Al-‘Aqeeq Valley and was buried in Al-Madeenah.

الجَوَابُ: مَاتَ فِي العَقِيقِ، وَدُفِنَ بِالمدِينَةِ.

40- Mention three of the Companions who narrated the greatest number of Hadeeths on the authority of the Prophet, sallallaahu ‘alayhi wa sallam?

40- اذكُر ثَلَاثَةً مِنَ الَّذِينَ أَكْثَرُوا رِوَايَةَ الحَدِيثِ مِنَ الصَّحَابَةِ؟

Answer:

الجَوَابُ:

1- Abu Hurayrah, May Allah Be Pleased with him.

1- أَبُو هُرَيرَةَ ﷺ.

2- Anas ibn Maalik, May Allah Be Pleased with him.

3- Abu Sa'eed Al-Khudri, May Allah Be Pleased with him.

41- What were the names of Abu-Hurayrah and Abu Sa'eed Al-Khudri?

Answer: The name of Abu Hurayrah was 'Abdul-Rahmaan ibn Sakhr Ad-Dawsi.

The name of Abu Sa'eed Al-Khudri was Sa'd ibn Maalik ibn Sinaan.

42- Who were the famous poets of the Messenger of Allah, sallallaahu 'alayhi wa sallam?

Answer: They were:

1- Ka'b ibn Maalik.
2- 'Abdullaah ibn Rawaahah.
3- Hassaan ibn Thaabit.

43- Who are the Muezzins of the Messenger of Allah, sallallaahu 'alayhi wa sallam?

Answer: They were:

1- Bilaal ibn Rabaah.

2- 'Amr ibn Umm Maktoom.

3- Sa'd Al-Qurath.

4- Abu Mahthoorah.

2- أَنَسُ بنُ مَالِكٍ رضي الله عنه.

3- أَبُو سَعِيدٍ الخُدْرِيّ رضي الله عنه.

41- مَا اسمُ أَبِي هُرَيرَةَ، وَأَبِي سَعِيدٍ الخُدْرِيّ؟

الجواب: اسمُ أَبِي هُرَيرَةَ عَبدُ الرَّحمَنِ بنُ صَخرٍ الدَّوسِيّ. واسمُ أَبِي سَعِيدٍ الخُدْرِيّ سَعِيدُ بنُ مَالِكِ بنِ سِنَان.

42- مَن شُعَرَاءُ الرَّسُولِ ﷺ المَشْهُورُونَ؟

الجواب: هُمْ:
1- كَعبُ بنُ مَالِك.
2- عَبدُ اللهِ بنُ رَوَاحَة.
3- حَسَّانُ بنُ ثَابِت.

43- مَن مُؤَذِّنُوا الرَّسُولِ ﷺ؟

الجواب: مُؤَذِّنُوا الرَّسُولِ ﷺ هُمْ:
1- بِلَالُ بنُ رَبَاح.
2- عَمَرو بنُ أُمِّ مَكتُوم.
3- سَعدُ القُرَظِ.
4- أَبُو مَحذُورَة.

44- Who were the three Muslim leaders who were martyred in the Battle of Mu'tah?

Answer:
1- Zayd ibn Haarithah.
2- Ja'far ibn Abi Taalib.
3- 'Abdullaah ibn Rawaahah.

45- Who was the Companion who gave up all his property in return for migrating in the Cause of Allah?
Answer: He was Suhayb Ar-Roomi.

46- Who was the scribe of the Messenger of Allah, sallallaahu 'alayhi wa sallam?
Answer: He was Zayd ibn Thaabit.

47-Who was the Prophet's secret keeper?
Answer: He was Huthayfah ibn Al-Yamaan.

48- Who was the first child born in Islam?
Answer: He was 'Abdullaah ibn Az-Zubayr.

49- Who was the Companion whose name was mentioned in the Quran?

٤٤- مَنِ القَادَةُ الثَّلَاثَةَ الَّذِينَ استُشهِدُوا فِي غَزوَةِ مَوتَةَ؟

الجواب:
١- زَيدُ بنُ الحَارِثَة.
٢- جَعفَرُ بنُ أَبِي طَالِبٍ (جَعفَرُ الطَّيَّار).
٣- عَبدُ اللهِ بنُ أَبِي رَوَاحَة.

٤٥- مَنِ الصَّحَابِيّ الَّذِي دَفَعَ جَمِيعَ مَالِهِ مُقَابِلَ الهِجرَةِ فِي سَبِيلِ الله؟

الجواب: هُوَ صُهَيبُ الرُّومِيّ.

٤٦- مَن هُوَ كَاتِبُ الرَّسُولِ ﷺ؟

الجواب: كَاتِبُ الرَّسُولِ ﷺ زَيدُ ابنُ ثَابِت.

٤٧- مَن صَاحِبُ سِرِّ النَّبِيّ ﷺ؟

الجواب: حُذَيفَةُ بنُ اليَمَان؟

٤٨- مَن أَوَّلُ مَولُودٍ فِي الإسلام؟

الجواب: عَبدُ اللهِ بنُ الزُّبَير.

مَنِ الصَّحَابِيُّ الَّذِي ذُكِرَ اسمُهُ فِي القُرآن؟

Answer: Zayd ibn Al-Haarithah.

الجواب: زَيدُ بنُ الحَارِثَة.

50- Who was the Companion who advised the Messenger of Allah, sallallaahu 'alayhi wa sallam, to dig the trench?

50- مَنِ الصَّحَابِيُّ الَّذِي أَشَارَ عَلَى الرَّسُولِ ﷺ بِحَفرِ الخَندَقِ؟

Answer: Salmaan Al-Faarisi.

الجواب: سَلمَانُ الفَارِسِيّ.

51- Who was the master of the martyrs?

51- مَن سَيِّدُ الشُّهَدَاءِ؟

Answer: Hamzah ibn 'Abd Al-Muttalib.

الجواب: حمَزَةُ بنُ عَبدِ المُطَّلِب.

52- Who was the first ambassador in Islam?

52- مَن أَوَّلُ سَفِيرٍ فِي الإسلامِ؟

Answer: Mus'ab ibn 'Umayr.

الجواب: مُصعَبُ بنُ عُمَير.

53- Who was the unsheathed Sword of Allah?

53- مَن سَيفُ اللهِ المَسلُول؟

Answer: Khaalid ibn Al-Waleed.

الجواب: خَالِدُ بنُ الوَلِيد.

54- Who are the two masters of the youth of Paradise?

54- مَن سَيِّدَا شَبَابِ أَهلِ الجَنَّة؟

Answer: They are Al-Hasan and Al-Husayn.

الجواب: الحَسَنُ وَالحُسَين.

55- Who is the most knowledgeable scholar of the Ummah?

55- مَن حَبرُ الأُمَّة؟

Answer: 'Abdullaah ibn 'Abbaas.

الجواب: عَبدُ اللهِ بنُ عَبَّاس.

56- Who was the first one who came to Al-Madeenah from the Muhaajiroon (immigrants)?

56- مَن أَوَّلُ مَن قَدِمَ المَدِينَةَ مُهَاجِرًا؟

Answer: Abu Salamah, May Allah Be Pleased with him.

الجواب: أَبُو سَلَمَة ﷺ.

57- Who was the Companion who wept when the Messenger of Allah, sallallaahu 'alayhi wa sallam, did not allow him to take part in Jihaad owing to his young age?

Answer: 'Umayr ibn Abi Waqqaas, May Allah Be Pleased with him.

58- Who was the Companion who was known as the seeker of truth?

Answer: Salmaan Al-Faarisi, May Allah Be Pleased with him.

59- How many polytheists did Al-Baraa' ibn Maalik, May Allah Be Pleased with him, kill in duel?

Answer: He killed one hundred polytheists.

60- Who used to lead the Muhaajiroon in prayer in Al-Madeenah?

Answer: It was Saalim, the freed slave of Abu Huthayfah.

61- Who killed Hamzah ibn 'Abd Al-Muttalib, May Allah Be Pleased with him?

Answer: Wahshiyy ibn Harb killed him.

62- What was the expiation that Wahshiyy offered for killing Hamzah?

٥٧- مَنْ بَكَى عِنْدَمَا رَدَّهُ النَّبِيُّ ﷺ عَنِ الْجِهَادِ لِصِغَرِ سِنِّهِ؟

الْجَوَابُ: عُمَيْرُ بْنُ أَبِي وَقَّاصٍ رضي الله عنه.

٥٨- مَنِ الصَّحَابِيُّ الَّذِي كَانَ بَاحِثًا عَنِ الْحَقِيقَةِ؟

الْجَوَابُ: هُوَ سَلْمَانُ الْفَارِسِيُّ رضي الله عنه.

٥٩- كَمْ مُشْرِكًا قَتَلَ الْبَرَاءُ بْنُ مَالِكٍ رضي الله عنه بِالْمُبَارَزَةِ؟

الْجَوَابُ: قَتَلَ مِائَةَ مُشْرِكٍ.

٦٠- مَنْ كَانَ يَؤُمُّ الْمُهَاجِرِينَ مِنْ مَكَّةَ إِلَى الْمَدِينَةِ؟

الْجَوَابُ: سَالِمٌ مَوْلَى أَبِي حُذَيْفَةَ.

٦١- مَنْ قَتَلَ حَمْزَةَ بْنَ عَبْدِ الْمُطَّلِبِ رضي الله عنه؟

الْجَوَابُ: قَتَلَهُ وَحْشِيُّ بْنُ حَرْبٍ.

٦٢- مَاذَا كَانَتْ كَفَّارَةُ وَحْشِيٍّ عَنْ قَتْلِ حَمْزَةَ؟

Answer: It was the killing of Musaylimah Al-Kaththaab (the liar).

الجواب: كَانَتْ كَفَّارَتُهُ قَتْلَ مُسَيْلِمَةَ الكَذَّاب.

63- Who was given the title "The Turjumaan (interpret-er) of the Quran"?

63- مَنْ كَانَ يُلَقَّبُ بِتُرْجُمَانِ القُرآن؟

Answer: 'Abdullaah ibn 'Abbaas, May Allah Be Pleased with him.

الجواب: عَبدُ اللهِ بنُ عَبَّاسٍ ﵁.

64- Who is known as the "Father of the needy"?

64- مَن أَبُو المَسَاكِين؟

Answer: Ja'far ibn Abi Taalib, May Allah Be Pleased with him.

الجواب: جَعفَرُ بنُ أَبِي طَالِبٍ ﵁؟

65- What was the color of the turban that Abu Dujaanah wore on the Day of Uhud?

65- مَا لَونُ العِمَامَةِ الَّتِي كَانَ يَلبَسُهَا أَبُو دُجَانَةَ ﵁ يَومَ أُحُد؟

Answer: It was red.

الجواب: كَانَ لَونُهَا أَحْمَر.

66- Who was the one who initiated the practice of offering two voluntary Rak'ahs before being killed?

66- مَنْ أَوَّلُ مَن سَنَّ الصَّلَاةَ قَبلَ القَتل؟

Answer: Khubayb ibn 'Adiyy.

الجواب: خُبَيبُ بنُ عَدَيّ.

67- Who were the two Muslims who killed Abu Jahl?

67- مَنْ قَاتِلَا أَبِي جَهل؟

Answer: They were Mu'aath ibn 'Amr ibn Al-Jamooh and Mu'aath ibn 'Afraa'.

الجواب: قَاتِلَا أَبِي جَهْلٍ مُعَاذُ بنُ عَمرِو بنِ الجُمُوحِ، وَمُعَاذُ بنُ عَفرَاء.

68- Who was the first of the inhabitants of Al-Madeenah to return to it from Makkah as a Muslim?

68- مَن أَوَّلُ مَن قَدِمَ المَدِينَةَ فِي الإسلام؟

Answer: As'ad ibn Zuraarah.

الجواب: أَسعَدُ بنُ زُرَارَةَ ﵁.

69- *Who are the four Companions about whom the Messenger of Allah, sallallaahu 'alayhi wa sallam said, "Learn the Quran from them."?*

Answer: They are:

1- Ubayy ibn Ka'b.

2- 'Abdullaah ibn Mas'ood.

3- Mu'aath ibn Jabal.

4- Saalim, the freed slave of Abu Huthayfah.

69- مَنِ الأَرْبَعَةُ الَّذِينَ قَالَ فِيهِم رَسُولُ اللهِ ﷺ: «خُذُوا مِنْهُمُ القُرآنَ»؟

الجواب:

1- أُبَيُّ بنُ كَعب.

2- عَبدُ اللهِ بنُ مَسعُود.

3- مُعَاذُ بنُ جَبَل.

4- سَالِمُ مَولَى أَبِي حُذَيفَة.

* * *

Part Two

Women Around the Messenger of Allah, Sallallaahu 'alayhi wa sallam

1- Mention the names of six of the wives of the Messenger of Allah, sallallaahu 'alayhi wa sallam.

Answer:

1- Khadeejah bint Khuwaylid, May Allah Be Pleased with her.

2- Sawdah bint Zam'ah, May Allah Be Pleased with her.

3- 'Aa'ishah bint As-Siddeeq, May Allah Be Pleased with her.

4- Hafsah bint 'Umar ibn Al-Khattaab, May Allah Be Pleased with her.

5- Zaynab bint Khuzaymah, May Allah Be Pleased with her

6- Umm Salamah; Hind bint Abu Umayyah, May Allah Be Pleased with her.

2- Who is the first female martyr in Islam?

Answer: Sumayyah the mother of 'Ammaar ibn Yaasir, May Allah Be Pleased with her.

3- Who is the 'Woman of the two belts'?

Answer: Asmaa' bint Abi

القِسمُ الثّاني

نِسَاءٌ حَولَ الرَّسُولِ ﷺ

1- اذكُرْ سِتَّةَ مِن أزوَاجِ النَّبِيِّ ﷺ؟

الجواب:

1- خَدِيجَةُ بِنتُ خُوَيلِد ▲ .

2- سَودَةُ بِنتُ زَمعَة ▲ .

3- عَائِشَةُ بِنتُ الصِّدِّيق ▲ .

4- حَفصَـةُ بِنتُ عُمَرَ بنِ الخَطَّابِ ▲ .

5- زَينَبُ بِنتُ خُزَيمَة ▲ .

6- أُمُّ سَلَمَة: هِندُ بِنتُ أَبِي أُمَيَّة ▲ .

2- مَن أَوَّلُ شَهِيدَةٍ فِي الإسلَام؟

الجواب: سُمَيَّةُ أُمُّ عَمَّارِ بنِ يَاسِر ▲ .

3- مَن ذَاتُ النِّطَاقَين؟

الجواب: أَسمَاءُ بِنتُ أَبِي بَكرٍ أُمُّ

Bakr, the mother of 'Abdullaah ibn Az-Zubayr, May Allah Be Pleased with them.

عَبْدِ اللهِ بنِ الزَّبَيرِ .

4- Who was the first woman to accept Islam?

4- مَنْ كَانَت أَوَّلُ امْرَأَةٍ أَسْلَمَت؟

Answer: She was Khadeejah bint Khuwaylid, May Allah Be Pleased with her.

الجَوَاب: هِيَ خَدِيجَةُ بِنتُ خُوَيْلِد ▲ .

5- Who is the mother of the daughters of the Messenger of Allah, sallallaahu 'alyhi wa sallam?

5- مَنْ هِيَ أُمُّ بَنَاتِ رَسُولِ الله ﷺ؟

Answer: Khadeejah bint Khuwaylid, May Allah Be Pleased with her.

الجَوَاب: هِيَ خَدِيجَةُ بِنتُ خُوَيْلِد ▲ .

6- What was the dowry of Umm Sulaym, the wife of Abu Talhah, May Allah Be Pleased with them?

6- مَاذَا كَانَ مَهرُ أُمِّ سُلَيمٍ زَوجَةِ أَبِي طَلْحَةَ ﷺ؟

Answer: Her dowry was his accepting Islam.

الجَوَاب: كَانَ مَهرُهَا اعْتِنَاقَ الإِسْلَام.

7- Who was the wet nurse of the Messenger of Allah, sallallaahu 'alayhi wa sallam?

7- مَنْ مُرضِعَةَ الرَّسُولِ ﷺ؟

Answer: Haleemah As-Sa'diyyah, May Allah Be Pleased with her.

الجَوَاب: هِيَ حَلِيمَةُ السَّعدِيَّة ▲ .

8- Who is the mother of Ash-Shaymaa'?

8- مَنْ أُمُّ الشَّيمَاء؟

Answer: Haleemah As-Sa'diyyah, May Allah Be Pleased with her.

الجَوَاب: هِيَ حَلِيمَةُ السَّعدِيَّة ▲ .

9- Who was the woman who complained to the Prophet,

9- مَنْ جَادَلَتِ النَّبِيَّ ﷺ فِي زَوجِهَا وَسَمِعَ اللهُ قَولَهَا؟ وَمَن زَوجُهَا؟

sallallaahu 'alayhi wa sallam, regarding her husband and Allah, The Almighty, Heard her statement? Who was her Husband?

Answer: She was Khawlah bint Tha'labah, May Allah Be Pleased with her. Her husband was Aws ibn As-Saamit.

الجواب: هِيَ خَوْلَةُ بِنْتُ ثَعْلَبَةَ ▲، وَزَوْجُهَا هُوَ أَوْسُ بْنُ الصَّامِتِ.

10- Who is the female Companion whose father, son and grandfather are Companions?

10- مَنِ الصَّحَابِيَّةُ الَّتِي كَانَ أَبُوهَا وَابْنُهَا وَجَدُّهَا مِنَ الصَّحَابَةِ؟

Answer: Asmaa' bint Abu Bakr As-Siddeeq, May Allah Be Pleased with her, since her father is Abu Bakr As-Siddeeq, her son is 'Abdullaah ibn Az-Zubayr and her grandfather is 'Uthmaan ibn 'Aamir (Abu Quhaafah), May Allah Be Pleased with him.

الجواب: هِيَ أَسْمَاءُ بِنْتُ أَبِي بَكْرٍ الصِّدِّيقُ ﷺ. لِأَنَّ أَبَاهَا أَبُو بَكْرٍ الصِّدِّيقُ ﷺ، وَابْنُهَا عَبْدُ اللهِ بْنُ الزُّبَيْرِ ﷺ... وَجَدُّهَا عُثْمَانُ بْنُ عَامِرٍ (أَبُو قُحَافَةَ).

11- Who is the female Companion who is known as Ar-Rumaysaa'?

11- مَنِ الصَّحَابِيَّةُ المَعْرُوفَةُ بِالرُّمَيْصَاءِ؟

Answer: Umm Sulaym bint Milhaan, wife of the noble Companion Abu Talhah and the mother of his son 'Abdullaah ibn Abu Talhah.

الجواب: هِيَ أُمُّ سُلَيْمٍ بِنْتُ مِلْحَانَ زَوْجُ الصَّحَابِيِّ الجَلِيلِ أَبُو طَلْحَةَ وَأُمُّ ابْنِهِ عَبْدِ اللهِ بْنِ أَبِي طَلْحَةَ.

12- Who is the female Companion who embraced Islam at the hands of her

12- مَنِ الصَّحَابِيَّةُ الَّتِي أَسْلَمَت عَلَى يَدِ زَوْجِهَا قَبْلَ دُخُولِ المُسْلِمِينَ بِدَارِ الأَرْقَمِ بْنِ أَبِي الأَرْقَمِ، وَتَزَوَّجَتْ خَلِيفَتَيْنِ مِن

husband even before the Muslims entered the house of Al-Arqam ibn Abi Al-Arqam for their gatherings. She was married to two of the Muslims' Caliphs (one after the other).

Answer: Asmaa' bint 'Umays, May Allah Be Pleased with her.

الجَواب: هِيَ أَسمَاءُ بِنتُ عُمَيسٍ ▲.

13- Who is the female Companion about whom 'Ali ibn Abi Taalib, May Allah Be Pleased with him, said, "He who longs for imminent martyrdom, let him marry her"?

13- مَن الصَّحَابِيَّة الَّتِي قَالَ عَنهَا عَلِيُّ بنُ أَبِي طَالِبٍ ﷺ: «مَن أَحَبَّ الشَّهَادَةَ الحَاضِرَةَ فَليَتَزَوَّجهَا....»؟

Answer: 'Aatikah bint Zayd, May Allah Be Pleased with her.

الجَواب: هِيَ عَاتِكَةُ بِنتُ زَيدٍ ▲.

14- What is the name of Umm Ayman, the nursemaid of the Messenger of Allah, sallallaahu 'alayhi wa sallam?

14- مَا اسمُ أَمِّ أَيمَن حَاضِنَةِ رَسُولِ اللهِ ﷺ؟

Answer: Her name is Barakah, May Allah Be Pleased with her.

الجَواب: اسمُهَا: بَرَكَة ▲.

15- What is the name of Umm Shareek who was said to have offered herself in marriage to the Prophet, sallallaahu 'alayhi wa sallam, who declined her offer?

15- مَا اسمُ أَمِّ شَرِيك الَّتِي قِيلَ: هِيَ الَّتِي وَهَبَت نَفسَهَا لِلنَّبِيَّ ﷺ فَلَم يَقبَلهَا؟

Answer: Her name is Ghuzayyah bint Jaabir Ad-Dawsiyyah, May Allah Be Pleased with her.

الجَواب: غُزَيَّةُ بِنتُ جَابِرٍ الدَّوسِيَّةُ ▲.

16- **What is the name of Umm 'Umaarah, May Allah Be Pleased with her, whose hand was cut off while performing Jihaad?**

Answer: Her name is Nusaybah bint Ka'b.

١٦- مَا اسمُ أُمّ عمَارَةَ (الَّتِي قُطِعَت يَدُهَا فِي الجِهَاد)؟

الجواب: اسمُهَا نُسَيبَةُ بِنتُ كَعَب.

أَدْعِيةٌ وَأَذْكَارٌ نَبويَّةٌ

Supplications and Invocations

Q1: What is the Du'aa (supplication) to be recited before engaging in sexual intercourse with one's spouse?

Answer: Bismillaah, Allaahumma Jannibna Ash-Shaytaan wa Jannib Ash-Shaytaan Ma Razaqtana (In the Name of Allah, O Allah keep the devil away from us and away from what You have blessed us with).

Q2: What is the Du'aa to be recited when one is angry?

Answer: A'oothu Billahi Min Ash-Shaytaan Ar-Rajeem (I seek refuge with Allah from the accursed devil).

Q3: What is the Du'aa to be recited when seeing an afflicted person?

Answer: Al-Hamdu lillaahi Allathi 'Aafaani Mimma Ibtalaaka Bihi wa Fadhalani 'Ala Katheerin Mimman Khalaqa Tafdheela (Praise be to Allah Who Kept me safe from what He Afflicted you with and Favored me over many of His Creatures).

Q4: What is the Du'aa to be recited at the end of a gathering?

Answer: Subhaanak Allaahumma wa Bihamdik,

س1: مَا الدُّعَاءُ قَبْلَ إِتْيَانِ الزَّوْجَةِ؟

جـ1: بِسْمِ اللهِ، اللَّهُمَّ جَنِّبْنَا الشَّيْطَانَ وَجَنِّبِ الشَّيْطَانَ مَا رَزَقْتَنَا.

س2: مَا دُعَاءُ الغَضَبِ؟

جـ2: أَعُوذُ بِاللهِ مِنَ الشَّيْطَانِ الرَّجِيمِ.

س3: مَاذَا يَقُولُ مَنْ رَأَى مُبْتَلًى؟

جـ3: الْحَمْدُ للهِ الَّذِي عَافَانِي مِمَّا ابْتَلَاكَ بِهِ، وَفَضَّلَنِي عَلَى كَثِيرٍ مِمَّنْ خَلَقَ تَفْضِيلًا.

س4: مَا دُعَاءُ كَفَّارَةِ المَجْلِسِ؟

جـ4: سُبْحَانَكَ اللَّهُمَّ وَبِحَمْدِكَ، أَشْهَدُ أَنْ لَّا إِلَهَ إِلَّا أَنْتَ، أَسْتَغْفِرُكَ

وَأَتُوبُ إِلَيْكَ.

Ash-hadu Alla Ilaaha illa Anta Astaghfiruka wa Atoobu Ilayk (O Allah, may You Be Exalted and Praised. I testify that none has the right to be worshipped except You. I seek Your Forgiveness and turn to You in repentance).

Q5: How should we answer the one who says, "Ghafara Allaahu lak (May Allah Forgive you)"?

س5: مَاذَا تَقُولُ لِمَنْ قَالَ غَفَرَ اللهُ لَكَ؟

Answer: Wa lak (May Allah Forgive you too).

جـ5: وَلَكَ.

Q6: What should we say to the one who did us a favor?

س6: مَاذَا تَقُولُ لِمَنْ صَنَعَ إِلَيْكَ مَعْرُوفًا؟

Answer: Jazaaka Allaahu Khayran (May Allah Reward you).

جـ6: جَزَاكَ اللهُ خَيْرًا.

Q7: What if someone tells you he loves you for the Sake of Allah, what should you say?

س7: مَاذَا تَقُولُ لِمَنْ قَالَ لَكَ إِنِّي أُحِبُّكَ فِي اللهِ؟

Answer: Ahabbak Allathi Ahbabtani lah (May Allah, for Whose Sake you love me, Love you).

جـ7: أَحَبَّكَ الَّذِي أَحْبَبْتَنِي لَهُ.

Q8: What is the Du'aa to be recited in favor of someone who offers you his money?

س8: مَا الدُّعَاءُ لِمَنْ عَرَضَ عَلَيْكَ مَالَهُ؟

Answer: Baarak Allaahu laka fi Ahlika wa Maalik (May Allah Bless your family and wealth).

جـ8: بَارَكَ اللهُ لَكَ فِي أَهْلِكَ وَمَالِكَ.

Q9: What is the Du'aa to be recited when one fears of

س9: مَا دُعَاءُ الخَوْفِ مِنَ الشِّرْكِ؟

أَسَاسِيَّاتٌ فِي التَّرْبِيَةِ الإِسْلَامِيَّةِ

committing Shirk (polytheism)?

Answer: Allaahumma Inni A'oothu Bika An Ushrika Bika wa Ana A'lam wa Astaghfiruka Lima La A'lam (O Allah, I seek refuge with You lest I should commit Shirk knowingly and I seek Your Forgiveness for what I commit thereof unknowingly).

جـ9: اللَّهُمَّ إِنِّي أَعُوذُ بِكَ أَنْ أُشْرِكَ بِكَ وَأَنَا أَعْلَمُ، وَأَسْتَغْفِرُكَ لِمَا لَا أَعْلَمُ.

Q10: How should we answer the one who says to us, "May Allah Bless you"?

Answer: Wa Feeka Baarak Allah (May Allah Bless you too).

س10: بِمَ تُجِيبُ لِمَنْ قَالَ بَارَكَ اللهُ فِيكَ؟

جـ10: وَفِيكَ بَارَكَ اللهُ.

Q11: What is the Du'aa to be recited when feeling that something is a bad omen?

Answer: Allaahumma La Tayra Illa Tayruk wa La Khayra Illa Khayruk wa La Ilaaha Ghayruk (O Allah, there is no omen but there is reliance on You, there is no good but Your Good and none is worthy of worship except You).

س11: مَا دُعَاءُ كَرَاهِيَةِ الطِّيَرَةِ؟

جـ11: اللَّهُمَّ لَا طَيْرَ إِلَّا طَيْرُكَ، وَلَا خَيْرَ إِلَّا خَيْرُكَ، وَلَا إِلَهَ غَيْرُكَ.

Q12: What is the Du'aa of riding an animal or any vehicle?

Answer: Bismillaah wa Al-Hamdu lillaah, Subhaan Allathi Sakhkhara Lana Haatha wa Ma

س12: مَاذَا يَقُولُ مَنْ رَكِبَ دَابَّةً أَوْ غَيْرَهَا مِنَ المَرْكُوبَاتِ؟

جـ12: بِسْمِ اللهِ، وَالْحَمْدُ للهِ ﴿سُبْحَانَ الَّذِي سَخَّرَ لَنَا هَذَا وَمَا

Kunna Lahu Muqrineen wa Inna Ila Rabbina Lamunqaliboon. Al-Hamdu Lillaah Al-Hamdu Lillaah Al-Hamdu Lillaah, Allaahu Akbar, Allaahu Akbar, Allaahu Akbar Subhaanak Allaahumma Inni Thalamtu Nafsi Faghfir Li Fa Innahu La Yaghfir Ath-Thunooba Illa Ant (In the Name of Allah and praise be to Allah. "Exalted is He who has subjected this to us, and we could not have [otherwise] subdued it. And indeed we, to our Lord, will [surely] return." Praise be to Allah (three times), Allah Is the Greatest (three times), O Allah, may You Be Exalted, I wronged myself so Forgive me, for, indeed, none can forgive sins but You).

Q13: What is the Du‘aa to be said when setting out on a journey?

Answer: Allaahu Akbar, Allaahu Akbar, Allaahu Akbar, Subhaan Allathi Sakhkhara Lana Haatha wa Ma Kunna Lahu Muqrineen wa Inna Ila Rabbina Lamunqaliboon, Allaahumma Inna Nas'aluka Fi Safarina Haatha Al-Birra wat Taqwa wa Min Al-'Amali Ma

كُنَّا لَهُ مُقْرِنِينَ، وَإِنَّا إِلَى رَبِّنَا لَمُنْقَلِبُونَ، ((الْحَمْدُ لِلَّهِ ، الْحَمْدُ لِلَّهِ ، الْحَمْدُ لِلَّهِ ، اللهُ أَكْبَرُ، اللهُ أَكْبَرُ، اللهُ أَكْبَرُ، سُبْحَانَكَ اللَّهُمَّ إِنِّي ظَلَمْتُ نَفْسِي فَاغْفِرْ لِي؛ فَإِنَّهُ لَا يَغْفِرُ الذُّنُوبَ إِلَّا أَنْتَ.

س13: مَا دُعَاءُ السَّفَرِ؟

ج ــ 13: اللهُ أَكْبَرُ، اللهُ أَكْبَرُ، اللهُ أَكْبَرُ، ﴿سُبْحَانَ الَّذِي سَخَّرَ لَنَا هَذَا وَمَا كُنَّا لَهُ مُقْرِنِينَ * وَإِنَّا إِلَى رَبِّنَا لَمُنْقَلِبُونَ﴾ اللَّهُمَّ إِنَّا نَسْأَلُكَ فِي سَفَرِنَا هَذَا الْبِرَّ وَالتَّقْوَى، وَمِنَ الْعَمَلِ مَا تَرْضَى، اللَّهُمَّ هَوِّنْ عَلَيْنَا سَفَرَنَا هَذَا وَاطْوِ عَنَّا بُعْدَهُ، اللَّهُمَّ أَنْتَ الصَّاحِبُ فِي السَّفَرِ،

وَالْخَلِيفَةِ فِي الْأَهْلِ، اللَّهُمَّ إِنِّي أَعُوذُ بِكَ مِنْ وَعْثَاءِ السَّفَرِ، وَكَآبَةِ الْمَنْظَرِ، وَسُوءِ الْمُنْقَلَبِ فِي الْمَالِ وَالْأَهْلِ.

Tardha, Allaahumma Hawwin 'Alayna Safarana Haatha Watwi 'Anna Bu'dah, Allaahumma Anta As-Saahibu Fi As-Safar wal Khaleefatu Fi Al-Ahl, Allaahumma Inni A'oothu Bika Min Wa'thaa' As-Safar wa Ka'aabat Al-Manthar wa Soo' Al-Munqalab Fi Al-Maali wa Al-Ahl (Allah Is The Greatest (three times). "Exalted Is He Who Has Subjected this to us, and we could not have [otherwise] subdued it. And indeed we, to our Lord, will [surely] return." O Allah, we ask You to Grant us piety and fear of You in this journey of ours and to Guide us to the kind of deeds that please You. O Allah, Make our journey easy for us and Let us cover its distance quickly. O Allah, You Are The Companion in journey and The Guardian over the family. O Allah, I seek refuge with You from the hardship of traveling, from seeing what is unpleasant and from an ill-fated outcome in wealth and family).

س14: مَا ذِكْرُ الرُّجُوعِ مِنَ السَّفَرِ؟

Q14: What is the Du'aa to be recited when returning from a journey?

Answer: La Ilaaha Illa Allaahu Wahdahu La Shareeka Lah, Lahul Mulku wa Lahul Hamdu wa Huwa 'Ala Kulli Shay'in Qadeer Aayiboon Taa'iboon 'Aabidoon Lirabbina Haamidoon, Sadaqa Allaahu Wa'dahu wa Nasara 'Abdahu wa Hazama Al-Ahzaaba Wahdah (There is none worthy of worship but Allah Who Has no partners. To Him belongs sovereignty and to Him belongs praise. We return repentant to our Lord, worshipping Him and praising Him. Allah Fulfilled His Promise, Granted His slave victory and Defeated the confederates Alone).

Q15: *What is the Du'aa to be said upon entering a village or a town?*

Answer: Allaahumma Rabb As-Samaawaati As-Sab'i wa Ma Athlaln wa Rabb Al-Aradheen As-Sab'i wa ma Aqlaln wa Rabb Ash-Shayaatenna wa Ma Athlaln wa Rabb Ar-Riyaah wa Ma Tharayn, As'aluka Khayra Haathihi Al-Qaryah wa Khayra Ahliha wa Khayra Ma Feeha wa A'oothu Bika Min Sharriha wa Sharri Ahliha wa Sharri Ma

جـ14: لَا إِلَـهَ إِلَّا اللهُ وَحْـدَهُ لَا شَرِيكَ لَـهُ، لَـهُ المُلْكُ وَلَـهُ الحَمْدُ وَهُوَ عَلَى كُلِّ شَيْءٍ قَدِيرٌ، آيِبُونَ، تَائِبُونَ، عَابِدُونَ، لِرَبِّنَا حَامِدُونَ، صَدَقَ اللهُ وَعْدَهُ، وَنَصَرَ عَبْدَهُ، وَهَزَمَ الأَحْزَابَ وَحْدَهُ.

س15: مَا دُعَاءُ دُخُولِ القَرْيَةِ أَوِ البَلْدَةِ؟

جـ15: اللَّهُـمَّ رَبَّ السَّـمَوَاتِ السَّبْعِ وَمَا أَظْلَلْنَ، وَرَبَّ الأَرَضِينَ السَّبْعِ وَمَا أَقْلَلْنَ، وَرَبَّ الشَّيَاطِينِ وَمَـا أَضْلَلْنَ، وَرَبَّ الرِّيَاحِ وَمَـا ذَرَيْنَ، أَسْأَلُكَ خَيْرَ هَذِهِ القَرْيَةِ، وَخَيْرَ أَهْلِهَا، وَخَيْرَ مَا فِيهَا، وَأَعُوذُ بِكَ مِنْ شَرِّهَا، وَشَرِّ أَهْلِهَا، وَشَرِّ مَا فِيهَا.

Feeha (O Allah, Lord of the seven heavens and everything they shade and Lord of the seven earths and everything they carry, Lord of the devils and all those they lead astray, Lord of the winds and everything they blow. I ask You the good of this town and the good of its people, and I seek refuge with You from its evil, the evil of its people and the evil of what is therein).

Q16: What is the Du'aa of entering the market?

Answer: La Ilaaha illa Allaah Wahdahu La Shareeka Lah Lahul Mulku lahul Hamdu Yuhyi wa Yumeet wa Huwa Hayyun La Yamoot Biyadihi Al-Khayru wa Huwa 'Ala Kulli Shay'in Qadeer (None is worthy of worship but Allah Alone, Who Has no partner. To Him belongs all sovereignty and praise. He Gives life and Causes death. He Is ever-living and never Dies. All good is in His Hand and He Is over everything Competent).

Q17: What is the Du'aa to be said when a mount stumbles?

Answer: Bismillaah (In the Name of Allah).

س١٦: مَا دُعَاءُ دُخُولِ السُّوقِ؟

جـ ١٦: لاَ إِلَـهَ إِلاَّ اللهُ وَحْـدَهُ لاَ شَرِيكَ لَهُ، لَهُ الْمُلْكُ، وَلَهُ الْحَمْدُ، يُحْيِي وَيُمِيتُ، وَهُوَ حَيٌّ لا يَمُوتُ، بِيَدِهِ الْخَيْرُ، وَهُوَ عَلَى كُلِّ شَيْءٍ قَدِيرٌ.

س١٧: مَا الدُّعَاءُ إِذَا تَعِسَ المَرْكُوبُ؟

جـ ١٧: بِسْمِ اللهِ.

Q18: What is the Du'aa of the traveler for the resident?

Answer: Astawdi'uka Allaaha Allathi La Tadhee'u Wadaa'i'uh (I leave you in the Trust of Allah Whose Trust is never lost).

Q19: What is the Du'aa of the resident for the traveler?

Answer: Zawwadaka Allaahu At-Taqwa wa Ghafara Thambak wa Yassara Laka Al-Khayra Haythu Ma Kunt (May Allah Provide you with piety, Forgive your sin, and Facilitate for you what is good wherever you are).

Q20: What do we say on alighting at a place?

Answer: A'oothu Bikalimaati-llaahi At-Taammaati Min Sharri Ma Khalaq (I seek refuge with the perfect Words of Allah from the evil of His Creatures).

Q21: What is to be said on receiving pleasant news?

Answer: Al-Hamdu Lillaahi Allathi Bini'matihi Tatimmu As-Saalihaat (All praise is due to Allah by Whose Blessing good deeds are accomplished).

Q22: What is to be said on receiving bad news?

س18: مَا دُعَاءُ المُسَافِرِ لِلْمُقِيمِ؟

جـ18: أَسْتَوْدِعُكَ اللهَ الَّذِي لاَ تَضِيعُ وَدَائِعُهُ.

س19: مَا دُعَاءُ المُقِيمِ لِلْمُسَافِرِ؟

جـ19: زَوَّدَكَ اللهُ التَّقْوَى، وَغَفَرَ ذَنْبَكَ، وَيَسَّرَ لَكَ الخَيْرَ حَيْثُ مَا كُنْتَ.

س20: مَاذَا تَقُولُ عِنْدَ نُزُولِكَ المَنْزِلَ؟

جـ20: أَعُوذُ بِكَلِمَاتِ اللهِ التَّامَّاتِ مِنْ شَرِّ مَا خَلَقَ.

س21: مَاذَا يَقُولُ وَيَفْعَلُ مَنْ أَتَاهُ أَمْرٌ يَسُرُّهُ؟

جـ21: الحَمْدُ لِلهِ الَّذِي بِنِعْمَتِهِ تَتِمُّ الصَّالِحَاتُ.

س22: مَاذَا يَقُولُ مَنْ أَتَاهُ أَمْرٌ يَكْرَهُهُ؟

Answer: Al-Hamdu Lillaahi ‘Ala Kulli Haal (All praise is due to Allah in all circumstances).

Q23: How should one return the disbeliever's greeting?

Answer: Wa ‘Alaykom (And upon you too).

Q24: What is the Du‘aa to be recited on hearing a rooster crow?

Answer: The Prophet, sallallaahu ‘alayhi wa sallam, said, "If you hear the crowing of a rooster, ask Allah for His Bounty for it has seen an angel."

Q25: What is the Du‘aa to be said on hearing a donkey bray?

Answer: The Prophet, sallallaahu ‘alayhi wa sallam, said, "If you hear the braying of a donkey, seek refuge with Allah from the devil for it has seen a devil."

Q26: What should a Muslim say when praised?

Answer: Allaahumma La Tu’aakhithni Bima Yaqooloon Waghfir Li Ma La Ya‘lamoon Waj‘alni Khayran Mimma Yathunnoon (O Allah, do not impose blame upon me because

جـ 22: الْحَمْدُ للهِ عَلَى كُلِّ حَالٍ.

س23: كَيْفَ يَرُدُّ السَّلَامَ عَلَى الْكَافِرِ إِذَا سَلَّمَ؟

جـ 23: وَعَلَيْكُمْ.

س24: مَا دُعَاءُ صِيَاحِ الدِّيكِ؟

جـ 24: قَالَ رَسُولُ اللهِ ﷺ: «إِذَا سَمِعْتُمْ صِيَاحَ الدِّيَكَةِ فَاسْأَلُوا اللهَ مِنْ فَضْلِهِ؛ فَإِنَّهَا رَأَتْ مَلَكاً».

س25: مَا دُعَاءُ نَهِيقِ الْحِمَارِ؟

جـ 25: قَالَ ﷺ: «إِذَا سَمِعْتُمْ نَهِيقَ الْحِمَارِ فَتَعَوَّذُوا بِاللهِ مِنَ الشَّيْطَانِ؛ فَإِنَّهُ رَأَى شَيْطَاناً».

س26: مَاذَا يَقُولُ الْمُسْلِمُ إِذَا زُكِّيَ؟

جـ 26: اللَّهُمَّ لَا تُؤَاخِذْنِي بِمَا يَقُولُونَ، وَاغْفِرْ لِي مَا لَا يَعْلَمُونَ، وَاجْعَلْنِي خَيْراً مِمَّا يَظُنُّونَ.

of what they say (about me), forgive my sins that they know nothing of and make me better than what they think).

Q27: What is the Talbiyah that the pilgrim should recite in Hajj (pilgrimage) or 'Umrah (minor pilgrimage)?

Answer: Labbayka Allaahumma Labbayk, Labbayka La Shareeka Laka Labbayk, Inn-al-Hamda Wanni'mata laka Wal Mulk, La Shareeka Lak (O Allah, here I am (in response to Your Call), here I am. You have no partner, here I am. All praise, praise and blessing belong to You and sovereignty are Yours. You Have no partner).

Q28: What is the Du'aa to be recited between the Yamaani Corner and the Black Stone?

Answer: Rabbana Aatina Fid-Dunya Hasanah wa Fi-l-Aakhirati Hasanah wa Qina 'Athaab An-Naar (Our Lord, Give us in this worldly life [that which is] good and in the Hereafter [that which is] good and Protect us from the punishment of the Hellfire).

Q29: What is the Du'aa to be recited when standing on Safa

س27: كَيْفَ يُلَبِّي الْمُحْرِمُ فِي الْحَجّ أَوِ الْعُمْرَةِ؟

جـ 27: لَبَّيْكَ اللَّهُمَّ لَبَّيْكَ، لَبَّيْكَ لاَ شَرِيكَ لَكَ لَبَّيْكَ، إِنَّ الْحَمْدَ، وَالنّعْمَةَ، لَكَ وَالْمُلْكَ، لاَ شَرِيكَ لَكَ.

س28: مَا الدُّعَاءُ بَيْنَ الرُّكْنِ الْيَمَانِيّ وَالْحَجَرِ الأَسْوَدِ؟

جـ 28: ﴿رَبَّنَا آتِنَا فِي الدُّنْيَا حَسَنَةً وَفِي الآخِرَةِ حَسَنَةً وَقِنَا عَذَابَ النَّارِ﴾.

س29: مَا الدُّعَاءُ عِنْدَ الْوُقُوفِ عَلَى الصَّفَا وَالْمَرْوَةِ؟

and Marwah?

Answer: La Illaaha Illa Allaah Wahadahu La Shareeka Lah, Lahul Mulku wa Lahul Hamdu wa Huwa 'Ala Kulli Shay'in Qadeer, La Illaaha Illa Allaahu Wahdah, Anjaza Wa'dahu wa Nasara 'Abdahu wa Hazama Al-Ahzaaba Wahdah (None is worthy of worship but Allah Alone, without a partner. Sovereignty and praise belong to Him and He Is over everything Competent. None is worthy of worship but Allah Alone. He fulfilled His Promise, granted His Slave victory and Defeated the confederates Alone (this is to be said three times)).

Q30: What is the Du'aa of the Day of 'Arafah?

Answer: La Ilaaha Illa Allaahu Wahdahu La Shareeka Lah, Lahul Mulku wa Lahul Hamdu wa Huwa 'Ala Kulli Shay'in Qadeer (None has the right to be worshipped except Allah Alone, without a partner. All sovereignty and praise belong to Him and He is over everything Competent.

Q31: What should one say when being amazed and on

ج ــ 29: لاَ إِلَــهَ إِلاَّ اللهُ وَحْـدَهُ لاَ شَرِيكَ لَهُ، لَهُ الْمُلْكُ وَلَهُ الْحَمْدُ وَهُوَ عَلَى كُلِّ شَيْءٍ قَدِيرٌ، لاَ إِلَهَ إِلاَّ اللهُ وَحْدَهُ، أَنْجَزَ وَعْدَهُ، وَنَصَرَ عَبْدَهُ، وَهَـزَمَ الأَحْـزَابَ وَحْـدَهُ. ثَلَاثَ مَرَّاتٍ.

س30: مَا دُعَاءُ يَوْمِ عَرَفَةَ؟

ج ــ 30: لاَ إِلَــهَ إِلاَّ اللهُ وَحْـدَهُ لاَ شَرِيكَ لَهُ، لَهُ الْمُلْكُ وَلَهُ الْحَمْدُ وَهُوَ عَلَى كُلِّ شَيْءٍ قَدِيرٌ.

س31: مَا الدُّعَاءُ عِنْدَ التَّعَجُّبِ وَالأَمْرِ السَّارِّ؟

receiving good news?

Answer: Subhaanallaah, Allaahu Akbar (Exalted Be Allah, Allah Is the Greatest).

Q32: What should be done on receiving good news?

Answer: One should fall in prostration out of gratitude to Allah, The Almighty.

Q33: What should one do when feeling pain in his body?

Answer: One should put his hand on the place of pain and say three times, "Bismillaah (In The Name of Allah)." Then say seven times, "A'oothu Billaahi wa Qudratihi Min Sharri Ma Ajidu wa Uhaathir (I seek refuge with Allah and His Omnipotence from the evil of what I feel and fear)."

Q34: What should one do to avoid harming himself or anyone with an evil eye?

Answer: The Prophet, sallallaahu 'alayhi wa sallam, said, "If anyone of you sees in his brother, in himself or in his wealth something that he finds impressive, let him ask Allah to Bless it, for the evil eye is indeed true."

Q35: What is to be said at times of fear?

جـ31: سُبْحَانَ اللهِ، اللهُ أَكْبَرُ.

س32: مَاذَا يَفْعَلُ مَنْ أَتَاهُ أَمْرٌ يَسُرُّهُ؟

جـ32: يَخِرُّ سَاجِداً شُكْراً لله تَبَارَكَ وَتَعَالَى.

س33: مَاذَا تَفْعَلُ إِذَا أَحْسَسْتَ بِوَجَعٍ في جَسَدِكَ؟

جـ33: ضَعْ يَدَكَ عَلَى الَّذِي تَأَلَّمَ مِنْ جَسَدِكَ وَقُلْ: بِسْمِ اللهِ، ثَلَاثاً، وَقُلْ سَبْعَ مَرَّاتٍ: أَعُوذُ بِاللهِ وَقُدْرَتِهِ مِنْ شَرِّ مَا أَجِدُ وَأَحَاذِرُ.

س34: مَاذَا يَفْعَلُ مَنْ خَشِيَ أَنْ يُصِيبَ شَيْئاً بِعَيْنِهِ؟

جـ34: قَالَ ﷺ: «إِذَا رَأَى أَحَدُكُمْ مِنْ أَخِيهِ، أَوْ مِنْ نَفْسِهِ، أَوْ مِنْ مَالِهِ مَا يُعْجِبُهُ، (فَلْيَدْعُ لَهُ بِالْبَرَكَةِ) فَإِنَّ الْعَيْنَ حَقٌّ».

س35: مَاذَا يُقَالُ عِنْدَ الْفَزَعِ؟

جـ35: لَا إِلَهَ إِلَّا اللهُ.

Answer: La Ilaaha Illa Allaah (None is worthy of worship but Allah).

س36: مَاذَا يُقَالُ عِنْدَ الذَّبْحِ أَوِ النَّحْرِ؟

Q36: What is to be said on slaughtering a sacrifice?

جـ36: بِسْمِ اللهِ وَاللهُ أَكْبَرُ (اللَّهُمَّ مِنْكَ وَإِلَيْكَ) اللَّهُمَّ تَقَبَّلْ مِنِّي.

Answer: Bismillaah Wallaahu Akbar, Allaahumma Minka wa Ilayk, Allaahumma Taqabbal Minni (In The Name of Allah, Allah Is the Greatest. O Allah, it is from You and belongs to You. O Allah, Accept it from me).

س37: مَا فَضْلُ التَّسْبِيحِ وَالتَّحْمِيدِ وَالتَّهْلِيلِ وَالتَّكْبِيرِ؟

Q37: What is the virtue of Tasbeeh (saying Subhaanallaah), Tahmeed (saying Alhamdulillaah), Tahleel (saying La Illaaha Illa Allaah) and Takbeer (saying Allahu Akbar)?

جـ37: قَالَ ﷺ: «لَأَنْ أَقُولَ سُبْحَانَ اللهِ، وَالْحَمْدُ للهِ، وَلَا إِلَهَ إِلَّا اللهُ، وَاللهُ أَكْبَرُ، أَحَبُّ إِلَيَّ مِمَّا طَلَعَتْ عَلَيْهِ الشَّمْسُ»

Answer: The Prophet, sallallaahu 'alayhi wa sallam, said, "Saying Subhaanallaah (Exalted is Allah), Alhamdulillaah (Praise be to Allah), la ilaaha Illa Allaah (None is worthy of worship but Allah) and Allaahu Akbar (Allah is the Greatest) is dearer to me than everything upon which the sun rises (the whole worldly life)."

وَقَالَ ﷺ: «كَلِمَتَانِ خَفِيفَتَانِ عَلَى اللِّسَانِ، ثَقِيلَتَانِ فِي الْمِيزَانِ،

The Prophet, sallallaahu 'alayhi wa sallam, also said, "Two

words are light on the tongue (i.e., easy to say), heavy on the Scale and loved by the Most Merciful: Subhaanallaahi wa Bihamdih, Subhaanallahi Al-'Atheem (Exalted Is Allah and praise be to Him, Exalted Is Allah, The Great)."

حَبِيبَتَانِ إِلَى الرَّحْمَنِ: سُبْحَانَ اللهِ وَبِحَمْدِهِ، سُبْحَانَ اللهِ الْعَظِيمِ».

أربعون حديثا من الصحيحين

40 Hadeeths
Excerpted from
Saheeh Al-Bukhaari
and Saheeh Muslim

40 Hadeeths excerpted from Saheeh Al-Bukhaari and Saheeh Muslim

Offering Acts of Worship to Allah with Full Sincerity:

1- It was narrated on the authority of 'Umar ibn Al-Khattaab, May Allah Be Pleased with him, that he said: «I heard The Messenger of Allah saying, «*The reward of deeds depends upon the intentions and every person will get the reward according to what he has intended. So whoever emigrated for worldly benefits or for a woman to marry, his emigration would be for what he emigrated for*». [Al-Bukhaari and Muslim]

Virtue of Seeking Knowledge:

2- It was narrated on the authority of Abu Hurayrah, May Allah Be Pleased with him, that the Messenger of Allah, sallallaahu 'alayhi wa sallam, said: «*Whoever seeks a way to acquire knowledge Allah Will Make easy for him a way to Paradise*». [Muslim]

أَربَعونَ حَدِيثًا مِنَ الصَّحِيحَين

إخلاص النية لله ﷻ:

1- عَنْ عُمَرَ بِنِ الخطَّابِ ﷺ قـال: سَمِعْتُ رَسُولَ اللَّهِ ﷺ يَقُولُ «إِنَّمَا الأَعْمَالُ بِالنِّيَّاتِ وَإِنَّمَا لِكُلِّ امْرِئٍ مَا نَوَى، فَمَنْ كَانَتْ هِجْرَتُهُ إِلَى اللهِ وَرَسُولِهِ فَهِجْرَتُهُ إِلَى اللهِ وَرَسُولِهِ، وَمَنْ كَانَتْ هِجْرَتُهُ لِدُنْيَا يُصِيبُهَا أَوْ إِلَى امْرَأَةٍ يَنْكِحُهَا فَهِجْرَتُهُ إِلَى مَا هَاجَرَ إِلَيْهِ». [مُتفق عليه].

فضل طلب العلم:

2- عَنْ أَبِي هُرَيْرَةَ ﷺ أن رسُولِ اللهِ ﷺ قـال: «وَمَنْ سَلَكَ طَرِيقًا يَلْتَمِسُ فِيهِ عِلْمًا؛ سَهَّلَ اللهُ لَهُ بِهِ طَرِيقًا إِلَى الْجَنَّةِ» [رواه مسلم].

Virtue of Learning and Teaching the Quran:

3- It was narrated on the authority of 'Uthmaan ibn 'Affaan, May Allah Be Pleased with him, that the Messenger of Allah, sallallaahu 'alayhi wa sallam, said: «*The best of you is he who learns the Quran and teaches it*». [Al-Bukhaari]

Virtue of Having a deep Understanding of the Religion:

4- It was narrated on the authority of Mu'aawiyah ibn Abi Sufyaan, May Allah Be Pleased with him, that the Messenger of Allah, sallallaahu 'alayhi wa sallam, said: «*The one for whom Allah Wills goodness, He Grants him a deep understanding of the religion*». [Al-Bukhaari and Muslim]

The Five Pillars of Islam:

5- It was narrated on the authority of Ibn 'Umar, May Allah Be Pleased with them, that the Messenger of Allah, sallallaahu 'alayhi wa sallam, said: «*Islam is built on five pillars: testifying that there is no deity but Allah and that Muhammad is the Messenger*

فَضْلُ تَعَلُّمِ القُرآنِ وتَعليمِهِ:

3- عَنْ عثمانَ بن عفانَ ﷺ قالَ: قالَ رسولُ الله ﷺ: «خَيْرُكُم مَنْ تَعَلَّمَ القُرْآنَ وَعَلَّمَهُ». [رواه البخاري]

فضل الفقه في الدين:

4- عَنْ مُعاويةَ، ﷺ، قالَ: قالَ رسولُ اللهِ ﷺ: «مَنْ يُرِدِ الله بِهِ خَيْراً يُفَقِّهْهُ في الدِّينِ» [متفق عليه].

أركان الإسلام الخمسة:

5- عن ابنِ عمرَ رضى الله عنهما قالَ: قالَ رسولُ الله ﷺ: «بُنِيَ الإسلامُ على خَمْسٍ: شَهادَةِ أَنْ لا إِلَهَ إلاَّ الله، وأنَّ مُحمداً رسولُ اللَّهِ، وإقام الصَّلاةِ، وإيتاءِ الزَّكاةِ، وحَجِّ البَيْتِ، وصَوْمِ رَمضانَ» [متفق عليه].

of Allah, performing the prayers, paying the Zakaah, making Hajj to the House (of Allah) and fasting (the month of) Ramadhaan». [Al-Bukhaari and Muslim]

The Pillars of Eemaan (Faith):

6- It was narrated on the authority of 'Umar ibn Al-Khattaab, May Allah Be Pleased with him, that he said: «*A man came to the Prophet, sallallaahu 'alayhi wa sallam, and said, 'O Messenger of Allah, what is Eemaan (Faith)?' The Prophet, sallallaahu 'alayhi wa sallam, said, 'It is to believe in Allah, His Angels, His Revealed Books, His Messengers, the Last Day and to believe in The Divine Decree, the good and evil thereof*». [Muslim]

Virtue of Testifying That There Is no Deity but Allah:

7- It was narrated on the authority of Abu Hurayrah, May Allah Be Pleased with him, that the Prophet, sallallaahu 'alayhi wa sallam, said: «*Whoever testifies that*

أركان الإيمان:

6- عن عُمَرَ بنِ الخطاب ﷺ قال: جاء رجل إلى النبي ﷺ فقال: يا رسول الله، ما الإيمان؟ فقال النبي ﷺ: «أَنْ تُؤْمِنَ بِاللَّهِ وملائِكَتِهِ، وكُتُبِهِ ورُسُلِهِ، واليوم الآخِرِ، وتُؤْمِنَ بِالْقَدَرِ خَيْرِهِ وشَرِّهِ» [رواه مسلم].

فضل لا إله إلا الله:

7- عن أَبي هُرَيْرَةَ ﷺ عن النبي ﷺ قال: «مَنْ شَهِدَ أَنْ لا إِلَـهَ إِلاَّ اللَّهُ مستيقنا بها قلبه فَبَشِّرْهُ بِالْجَنَّةِ» [رواه مسلم].

there is no deity but Allah with certainty, give him the glad tidings of entering Paradise». [Muslim]

Virtue of the Five Prayers:

8- It was narrated on the authority of Jaabir, May Allah Be Pleased with him, that he said that the Messenger of Allah, sallallaahu 'alayhi wa sallam, said: «*The similitude of the five prayers is like an overflowing river passing by the gate of one of you in which he washes five times daily».* [Muslim]

Virtue of the Fajr and 'Asr Prayers:

9- It was narrated on the authority of Abu Moosa Al-Ash'ari, May Allah Be Pleased with him, that he said that the Messenger of Allah, sallallaahu 'alayhi wa sallam, said: «*Whoever prays Al-Bardayn (the Fajr and 'Asr prayers) will enter Paradise».*

Virtue of the 'Ishaa' and Fajr Prayers:

10- It was narrated on the authority of 'Uthmaan ibn 'Affaan, May Allah Be Pleased with him, that he said that he heard the Messenger of Allah,

فضل الصلوات الخمس:

8- وعَـنْ جَـابِرٍ ﷺ قَـالَ: قَـالَ رسُـولُ اللهِ ﷺ: «مثَـلُ الصَّـلواتِ الخَمْسِ كمثَلِ نهرٍ غمْرٍ جارٍ عَلى بابِ أَحَدِكُم يغْتَسِلُ مِنْـهُ كُلَّ يَوْمٍ خمْسَ مرَّاتٍ» [رواه مسلم].

فضل صلاة الفجر والعصر:

9- عَنْ أَبِي موسَى الأشْعَرِيّ ﷺ قال: قال رسول اللهِ ﷺ قال: «مَنْ صَـلَّى البرْ دين دَخَـلَ الجنَّـة» [متفقٌ عليه].

فضل صلاة العشاء والفجر:

10- عن عثمانَ بن عفانَ ﷺ قالَ: سمعتُ رسولَ اللهِ ﷺ يقولُ: «مَنْ صَـلَّى العِشَـاءَ في جـمَاعَةٍ، فَكَأَنَّمـا قَامَ نِصْفَ اللَّيْلِ وَمَنْ صَلَّى الصبح في جمَاعَةٍ، فَكَأَنَّمـا صَلَّى اللَّيْلَ

sallallaahu 'alayhi wa sallam, saying: «*He who prays the 'Ishaa' in congregation is as if he has prayed half the night. As to him who prays the Fajr in congregation, it is as if he has prayed all night*». [Muslim]

Virtue of Fasting:

11- It was narrated on the authority of Abu Hurayrah, May Allah Be Pleased with him, that the Messenger of Allah, sallallaahu 'alayhi wa sallam, said: «*He who observed the fast of Ramadhaan out of faith and seeking reward (from Allah), all his previous sins would be forgiven*». [Al-Bukhaari and Muslim]

Virtue of The Night of Al-Qadr:

12- It was narrated on the authority of Abu Hurayrah, May Allah Be Pleased with him, that the Messenger of Allah, sallallaahu 'alayhi wa sallam, said: «*He who observed prayer on the Night of Al-Qadr out of faith and seeking reward (from Allah), all his previous sins would be forgiven*». [Al-Bukhaari and Muslim]

كُلَّهُ» [رواه مسلم].

فضل الصوم:

11- عَنْ أَبِي هُرَيرةَ ﷺ، عَنِ النَّبِيِّ ﷺ قَالَ: «مَنْ صَامَ رَمَضَانَ إِيمَاناً وَاحْتِسَاباً، غُفِرَ لَهُ مَا تَقَدَّمَ مِنْ ذَنْبِهِ» [متفقٌ عليه].

فضل ليلة القدر:

12- وَعَنْ أَبِي هُرَيرةَ ﷺ عَنِ النَّبِيِّ ﷺ قال: «مَنْ قَامَ لَيْلَةَ القَدْرِ إِيمَاناً وَاحْتِسَاباً، غُفِرَ لَهُ مَا تقدَّم مِنْ ذَنْبِهِ» [متفقٌ عليه].

Virtue of Performing Hajj:

13- It was narrated on the authority of Abu Hurayrah, May Allah Be Pleased with him, that the Messenger of Allah, sallallaahu 'alayhi wa sallam, said: «*He who came to this House (Ka'bah) (with the intention of performing Hajj), and neither spoke indecently nor acted wickedly would return (free from sin) as on the very first day his mother gave birth to him*».
[Al-Bukhaari and Muslim]

The Worldly Life Is the Believer's Prison:

14- It was narrated on the authority of Abu Hurayrah, May Allah Be Pleased with him, that the Messenger of Allah, sallallaahu 'alayhi wa sallam, said: «*The worldly life is a prison-like abode for the believer and a paradise for the disbeliever*». [Muslim]

Manners of Eating:

15- It was narrated on the authority of 'Umar ibn Abu Salamah, May Allah Be Pleased with him, that he said that the Messenger of Allah, sallallaahu 'alayhi wa sallam,

فضل الحج:

13- عَنْ أَبِي هُرَيْرَةَ ﵁ قَالَ رَسُولَ اللَّهِ ﷺ يَقُولُ: «مِنْ حَجَّ فَلَمْ يَرْفُثْ، وَلَمْ يَفْسُقْ، رَجَعَ كَيَوْمِ وَلَدَتْهُ أُمُّهُ». [مُتَّفَقٌ عَلَيْهِ].

الدُّنْيَا سِجْنُ المُؤْمِنِ:

14- عَنْ أَبِي هُرَيْرَةَ ﵁ قَالَ رَسُولُ اللَّهِ ﷺ: «الدُّنْيَا سِجْنُ المُؤْمِنِ وجَنَّةُ الكَافِرِ» [رواه مسلم].

آداب الأكل:

15- عن عُمَرَ بنِ أَبِي سَلَمَة رَضِي اللَّه عنهما قَالَ: قَالَ لِي رَسُولُ اللَّه ﷺ: «سَمِّ اللَّه وكُلْ بِيَمِينِكَ، وكُلْ مِمَّا يَلِيكَ» [مُتَّفَقٌ عَلَيْهِ].

said to him: «*O Boy, mention The Name of Allah, and eat with your right hand and eat from what is near you*». [Al-Bukhaari and Muslim]

The Blessing of Eating in a Group:

16- It was narrated on the authority of Abu Hurayrah, May Allah Be Pleased with him, that he said that the Messenger of Allah, sallallaahu 'alayhi wa sallam, said: «*Food for two persons suffices three persons and food for three persons suffices four persons*». [Al-Bukhaari and Muslim]

The Believer Eats in One Intestine:

17- It was narrated on the authority of Ibn 'Umar, May Allah Be Pleased with them, that he said that the Messenger of Allah, sallallaahu 'alayhi wa sallam, said: «*The believer eats in one intestine, whereas the disbeliever —or a hypocrite— eats in seven intestines*». [Al-Bukhaari and Muslim]

Virtue of Remaining Silent:

18- It was narrated on the authority of Abu Hurayrah, May Allah Be Pleased with

بركة الاجتماع على الطعام:

16- عن أبي هريرة رضيَ الله تعالى عنه قالَ: قال رسولُ الله ﷺ: «طَعَامُ الإثنَين كَافِي الثَّلاثَةِ، وطَعَامُ الثَّلاثَةِ كَافِي الأربعَةِ» [متفقٌ عليه].

المؤمن يأكل في معي واحد:

17- عَنِ ابنِ عُمَرَ قَالَ: قَالَ رَسُولُ اللهِ ﷺ: «إنَّ المُؤمِنَ يَأكُلُ فِي مِعًي وَاحِدٍ وإنَّ الكَافِرَ - أوِ المُنَافِقَ - يَأكُلُ فِي سَبعَةِ أمعَاءٍ» [متفق عليه].

فضل الصمت:

18- عن أبي هُرَيرَةَ ﷺ عَن النبي ﷺ قَالَ: «مَنْ كَانَ يُؤمِنُ بِاللهِ وَاليَومِ الآخِرِ فَليقُلْ خَيرًا، أو

him, that he said that the Messenger of Allah, sallallaahu 'alayhi wa sallam, said: «*He who believes in Allah and the Last Day let him speak good or remain silent*». [Al-Bukhaari and Muslim]

Prohibition of Insulting a Muslim:

19- It was narrated on the authority of Ibn Mas'ood, May Allah Be Pleased with him, that he said that the Messenger of Allah, sallallaahu 'alayhi wa sallam, said: «*Insulting a Muslim is evildoing and fighting him is disbelief*». [Al-Bukhaari and Muslim]

Threats of Punishment for a Muslim Who Accuses a Fellow Muslim of Disbelief:

20- It was narrated on the authority of Ibn 'Umar, May Allah Be Pleased with them, that he said that the Messenger of Allah, sallallaahu 'alayhi wa sallam, said: «*Any person who calls his brother 'O disbeliever' has in fact done an act by which this accusation would return to one of them*». [Al-Bukhaari and Muslim]

لِيَصْمُتْ» [متفقٌ عليه].

تحريم سب المسلم:

19- وعَنِ ابنِ مَسـعودٍ ﷺ قـالَ: قال رسُولُ اللهِ ﷺ: «سِبـاب المُسْلِم فُسوقٌ، وقِتَالُهُ كُفْرٌ» [متفقٌ عليه].

وعيد من كفر أخاه المسلم:

20- عَن عَبدِاللهِ بن عُمَرَ قَالَ: قَالَ رَسُـولُ اللهِ ﷺ: «أيَّمَـا رَجُـلٍ قَـالَ لأخِيــهِ: يَـا كَـافِرٍ فَقَـد بَـاءَ بِهَـا أَحَدُهُمَا» [متفق عليه].

Prohibition of Pointing a Weapon at a Muslim:

21- It was narrated on the authority of Abu Hurayrah, May Allah Be Pleased with him, that he said that the Messenger of Allah, sallallaahu 'alayhi wa sallam, said: «*None amongst you should point a weapon towards his brother, for he does not know that the devil might cause the weapon (to slip) from his hand and (he may injure anyone) and thus he may fall into Hellfire*». [Al-Bukhaari and Muslim]

Warning Against the Temptation Caused by Women:

22- It was narrated on the authority of Usaamah ibn Zayd, May Allah Be Pleased with him, that he said that the Messenger of Allah, sallallaahu 'alayhi wa sallam, said: «*I have not left after me any temptation more harmful to men than women*». [Al-Bukhaari and Muslim]

The Punishment of Lowering the Garment Below the Ankles:

23- It was narrated on the authority of Abu Hurayrah,

النهي عن الإشارة بالسلاح:

21- عَنْ أَبِي هُرَيْرَةَ ﷺ عَنْ رَسُولِ اللهِ ﷺ قَالَ: «لاَ يُشِرْ أَحَدُكُمْ إِلَى أَخِيهِ بِالسِّلاَحِ، فَإِنَّهُ لاَ يَدْرِي لَعَلَّ الشَّيْطَانَ يَنْزِعُ فِي يَدِهِ، فَيَقَعَ فِي حُفْرَةٍ مِنَ النَّارِ» [متفقٌ عليه].

التحذير من فتنة النساء:

22- عن أُسَامَةَ بنِ زيدٍ رضي الله عنهما عن النبيِّ ﷺ قَالَ: «مَا تركْتُ بعْدِي فِتْنَةً هِيَ أَضَرُّ عَلَى الرِّجَالِ: مِنَ النِّسَاءِ» [متفقٌ عليه].

ما في الإسبال من الوعيد:

23- عن أبي هُرَيْرَةَ ﷺ عَنِ النبي ﷺ قَالَ: «مَا أَسْفَلَ مِنَ الْكَعْبَيْنِ

May Allah Be Pleased with him, that he said that the Messenger of Allah, sallallaahu 'alayhi wa sallam, said: «*The part of an Izaar (lower garment) which hangs below the ankles is in Hellfire*». [Al-Bukhaari]

Prohibition of Producing Images of Living Beings:

24- It was narrated on the authority of Ibn 'Umar, May Allah Be Pleased with them, that he said that the Messenger of Allah, sallallaahu 'alayhi wa sallam, said: «*Those who produce these images would be punished on the Day of Resurrection and it would be said to them, 'Breathe soul into what you have created*». [Al-Bukhaari and Muslim]

Houses That the Angels Do Not Enter:

25- It was narrated on the authority of Abu Talhah, May Allah Be Pleased with him, that he said that the Messenger of Allah, sallallaahu 'alayhi wa sallam, said: «*Angels do not enter a house wherein there is a dog or a picture of a living creature (a human being or an animal)*». [Al-Bukhaari and

مِـــنَ الإزار فَفِــي النَّـــار» [رواه البخاري].

تحريم تصوير ذوات الأرواح:

24- عَـن ابْـن عُمَـر رضـي الله عَنْهُما أنَّ رَسُولَ اللهِ ﷺ قَالَ: «إنَّ الَّـذِين يَصْـنَعونَ هـذِه الصُّـورَ يُعَـذَّبُونَ يَـوْمَ القِيَامَـة، يُقَـالُ لَهُـمْ: أحْيُوا مَا خَلَقْتُمْ» [متفقٌ عليه].

بيوت لا تدخلها الملائكة:

25- عَنْ أبي طَلْحَة ﷺ أنَّ رَسُولَ اللهِ ﷺ قَـالَ: «لا تَـدْخُلُ المَلائِكَـةُ بَيْتاً فِيهِ كَلْبٌ وَلا صُورَةٌ» [متفقٌ عليه].

Muslim]

Places That Are the Dearest to Allah, The Almighty:

26- It was narrated on the authority of Abu Hurayrah, May Allah Be Pleased with him, that he said that the Messenger of Allah, sallallaahu ‘alayhi wa sallam, said: «*The dearest places to Allah are mosques, and the most hateful places to Allah are markets*». [Muslim]

The Signs of a Hypocrite:

27- It was narrated on the authority of Abu Hurayrah, May Allah Be Pleased with him, that the Messenger of Allah, sallallaahu ‘alayhi wa sallam, said: «*There are three signs of the hypocrite: when he speaks, he tells a lie, when he makes a promise, he acts treacherously, and when he is trusted, he betrays*». [Al-Bukhaari and Muslim]

Virtue of Maintaining Kinship Ties:

8- It was narrated on the authority of Anas, May Allah Be Pleased with him, that the Messenger of Allah, sallallaahu

أحب الأماكن إلى الله تعالى:

٢٦- عَنْ أَبِي هُرَيْرَةَ ﷺ عَنِ النبي ﷺ قَالَ: «أَحَبُّ الْبِلَادِ إِلَى اللهِ مَسَاجِدُهَا، وَأَبْغَضُ الْبِلَادِ إِلَى اللهِ أَسْوَاقُهَا» [رَوَاهُ مُسْلم].

علامات المنافق:

٢٧- عَنْ أَبِي هريرة ﷺ، أن رسولَ الله ﷺ قَالَ: «آيَةُ الْمُنَافِقِ ثَلَاثٌ: إِذَا حَدَّثَ كَذَبَ، وَإِذَا وَعَدَ أَخْلَفَ، وَإِذَا اؤْتُمِنَ خَانَ» [متفقٌ عليه].

فضل صلة الرحم:

٢٨- عن أنسٍ ﷺ أن رسولَ الله ﷺ قال: «مَنْ أَحَبَّ أَنْ يُبْسَطَ لـه فِي رِزْقِهِ، وَيُنْسَأَ لَهُ فِي أَثَرِهِ،

‘alayhi wa sallam, said: «*He who likes his sustenance to be expanded and his age to be lengthened should maintain the tie of kinship*» [Al-Bukhaari and Muslim]

Obligation of Marrying a Religious Woman:

29- It was narrated on the authority of Abu Hurayrah, May Allah Be Pleased with him, that the Messenger of Allah, sallallaahu ‘alayhi wa sallam, said: «*The woman is married for four things: her wealth, her noble family background, her beauty and her religion. So, you should marry the religious woman otherwise you will be a loser*». [Al-Bukhaari and Muslim]

The Reward of a Judge:

30- It was narrated on the authority of ‘Amr ibn Al-‘Aas, May Allah Be Pleased with him, that he heard the Messenger of Allah, sallallaahu ‘alayhi wa sallam, saying: «*If the judge gives a decision, having tried his best to decide correctly and is right, there will be two rewards for him;*

فَلْيَصِلْ رحِمهُ» [متفقٌ عليه].

وجوب نكاح ذات الدين:

29- عَنْ أبي هُرَيْرَةَ ﷺ عَنِ النبي ﷺ قَالَ: «تُنْكَحُ الْمَرْأَةُ لأرْبَعٍ: لِمالِهَا، وَلِحَسَبِهَا، وَلِجَمَالِهَا، وَلِدِينِهَا، فَاظْفَرْ بِذَاتِ الدِّينِ تَرِبَتْ يَدَاك» [متفقٌ عليه].

أجر الحاكم:

30- عَنْ عمْرو بْنِ الْعَاصِ ﷺ أنَّهُ سَمِعَ رسُولَ اللَّه ﷺ يَقُولُ: «إذَا حَكَمَ الْحَاكِمُ، فَاجْتَهَدَ، ثُمَّ أصَابَ، فَلَهُ أجْرَانِ وإنْ حَكَمَ وَاجْتَهَدَ، فَأَخْطَأَ، فَلَهُ أجْرٌ» [متفقٌ عَلَيْهِ].

and if he gave a judgment after having tried his best (to arrive at a correct decision) but erred, there would be one reward for him». [Al-Bukhaari and Muslim]

The Obedience to a Ruler as long as no Sin Is Involved:

31- It was narrated on the authority of Abu Hurayrah, May Allah Be Pleased with him, that the Messenger of Allah, sallallaahu 'alayhi wa sallam, said: «*Whoever obeys me, obeys Allah, and whoever disobeys me, disobeys Allah, and whoever obeys the ruler I appoint, obeys me, and whoever disobeys him, disobeys me*». [Al-Bukhaari and Muslim]

The Believers Are Like the Bricks of a Wall:

32- It was narrated on the authority of Abu Moosa Al-Ash'ari, May Allah Be Pleased with him, that the Messenger of Allah, sallallaahu 'alayhi wa sallam, said: «*The believer to the believer is like the bricks of a wall, reinforcing each other*». While (saying that) the

طاعة الأمير ما لم تكن معصية:

31- عن أبي هُرَيْرَةَ ﷺ قال: قال رسُولُ اللهِ ﷺ: «مَنْ أَطَاعَني فَقَدْ أَطَاعَ اللهَ، وَمَنْ عَصَاني فَقَدْ عَصَى اللهَ، وَمَنْ يُطِعِ الأميرَ فَقَدْ أَطَاعَني، ومَنْ يعْصِ الأميرَ فَقَدْ عَصَاني» [متفقٌ عليه].

المؤمن للمؤمن كالبنيان:

32- وعن أبي موسى ﷺ قال: قال رسُولُ اللهِ ﷺ: «المُؤمنُ للمُؤمِن كالبُنْيَانِ يَشدُّ بعْضُهُ بعْضاً» وَشَبَّكَ بَيْنَ أَصَابِعِه. [متفق عليه].

Prophet, sallallaahu 'alayhi wa sallam, clasped his hands, by interlacing his fingers». [Al-Bukhaari and Muslim]

The Muslim's Right Over His Fellow Muslim:

33- It was narrated on the authority of Abu Hurayrah, May Allah Be Pleased with him, that he heard the Messenger of Allah, sallallaahu 'alayhi wa sallam, saying: «*The rights of the Muslim over his fellow Muslim are five: to answer the greeting of peace, to visit the sick, to follow the funeral processions, to accept invitation and to reply to the sneezer*». [Al-Bukhaari and Muslim]

Dutifulness to Parents:

34- «*A man came to the Messenger of Allah, sallallaahu 'alayhi wa sallam, and said, 'O Messenger of Allah! Who is most entitled to my good companionship?' The Prophet, sallallaahu 'alayhi wa sallam, said, 'Your mother.' The man said, 'Who is next?' The Prophet, sallallaahu 'alayhi wa sallam, said, 'Your mother.' The man further said, 'Who is next?'*

حق المسلم على المسلم:

33- عَنْ أَبِي هريرة ﷺ أَنَّ رسول الله ﷺ قال: «حقُّ الْمُسْلِمِ عَلَى الْمُسْلِمِ خمسٌ: رَدُّ السَّلامِ، وَعِيَادَةُ الْمريضَ، واتِّبَاعُ الْجنَائِزِ، وإجابةُ الدَّعوةِ، وتَشْمِيت الْعَاطِسِ» [متفق عليه].

بر الوالدين:

34- جَاءَ رَجُلٌ إلى رسول الله ﷺ فقال: يا رسول الله مَنْ أَحَقُّ النَّاسِ بحُسنِ صَحَابتي؟ قَالَ: «أُمَّكَ» قال: ثُمَّ مِنْ؟ قال: «أُمَّكَ» قال: ثُمَّ مَنْ؟ قال: «أُمَّكَ» قال: ثُمَّ مَنْ؟ قال: «أَبُوكَ» متفقٌ عليه.

The Prophet, sallallaahu ‘alayhi wa sallam, said, 'Your mother.' The man asked for the fourth time, 'Who is next?' The Prophet, sallallaahu ‘alayhi wa sallam, said, 'Your father».[Al-Bukhaari and Muslim]

Prohibition of Envy and Other Evil Morals:

35- It was narrated on the authority of Anas, May Allah Be Pleased with him, that the Prophet, sallallaahu ‘alayhi wa sallam, said: «*Do not hate one another, do not envy one another, do not desert each other, and be, O slaves of Allah! brothers. Lo! It is not permissible for any Muslim to desert (not talk to) his brother (Muslim) for more than three days*». [Al-Bukhaari and Muslim]

Charity Causes the Blessing of Property:

36- It was narrated on the authority of Abu Hurayrah, May Allah Be Pleased with him, that the Messenger of Allah, sallallaahu ‘alayhi wa sallam, said: «*O son of Aadam, spend and I Will Spend on*

النهي عن الحسد وأمثاله:

35- وعَنْ أَنَسٍ ﷺ أَنَّ النبِيَّ ﷺ قال: «لا تَبَاغَضُوا، ولا تَحَاسَدُوا، ولاَ تَدَابَرُوا، ولا تَقَاطعُوا، وَكُونُوا عِبَادَ اللهِ إخوانـاً، ولا يَحِلُّ لِمُسْلِم أَنْ يهْجُرَ أَخَاه فوقَ ثلاثٍ» [متفق عليه].

الصدقة سبب لبركة المال:

36- عـنْ أبـي هُريـرَةَ ﷺ أن رسـولَ اللهِ ﷺ قـال: «قـال الله تعـالى: أنفِـق يـا ابـنَ آدمَ يُنْفَـقْ عَلَيْكَ» [متفقٌ عليه].

you». [Al-Bukhaari and Muslim]
Manners of Greeting:

37- It was narrated on the authority of Abu Hurayrah, May Allah Be Pleased with him, that the Messenger of Allah, sallallaahu 'alayhi wa sallam, said: «*The mounting greets the walking, the walking greets the sitting and the few greet the many*». [Al-Bukhaari and Muslim]

The Characteristic of the Believer:

38- It was narrated on the authority of Anas, May Allah Be Pleased with him, that the Messenger of Allah, sallallaahu 'alayhi wa sallam, said: «*None of you will have faith till he wishes for his (Muslim) brother what he wishes for himself*». [Al-Bukhaari and Muslim]

Good Health and Free Time:

39- It was narrated on the authority of Ibn 'Abbaas, May Allah Be Pleased with him, that the Messenger of Allah, sallallaahu 'alayhi wa sallam, said: «*There are two blessings which many people fail to make use of: (They are) good health and free time for doing*

آداب السلام:

37- عَنْ أبِي هريرة ﷺ أن رسول الله ﷺ قال: «يُسَلِّمُ الرَّاكِبُ عَلَى الْمَاشِي، وَالْمَاشِي عَلَي الْقَاعِدِ، وَالْقَلِيلُ على الْكَثِيرِ» [متفق عليه].

صفة المؤمن:

38- عَنْ أَنَس ﷺ عن النبيّ ﷺ قال: «لاَ يُؤْمِنُ أَحَدُكُمْ حَتَّى يُحِبَّ لأَخِيهِ مَا يُحِبُّ لِنَفْسِهِ» [متفقٌ عليه].

الصَّحَّةُ وَالفَرَاغُ:

39- عَنِ ابن عَبَّاسٍ ﷺ قَالَ: قَالَ رَسُولُ اللَّهِ ﷺ: «نِعْمَتَانِ مَغْبُونٌ فِيهِمَا كَثِيرٌ مِنَ النَّاسِ: الصَّحَّةُ وَالفَرَاغُ» [رواه مسلم].

good». [Al-Bukhaari]

Two Words that Are Weighty in the Scale:

كَلِمَتَانِ ثَقِيلَتَانِ فِي المِيزَانِ

40- It was narrated on the authority of Abu Hurayrah, May Allah Be Pleased with him, that the Messenger of Allah, sallallaahu 'alayhi wa sallam, said: «*Two are the words which are light on the tongue, but heavy in the Scale, dear to The Most Merciful: Subhaanallaahi wa Bihamdihi, Subhaanallaahi Al-'Atheem (Most Exalted and Praised Is Allah, Exalted Is Allah The Most Great)*». [Al-Bukhaari]

40- وَعَنْ أَبِي هُرَيرَةَ، ﷺ، قَالَ: قَالَ رَسُولُ اللَّهِ ﷺ: «كَلِمَتَانِ خَفِيفَتَانِ عَلَى اللِّسَانِ، ثَقِيلَتَانِ فِي المِيزَانِ، حَبِيبَتَانِ إِلَى الرَّحْمَنِ: سُبْحَانَ اللَّهِ وَبِحَمْدِهِ، سُبْحَانَ اللَّهِ العَظِيمِ» [متفقٌ عليه].

Conclusion

This was what I managed to compile and arrange by the Aid of Allah. I ask Allah, The Most Generous, Lord of the Mighty Throne to Grant success to all Muslims to return to The Book of their Lord and the Sunnah of their Prophet Muhammad, sallallaahu 'alayhi wa sallam.

[Our Lord, Give us in this worldly life [that which is] good and in the Hereafter [that which is] good and Protect us from the punishment of the Fire.] [Al-Baqarah:201]

Exalted Is your Lord, The Lord of Might, above what they describe. And peace be upon the Messengers.
And praise be to Allah, Lord of the Worlds

Abdullahi Hassan Farah
San'aa'-30/8/2008

الخاتمة:

هَذَا مَا وَفَّقَنِي اللهُ لَجمعِهِ وَتَرْتِيبِهِ، فَأَسْأَلُ اللهَ الْكَرِيمَ رَبَّ الْعَرْشِ الْعَظِيمِ أَنْ يُوَفِّقَ الْمُسْلِمِينَ جَمِيعًا الرُّجُوعَ إِلَى كِتَابِ رَبِّهِم وَسُنَّةِ نَبِيِّهِم مُحَمَّدٍ ﷺ.

﴿ رَبَّنَا آتِنَا فِي الدُّنْيَا حَسَنَةً وَفِي الْآخِرَةِ حَسَنَةً وَقِنَا عَذَابَ النَّارِ ﴾ [البقرة: 201].

سُبْحَانَ رَبِّكَ رَبِّ الْعِزَّةِ عَمَّا يَصِفُونَ، وَسَلَامٌ عَلَى الْمُرْسَلِينَ، وَالْحَمْدُ للهِ رَبِّ الْعَالَمِينَ.

عبدالله حسن فارح
2008/8/30م.

المصادر والفهرس

References & Index

References

1- The Noble Quran.

2- Saheeh Al-Bukhaari.

3- Saheeh Muslim.

4- Saheeh Sunan At-Tirmithi by Al-Albaani.

5- Saheeh Sunan Abu Daawood by Al-Albaani.

6- Saheeh Sunan Ibn Maajah by Al-Albaani.

7- Musnad Ahmad.

8- Ad-Duroos Al-Muhimmah Li 'Aammat Al-Ummah by Ibn Baaz.

9- Al-Anwaar fi Seerat An-Nabiyy Al-Mukhtaar by Sulaymaan Al-Luhaymeed.

10- Qasas Al-Anbiyaa' by Sulaymaan Al-Luhaymeed.

11- Al-'Aqeedah Al-Islaamiyyah by Muhammad Jameel Zeeno.

12- Mawsoo'at Al-Musaabaqaat Al-Islaamiyyah by Zaghlool Siddeeq Burhaam.

13- Musaabaqaat wa Thaqaafaat by Usaamah Banjar.

14- Mawsoo'at Kanz Al-Ma'loomaat Al-Islaamiyyah by 'Ali Badawi.

15- Hisn Al-Muslim by Sa'eed ibn 'Ali Al-Qahtaani.

16- Kitaab At-Tifl Al-Muslim by 'Awadh ibn Lutfi Al-Jazzaar.

المَصَادِر

1- القُرآن الكَريم.

2- صَحِيحُ الإمَام البخاري.

3- صَحِيحُ الإمَام مُسلِم.

4- صَحِيحُ سُنَنِ التَّرمِذيّ لِلشَّيخ الأَلبَانيّ.

5- صَحِيحُ سُنَنِ أَبِي دَاوُدَ لِلشَّيخ الأَلبَانيّ.

6- صَحِيحُ سُنَنِ ابنِ مَاجَة لِلشَّيخِ الأَلبَانيّ

7- مُسنَدُ الإمَام أَحمَد.

8- الدُّرُوسُ المُهِمَّةُ لعَامَّةِ الأُمَّةِ لِلشَّيخِ بنِ بَاز.

9- الأَنوَارُ في سِيرَةِ النَّبِيّ المُختَارِ لِلشَّيخ سُلَيمَان اللهيمِيد.

10- قَصَصُ الأَنبيَاءِ لِلشَّيخ سُلَيمَان اللهيمِيد.

11- العَقِيدَةُ الإسلَامِيَّةُ لِلشَّيخ مُحَمَّد بن جَمِيل زينُو.

12- مَوسُوعَةُ المُسَابَقَاتِ الإسلَامِيَّةِ، زَغلُول صَدِّيق برهَام.

13- مُسَابَقَاتٌ وَثَقَافَات، أُسَامَة بَنجَر.

14- مَوسُوعَةُ كَنزِ المعلومَاتِ الإسلَامِيَّة، عَلي بَدَوي.

15- حِصنُ المُسلِم، سَعِيدُ بنُ عَلِيّ القَحطَانيّ.

16- كِتَابُ الطِّفلِ المُسلِمِ، لِلشَّيخِ عَوَض بن لُطفِي الجَزَّار.

Table of Contents

فهرس الموضوعات

تم بحمد الله

أَلَا بِذِكْرِ اللَّهِ تَطْمَئِنُّ الْقُلُوبُ